MW00413221

What people are saying about *Omali Yeshitela Speaks*

What Omali Yeshitela presents in this book is "African Internationalism." What is at the core of Yeshitela's speeches is an all-out assault on the White Empire...and its various neocolonies.

These are fighting words, and as such, some will be upset with Yeshitela's opinions and speeches. So be it. The condition of black America, and indeed, every community of African life, is so grave, so dire, so horrendous, that to move folks from quiet acquiescence to action will take some upsetting.

From his ideas of African Socialism, to his anti-war and anti-imperialist speech against the (latest) war, to his remembrances of Malcolm X, Fred Hampton and African resistance fighters, Yeshitela gives us food for thought and, hopefully, fuel for action.

It is hoped that young people, especially, will take the time to read this book, so that it can feed their heads about the World, about Empire and about the necessity for Revolution.

—Mumia Abu Jamal, award-winning journalist, death row inmate, author of *We Want Freedom: A Life in the Black Panther Party*

In reading *Omali Yeshitela Speaks*, one can perceive the urgency and significance of the well-known author's dynamic presentation of politics, history and the black struggle in America.

Yeshitela's comments are bold. He shows that he is not afraid of the PATRIOT Act, new laws on civil rights, the FBI, CIA or the Bush family. He spells it out clearly with no holds barred.

Omali Yeshitela Speaks is an up-to-date chronicle of U.S. history from the U.S. robbery of Mexican land, forcing the Indigenous on to reservations, to the current war on Iraq. It is a must-read for movement activists, internationalists, socialists, but also for non-activists, scholars and mainstream politicians.

—Yuri Kochiyama, lifelong activist for social justice, close friend and supporter of Malcolm X who was by his side at his assassination in 1965

Omali Yeshitela Speaks is a remarkable collection of revolutionary analysis and thought. After reading this book, one must conclude that without a doubt the Chairman (as he is known to many of us) is one of the major revolutionary theoreticians in the world today.

Unión del Barrio, a Mexican-Indigenous liberation organization founded in 1981, first came into contact with Omali Yeshitela and the African People's Socialist Party in 1985. As we studied the writings of the Chairman, it became more and more apparent that his political theories applied to our struggle as well.

In *Omali Yeshitela Speaks,* with exact precision and clarity, which is characteristic of his writing and speaking (he is the best speaker I have ever heard), the Chairman puts forth his political philosophy. It is a philosophy based on the point of view of the oppressed.

Time and time again, within the pages of *Omali Yeshitela Speaks*, the Chairman expresses unity with the Mexican-Indigenous, Filipino and other oppressed peoples. But it is not any ordinary unity. It is a type of unity that respects and unconditionally supports other peoples' right to self-determination.

The Chairman's experiences and ideas are not only written in the pages of *Omali Yeshitela Speaks,* but are alive in the world. They are alive in the African People's Socialist Party and the African Socialist International. They are also alive among the masses—the workers, poor, students and prisoners of all nationalities. And they are certainly alive within my own organization, Unión del Barrio.

—Ernesto Bustillo, educator, community organizer and founding member of Unión del Barrio

During the 1960s, African people in the United States mounted an insurgency that threatened the system of domestic colonialism under which we live. This led to a ferocious counter-insurgency, which included the assassinations of some of our most important leaders, such as Malcolm X, Dr. Martin Luther King, Jr., Fred Hampton, Alprentice "Bunchy" Carter and John Huggins.

Unlike those who sought to retreat from the radicalism of groups like the Black Panther Party and the Revolutionary Action Movement (RAM), Omali Yeshitela and his comrades in the African People's Socialist Party sought to deepen and carry forward that radical tradition in both theory and practice.

Omali Yeshitela Speaks highlights the contributions of one of the most important revolutionary thinkers and leaders operating within U.S. borders today. Yeshitela's contribution to revolutionary theory deepens the insights brought to revolutionary theory by Frantz Fanon in *The Wretched of the Earth*.

While Yeshitela operates in the broad arena of revolutionary struggle against world capitalism in which Marx and Engels were such important theoreticians, he brings what he calls the "viewpoint of the slave" to our attention, which is an important—indeed a crucial—corrective to Marx and Engels' conception of the world capitalist system.

Marx wrote from the perspective of Europeans seeking to explain the impact of Africa's stolen wealth on European history. Yeshitela focuses on a much more comprehensive understanding of the relationship of the history of Africa and African people throughout the world to the history and development of capitalism. He focuses on the challenge to the capitalist world order and imperialist order, which can best be constructed from the "viewpoint of the slave." This standpoint will not be a new concept for many of us, but there is all too little discussion of this issue among intellectuals.

Yeshitela talks about the meaning of the fundamental crisis of imperialism in which we are now living and how we might engage effectively in a struggle for our own liberation. *Omali Yeshitela Speaks* is about a struggle to transform the earth by engaging in a common revolutionary front with all of the enemies of imperialism, but with an eye toward uniting most closely with those social forces in the working class and the peasantry who will be the most unflinching and constant foes of imperialism.

—Dr. Rod Bush, Associate Professor of Sociology and Anthropology at St. John's University. A long-time activist in the movement for social change and Black liberation, his most recent book is *We Are Not What We Seem: Black Nationalism and Class Struggle in the American Century*

Omali Yeshitela

Omali Yeshitela Speaks

African Internationalism
Political theory for our time

Preface by Luwezi Kinshasa

St. Petersburg, Florida, USA
burningspearmarketplace.com

Dedication

To Sundiata Acoli who,
along with his comrades in arms
has given us a glimpse of our strength and potential,
and whose continued imprisonment
represents our current impotency and shame.

To Marcus Garvey, Malcolm X, Dedan Kimathi,
Patrice Lumumba, Osagyefo Kwame Nkrumah
and Mangaliso Sobukwe,
whose extraordinary vision,
love for our people and works
have brought us thus far.

And to the brutalized and slandered
African workers and poor peasants
who, upon becoming organized
into our own revolutionary party
and conscious of our own selfish interests,
will liberate and unite Africa and
all our people scattered around the world.

Izwe Lethu i Afrika!

Contents

Articles

Interviews

Preface

Omali Yeshitela, leader for our times

I am one of the millions of Africans who has been profoundly touched and transformed by the philosophy and work of Chairman Omali Yeshitela.

Before I met the Uhuru Movement, like many Africans and colonized people, I spent a lot of time trying to understand the world and the role and place of African people in it. I first saw *The Burning Spear,* the official newspaper of the Uhuru Movement, in a London shop in 1989, but I did not buy it. I thought it was a newspaper of the reggae group Burning Spear. I said to myself, "Keep buying their records, not their papers."

A year later, my wife Patricia and I traveled to Paris, where we went to the *Presence Africaine* bookshop. I spotted a book in English by Omali Yeshitela with the title *Reparations Now!* I picked it up, read a few lines and my mind was blown. It talked about African people putting the U.S. government on trial for crimes against Africans in the U.S. The demand for reparations for our stolen resources struck a chord with me. The African working class must be brought back into political life. African workers must lead the struggle to complete the Black Revolution. That was powerful!

This book instantly helped me have a better summation of the defeat and state of the African Revolution in Congo, where I was born. It was the beginning of a qualitative leap forward in my own development. I bought the book, and my wife mentioned she had copies of *The Burning Spear* newspaper at home, back in

London. I asked how many she had. She replied, "quite a few." I said I wanted all those newspapers!

I immediately subscribed to *The Burning Spear,* which was then published in Oakland, California. I wanted to know more about completing the African Socialist Revolution. Whenever I had read and studied books written by European rhetoricians and practitioners of socialist philosophy, I never got a sense of the significance of African people and the African Revolution. I never had a feeling of belonging with European-centered socialist books.

Discovering the work of Omali Yeshitela was like opening up a boundless universe of ideas in defense of the African proletariat against white imperialism's vast world media. Yeshitela is the leader for our times. His growing influence is becoming the cement that unifies our contemporary understanding and practice of the forward motion towards the final offensive of the struggle for African liberation. Because of Yeshitela we see unity emerging before our eyes.

Omali Yeshitela's work gave me a true sense of the meaning of the international African Revolution. I began to understand it as a movement of African workers and peasants taking place throughout the world. Yeshitela teaches us that our struggle is informed by our own selfish interest to build a redeemed Africa by creating a continental socialist African State under the leadership of the international African working class.

The indescribably brutal attacks on Africa require an urgent response. Yeshitela's call to build the African Socialist International represents the most meaningful urgent response to defend African people and, indeed, the most urgent task of our time. Through Yeshitela, I have now learned that the fate and destiny of all Africans is the same wherever we are located under the parasitic capitalist system. I can now easily see that African masses fighting in Haiti, Martinique or Venezuela, or in Congo,

Ghana or the U.S. are all objectively fighting for Africa and Africans everywhere.

Omali Yeshitela represents the voice of the African enslaved in the Americas, who is speaking directly to the enslaved African proletariat living in Africa and elsewhere around the world. His philosophical work takes the socialist theory of liberation out of the hands of the self-serving European and North American left, and puts it firmly into the hands of African and all other colonized peoples, who are the driving forces for human progress and socialism in the real world. Challenging the opportunistic white left has never been so easy and rewarding!

I have been privileged to witness in action the impact of Omali Yeshitela's theory of African Revolution on Africans every-where—in France, South Africa, Holland, Britain, Congo, Guyana, Brazil, Germany, etc. The result has been almost the same for all: excitement and enthusiasm, a sense of increased self-confidence, and a forward-looking vision of a liberated and united African Continent.

The Chairman is never short of humor and jokes whenever he is addressing an audience or when he is having a simple con-versation with friends or Africans he just met for the first time. Everyone is touched by his profound revolutionary love for life and his vision of a world with no oppression and exploitation of any kind for African people and all oppressed and colonized peoples.

His philosophy from the point of view of the slave provides the only satisfactory explanation that I have ever seen of the fall of European communist regimes and the current ongoing crisis of imperialism. He shows us that the colonial peoples are the main progressive forces ushering in a new era of humanity and socialism.

Contrary to most of the present day followers of Garvey, Malcolm X, Lumumba, Nkrumah and other giant leaders of the

African Revolution, Chairman Omali is able to complete the work of his illustrious predecessors, weaving it into one coherent and continuously developing body of thought and action for this century. The universality of his analysis, known as African Internationalism or Yeshitelism, is a moving force that lifts all African and colonized peoples up from under the yoke of white imperialism.

Because he shows us how to fight imperialism on our own terms and in our own interests, Omali Yeshitela is truly loved not only by African people everywhere, but by Mexican, Filipino and other colonized peoples as well.

Chairman Omali travels thousands of miles, continuously and consistently seeking out African revolutionaries around the world to build the African Socialist International. I have never met anyone or any organization within the existing Black Liberation Movement, who will tirelessly go anywhere, regardless of comfort or safety, in order to meet African revolutionaries and progressive forces who could be won to the process of liberating Africa and African people.

I am writing this piece with the understanding that African revolutionary struggles taking place anywhere in the world will be guided by African Internationalism. Anyone looking for an advanced understanding of the African struggle need look no further than the African People's Socialist Party and its leader Chairman Omali Yeshitela. As the growing international voice of the slandered African masses, Chairman Omali represents a profound vision for the future of one, united and liberated Africa under the leadership of African workers and poor peasants.

Izwe Lethu i Afrika!

Luwezi Kinshasa
London, March 2005

Introduction

Omali Yeshitela speaks to us

Attacked and suppressed by white power, the white left and the black middle class alike, the revolutionary theory of Omali Yeshitela is bold, empowering and ahead of its time. In this long-overdue collection of speeches, articles and interviews, Yeshitela emerges as the most important and innovative political thinker of this era.

As we know, the world looks very different depending on which side of the capitalist equation you are on. TV, newspapers, movies and the music industry blast us daily with the worldview of white power. Only Omali Yeshitela speaks from our own point of view, talking directly to us, African workers wherever we are located, and all our comrades among the oppressed, the colonized and the enslaved of the world.

On these pages, in every day, down-to-earth language Yeshitela reveals to us how capitalism was born at our expense through slavery, genocide and colonial domination. Yeshitela is witty, sharp and passionate as he speaks about the ravenous hunger of capitalism, which he likens to a parasitic tapeworm that can only thrive by sucking our blood—stealing our land, labor, resources, culture and political independence.

As the white world gets richer, fatter and more powerful, we become poorer, more oppressed and powerless in the face of the incessant political, economic and military violence of imperialism. This is the dialectic of capitalism that Yeshitela brings to life for us.

Known as African Internationalism, the theory of Omali Yeshitela was forged in the heat of struggle. As Chairman of the African People's Socialist Party and leader of the fighting Uhuru Movement, Yeshitela has never had the luxury of developing his theoretical works in the quiet of a study or a library.

African Internationalism came out of the streets of the African community, from the campaigns for the liberation of African workers. This book reflects the demands of a vibrant mass movement on the ground in the Party's home base of St. Petersburg, Florida. The Chairman is working relentlessly to build the African Socialist International while he gives leadership to our Party organizations, institutions, publications, campaigns and growing influence throughout the U.S., Europe, Africa and South America. It seems amazing that he could find the time to write anything at all.

Those who read *Omali Yeshitela Speaks* can't help but be struck by the significance of the Chairman's theory not only for the future of Africa, but for the future of all the oppressed of this planet. Indeed the fate of the planet itself may rest on the success of Yeshitela's ambitious aim of wiping imperialism off the face of the earth and building a united and liberated Africa under the leadership of African workers and peasants.

In the African People's Socialist Party, we are very clear about the theoretical vacuum that African Internationalism fills as the Chairman carries on the legacy of Marcus Garvey, Malcolm X and Kwame Nkrumah.

Yeshitela is well versed in the works of the nineteenth century European revolutionary, Karl Marx, and the twentieth century Russian, V.I. Lenin. He used their theories as a foundation, not to try to learn about revolution but as tools to try to make sense of the brutal conditions faced by him and the majority of our African brothers and sisters.

Through the development of African Internationalism however, Chairman Omali has shown how the Euro-centric flaws of Marx and Lenin are not just incorrect when looked at through the lens of scientific African Internationalism. These flaws have proved *fatal* for the revolutionary movements led by colonized forces who attempted to adopt the theories of Marx and Lenin in their struggle to win national liberation. Without the right medicine, the Chairman tells us, we can never get rid of that tapeworm.

Fundamental to Yeshitela's theory: capitalism is parasitic

From the time he was a very young man, whose leadership was emerging during the Black Power Movement in the U.S. South, Yeshitela studied the works of Marx and Lenin, mulling over at length Marx's recognition of the "primitive accumulation of capital." Way in the back of *Capital,* Marx's eleven-hundred-page work written in 1867, the Chairman had noted this statement:

"The discovery of gold and silver in America, the extirpation, enslavement and entombment in mines of the aboriginal population, the beginning of the conquest and looting of the East Indies, the turning of Africa into a warren for the commercial hunting of black skins, signalized the rosy dawn of the era of capitalist production. These idyllic proceedings are the chief momenta of primitive accumulation, the necessary condition for capitalist production."

Marx answers the question of where the accumulation of start-up capital came from to kick off the capitalist system in backwards and poverty-ridden Europe: from the primitive (or first) accumulation of capital, which was "not the result of the capitalist mode of production but its *starting point.*"

Primitive accumulation, Chairman Omali asserts is *us*! It's the enslavement of the African and the theft of our resources; it's the genocide of the Indigenous population and the theft of their land; it's the colonization of Africa, Asia and the Americas for the benefit of the white world. So, if Marx understood the question of primitive accumulation, why did he come to the incorrect conclusion that capitalism as a world system would be overturned by development within Europe?

Yeshitela also noted that Lenin had written in 1916 in *Imperialism and the Split in Socialism* that "Imperialism is a specific historical stage of capitalism. Its specific character is threefold: imperialism is (1) monopoly capitalism; (2) parasitic, or decaying capitalism; (3) moribund capitalism."

In his pivotal early works, the Chairman shows that Lenin's definition of imperialism was *exactly the same thing* as Marx's discussion of primitive accumulation.

In *The Road to Socialism is Painted Black,* published in 1987, the Chairman explains of Marx's concept of primitive accumulation, "Like Lenin, his was a definition of the significance of the enslavement of African people only as it impacted on development inside Europe, a development which necessarily meant what has come to be called the underdevelopment of Africa, Asia and Latin America...

"Marx and Lenin's world was white. The enslaved Asian, African and 'Indian' of North and South America were essentially objects of history which had more or less significance for European development."

Capitalism did not become parasitic sometime in the nineteenth century with what is called imperialism, Chairman Omali proves. Capitalism was *born* parasitic. And it remains parasitic.

The loot from slavery and colonialism, from the stolen resources, land and labor of African and other oppressed peoples that flowed into Europe, creating the wealth and power of today's U.S. and Western imperialism, is almost unfathomable. The violence and brutality that it has taken to do that to us is chilling.

Chairman Omali's definition of parasitic capitalism is perhaps the most fundamental point that must be understood in his theory. Only from that point was he able to come to the correct conclusion that the struggle to defeat capitalism and imperialism can never be led from within the confines of Europe, the white world or the former Soviet Union as it was configured.

This is simply not possible because the entire white population, including white working people, is the beneficiary of parasitic capitalism at our expense. The white world sits on the pedestal of our oppression. Their children thrive because our children die. Their children get good jobs because our children are forced into colonial prisons.

The struggle to defeat parasitic capitalism must be led by us, the African working class. We are the pedestal of the capitalist system, and we must rise up to destroy capitalism that is sitting on our backs. We must rid the world of this monster in the process of liberating Our Africa for the benefit of our children and our children's children.

Broad range of Chairman's analysis

There are many other aspects of the Chairman's theory that he addresses in this book so brilliantly and creatively, in so many different situations to so many varied audiences. *Omali Yeshitela Speaks* is a profound and lively political education for anyone who wants to understand the world as it is and how we can transform it.

In this collection, the reader will see Yeshitela's sharp critique of the white left as apologists for parasitic capitalism. Because of this, the African People's Socialist Party formed the African People's Solidarity Committee in 1976, which organizes political and material solidarity in the white communities under the Party's leadership.

Readers will appreciate the Chairman's profound analysis of the historical conditions that created the Civil Rights Movement of the 1950s and how, as the leadership of African workers emerged, this movement was transformed into the revolutionary Black Power Movement of the '60s.

The Chairman's astute summation of the U.S. government's counterinsurgency, the military defeat of the Black Revolution of the Sixties is expounded on throughout these pages. Yeshitela shows us how once our movement was destroyed, the government turned this counterinsurgency against our entire African people, flooding our communities with deadly drugs and imposing on us brutal police containment policies, which take away our rights, brutalize us and fill the U.S. prisons with African people.

Chairman Omali shows us why we need our own Party that represents the selfish interests of the African working class, and why we must be organized into an advanced detachment as professional revolutionaries if we are to win our liberation. He lays out the serious flaws of the concept of Pan-Africanism and stresses the urgent need to build the African Socialist International (ASI). As an international party of African workers from around the world, the ASI is bent on destroying the imposed colonial borders in Africa and liberating our homeland.

These and so many other questions are taken up in this rich and powerful book *Omali Yeshitela Speaks* in which the Chairman analyzes everything from the September 11th attacks in the U.S. to the struggle for reparations, to the history of Africans in boxing, to the current situation in Zimbabwe and more.

All of the speeches contained in this volume have been copy edited. Chairman Omali generally does not speak from written manuscripts. His amazing presentations spring directly from his brain. We turned his electrifying spoken word into pieces that were more suitable for reading. If you have heard some of the same presentations on CD or video, you may recognize some of the changes. All of these presentations, however, have been carefully gone over and approved by Chairman Omali who in some cases added his own comments in footnote form.

As Omali Yeshitela makes clear in this book, his theory is not for armchair revolutionaries. If you are moved by the revelations here, you are bound by principle take up the struggle.

To find out more about the African People's Socialist Party and the various organizations it leads, or to bring the Chairman to your campus or town to speak, contact the Party at the Uhuru House, 1245 18th Avenue South, St. Petersburg, FL 33713. Call 727-821-6620 in the U.S., or 0208 265 1731 in Great Britain. You can visit the Party's website at www.apspuhuru.org and check out the Uhuru Africa Club at www.uhuruafrica.org. Send email to info@apspuhuru.org.

Uhuru!

Burning Spear Uhuru Publications
www.burningspearuhuru.com
info@burningspearuhuru.com

Omali Yeshitela

An insufficient biography

This short biography gives only a glimpse of the life lived thus far by Omali Yeshitela. It does not do justice to his almost nonstop pace of political work, leading campaigns to bring African people another step closer to political independence.

It does not give a full sense of Chairman Omali's stature as a thinker, a political theoretician who has unraveled and demystified the most profound concepts of the source of imperialist power, and made them easily accessible to the masses of the people as a tool for revolutionary struggle.

This little bio fails to convey Chairman Omali's limitless aspirations and ambition for justice for Africa and African workers and all oppressed peoples everywhere, who have suffered under this parasitic system for so long.

This biography gives no real picture of the Chairman's humanity and love for the people, his immense presence as a person, his leadership in every situation, his unmatched power to move an audience with his speaking ability, his sense of humor, talent for singing freedom songs, prowess at weight lifting or passion for vegetarianism and healthy living.

The fact that Omali Yeshitela is a giant among human beings, a man who stands with the greatest of African leaders past and present is *evident to all who come in contact with him. This biography just scratches the surface.*

Omali Yeshitela, formerly known as Joseph Waller, was born on October 9, 1941 in St. Petersburg, Florida.

Having learned to read as a toddler, Yeshitela's formative years were deeply influenced by his grandmother. She taught him Bible stories, especially emphasizing the story of Joseph who, after being sold into bondage by his brothers, became a great leader who rescued his people from disaster.

At eighteen, he joined the army and was stationed in Berlin, Germany. In 1962, at the height of the Civil Rights Movement, Yeshitela began organizing resistance to the anti-black practices of the military. As a result Yeshitela was thrown out of the army after being forced to see a military psychiatrist, who told him he was "a Garveyite."[1]

Following his discharge, Yeshitela returned to his hometown where he worked in construction and carpet laying before being hired by the *St. Petersburg Times* as a "copy boy," proofreader and later an apprentice printer.

In 1966 he joined the Student Nonviolent Coordinating Committee (SNCC).

In December of that year as a SNCC organizer, Yeshitela led a group of young African people into the St. Petersburg City Hall. In a courageous, now-famous act, Yeshitela ripped down from the walls of city hall a demeaning mural that had hung for thirty years on the first landing, in full view of every visitor to the building.

Depicting African people in offensive caricature, playing musical instruments while white people partied on the beach, the mural made very clear the subservient position forced on African people as colonial subjects in the U.S. South. For removing this despicable painting, Yeshitela was given a five-year prison sentence, of which he served two years.

While in prison in 1968, Yeshitela formed JOMO, the Junta of Militant Organizations. Four years later in the wake of the U.S. government's attack against the Black Power Movement of the '60s, Yeshitela organized the African People's Socialist Party, which built the Uhuru Movement, waging struggles throughout Florida, the South and elsewhere. In 1976 the Party formed the African People's Solidarity Committee, an organization of North American or white people who work under the Party's leadership.

By the late 1970s the Party's work had expanded to California, and within a few years Yeshitela moved the headquarters of the Party to Oakland. In 1979 the Chairman built the African National Prison Organization (ANPO). Opening up a front in New York in 1982, the Party held the first World Tribunal on Reparations for African People in Brooklyn and formed the African National Reparations Organization (ANRO).

In the face of massive African community homelessness in Oakland, the Uhuru Movement launched the Community Control Housing Initiative in 1984. Known as Measure O, the ballot initiative mandated rents to be no higher than twenty-five percent of the average income of a neighborhood. Despite a million dollar "No on O" campaign waged by landlords and businessmen that defeated the initiative, Measure O won 25,000 votes in the Oakland election.

In the heat of tireless struggles on many fronts during more than a decade in Oakland, Chairman Omali edited *The Burning Spear* newspaper, published books and pamphlets, and made groundbreaking advances in his political theory.

Known as African Internationalism, or Yeshitelism, the Chairman's theory defines capitalism as a parasitic system that was born from the enslavement of African people and the oppression of colonized peoples worldwide. Parasitic capitalism builds a pedestal of affluence and democracy for the white population upon a foundation of the colonial domination of African and oppressed peoples around the world.

While he was in Oakland, Chairman Omali initiated working relationships with Mexican, Filipino and Arab liberation movements based in California. During this period the Party built some of its most successful and popular economic and political institutions including the Uhuru House and Spear Graphics, as well as the Uhuru Bakery Cafe and Uhuru Furniture stores in Oakland followed by an Uhuru Furniture store in Philadelphia a few years later.

In 1991 the Chairman founded the International People's Democratic Uhuru Movement, a mass organization with the specific purpose of stopping the U.S. government's counterinsurgency against the African community.

The Party relocated its national office to St. Petersburg, Florida in 1993 and the Chairman returned to his oldest and deepest base, opening up an Uhuru House in the center of the impoverished African community. Since that time a successful fitness gym and the third Uhuru Furniture store have been established.

On October 24, 1996, the police killed an eighteen-year-old African motorist, TyRon Lewis, during a traffic stop on the busiest corner of the African community. The murder of Lewis took place only three blocks from the Uhuru House, and Party organizers were immediately on the scene.

That night the African working class of St. Petersburg rose up in rebellion, fusing scientific analysis and revolutionary theory into the militant mass uprising. Hundreds of African workers fought police in pitched battles in the streets. The Uhuru Movement went into immediate action, holding vigils, demonstrations, community meetings and a tribunal that put the city and killer police on trial by the people.

On November 13, the day the grand jury exonerated the killer cops, several municipal, state, county and local police forces attacked the Uhuru House, pepper spraying Chairman Omali and other Uhuru Movement organizers, and tear gassing over a hundred people who had gathered there for a regularly scheduled meeting. In the attack the police used all its reserves of tear gas.

In response, the African working class rose up in a second rebellion that brought down a police helicopter and pushed back the militarized police presence of over 300 highly armed cops in riot gear.

Following these uprisings, Chairman Omali and the Uhuru Movement became the recognized representatives of the African community. The Party embarked on its most prolonged period of multi-faceted mass work, successfully uniting the African petty bourgeoisie and a significant sector of the white population to the interests of the African working class.

This strategy forced the city for the first time to acknowledge the economic and political needs of African workers. It also made it difficult for the city to isolate and attack the Uhuru Movement. Yeshitela led the call for genuine economic development for the African community and an end to the repressive police containment policies that brutalize and terrorize African people daily.

As part of this mass strategy Chairman Omali ran for Mayor of St. Petersburg in 2001, winning every black and mixed precinct but one with his platform of "St. Petersburg united in shared prosperity."

Following his campaign, the Chairman formed Citizens United for Shared Prosperity (CUSP), a powerful citywide community organization that provided a strategic relationship between the African and white communities. Based on the commitment to genuine economic development for African people, CUSP took on a broad range of issues.

In 2001, following the September 11th attacks inside the U.S., the Chairman organized the Florida Alliance for Peace and Social Justice (FAPSJ) in the face of the threat of U.S. wars of colonial aggression against the peoples of Afghanistan, Iraq and other Middle Eastern militants and people. FAPSJ was a state-wide anti-war organization formed on the principle that true peace is only possible through national liberation for oppressed peoples.

In recent years the Chairman has been travelling and speaking tirelessly to fulfill his lifelong aim of building the African Socialist International (ASI), committed to the struggle to liberate and unify Africa as the birthright of African people everywhere.

Today various fronts of the Uhuru Movement are active in cities throughout North America, Africa and Europe, with a growing base in South America. Chairman Omali Yeshitela carries on the legacy of Marcus Garvey, Malcolm X and Kwame Nkrumah[2] as he leads the fight for one united and liberated Africa under the leadership of the African working class.

1 A follower of Marcus Garvey, 1887–1940, organized the Universal Negro Improvement Association (UNIA) and its coordinating body, the African Communities League. He published the newspaper the *Negro World* in several languages and toured the Americas speaking to large audiences of African people about his vision of African independence. The UNIA had millions of members in eleven hundred branches in more than forty countries. Garvey launched ambitious business ventures, notably the Black Star Line shipping company.

2 Marcus Garvey (cited in endnote 1), Malcolm X and Kwame Nkrumah were all twentieth century giants in the struggle for African liberation. Malcolm X, who was assassinated by the U.S. government in 1965, was the uncontested leader and spokesman of the African working class-led movement for Black Power in the 1960s. Kwame Nkrumah, who died in 1972, was the president of independent Ghana and tireless proponent for "the total liberation and unification of Africa under an All-African socialist government."

Presentations

The right kind of medicine
The science of defeating parasitic white power

This presentation is an entire political education in itself. "The right kind of medicine" contains the main points of African Internationalism or Yeshitelism, Omali Yeshitela's political theory. Yeshitelism exposes the origins of the parasitic capitalist system that was built and maintained on the enslavement and oppression of African and oppressed peoples around the world. The Chairman brilliantly answers the question of why African people face such brutal conditions today no matter where we are located.

Chairman Omali gave this presentation at the University of the District of Columbia on December 5, 1991, as part of a national speaking tour. The event was sponsored by the student groups Kiamsha and the Pan African Student Union. It was originally published as a supplement to the March/April 1992 issue of The Burning Spear *newspaper as "Black Power to the African Community."*

To the Pan African Student Union and Kiamsha, Brothers and Sisters, Comrades, Uhuru!

We say "Uhuru" when we greet each other. Uhuru means "freedom" and we think that freedom should be on the minds of African people twenty-four hours a day.

We say "Uhuru," as opposed to simply saying "freedom," because it is important, we believe, to understand and remember that we are African people. We're not just talking about freedom; we are talking about freedom as a people, as African people.

I think that the question of who we are is significant culturally and psychologically. More than that, we believe the question

21

of who we are as African people is central to our understandings of the entire world, why the world is as it is and why we are in the shape we are in as a people.

Since the defeat of the Black Revolution of the Sixties, reaction has set in throughout this country. There has been more than a suggestion that African people, black people if you will, are simply marginal to human civilization and society.

This is a misstatement of things as they really are in the world. The truth of the matter is that not only are we *not* marginal to human society and civilization, but modern history on the planet Earth has been forged from the relationship that Africa has had with the rest of the world. In most instances that relationship has been against our will.

When we talk about being African people, we're not just trying to make ourselves feel good. We believe that it is key to understanding political economy in the whole world and the structure of the world economy as it exists today.

In the final analysis when we talk about what is happening to us here in Washington, D.C., or Brooklyn, New York, or in Trinidad or Jamaica or anywhere, we're talking about the world economy. It is an economy that was built on the enslavement of black people.

It is no coincidence that the African is oppressed everywhere you look on the planet. All over the world African people are suffering from hunger, from homelessness, from drugs in our communities.

We need to understand how it got to be this way. Why is it that when you walk down the street in Washington, D.C., today you see a black man, sometimes with his entire family, who has been robbed of his identity and his dignity, standing up asking for pennies? What the hell has happened to us? We have to come to grips with it and understand it. You must understand history to understand how it got this way.

There are only two explanations for the conditions African people face. The most familiar explanation that's been handed down to us teaches us that things are as they are in the world simply because white people are civilized, thrifty and live reasonable lives, while black people everywhere are just the opposite. We are less civilized, in fact, the least civilized of all the people on the planet Earth. We live riotous lives and don't save money. That's what they tell us.

The white nationalist, reactionary ruling class philosophers and pundits put out this explanation. Even some black nationalist, so-called leaders parrot the same line. They say that if we just stopped living so riotously and saved our money, then sometime, somehow our circumstances would be transformed.

That idea obviously comes from the white nationalist imperialists. It even comes from forces who call themselves Marxists,[1] who represent the highest expression of European progressive philosophical thought.

The imperialists and the Marxists get to the same conclusion in a different way. Marxists don't say that we are in this shape because of some inherent defect in African people. They say it is a consequence of some historical process that they don't quite understand. Somehow white people are now at the top of the process and African and other peoples are at the bottom.

Capitalism built on the backs of Africans

We say that this explanation is nonsense. We have a scientific explanation. What we are looking at, experiencing and living in is a world that was constructed on the enslavement of the African and the dispersal of Africans throughout the world.

Slavery is not simply something that happened a long time ago, has now ended and no longer has any relevance for us today. As a process slavery created a political economy that is a parasitic economy. It is an economy that, of necessity, must suck the blood of Africa and African people and the oppressed peoples of the world in order to survive.

Even Marx was forced to say that capitalist society and what he called the "veiled wage slavery" of Europe needed as its pedestal "slavery pure and simple" in what he called the "New World." In other words, the entire capitalist world rests on the pedestal of the enslavement of African and other peoples.

History bears this out. History shows that famine, poverty and disease chased Europeans out of Europe into the rest of the world. I know they don't teach this at the University of the District of Columbia and most of the universities that we attend. They tell us about the noble explorers that came out of Europe.

We are accused of being barbarians and vandals. All over the U.S. we see Africans—our children—being locked up. There are four times more Africans in prison in this country than there are in what they call South Africa right now. Sharon Pratt Dixon, the honorable mayor of Washington D.C., has come forward with a program that she calls a "struggle for values" that will result in locking up fourteen-year-old children as adults.

The truth of the matter is that the Vandals and Barbarians were northern Europeans. Check your history. They were people who made their living by robbing and looting other people. They weren't farmers or philosophers. They were thieves, looters, robbers, pirates, pillagers and the rest of it.

Disease and poverty chased the European out of Europe. He left with a vengeance and set out on an attack against the world. Europe enslaved Africa.

You must understand how profound this was because it is the most understated contradiction in all of human history. There has never occurred anything in the history of humanity that compares to the enslavement of the African. It was so profound that during some periods Africa was literally sur-rounded by ships that were there to take black people away.

By the year 1500, Portugal—which is now a backwater of Europe—had alone brought out more than seven hundred tons of gold from Africa.

We're talking about Europe going out, enslaving the African, and in the process creating colonies all throughout the Americas. The creation of colonies throughout the Americas meant that there was a world economy for the first time in history.

People had traded with each other in history before. Look at the evidence in southern Mexico and parts of Central America where you see the Olmec heads.[2] Africans had been to the Americas hundreds and thousands of years before the Europeans. We didn't come as looters. We didn't come to commit genocide against the populations of the Indigenous peoples.

There had been trade by peoples around the world before, but there had never been a single world economy. The forging of one world economy that linked up the entire world into a single process was a precondition for the rise of capitalism. Capitalism was born as a *world* system. It is not something that just happened in England or Holland.

Capitalism was born parasitic and it was born as white power in the world. When I say parasitic, I'm talking about something like a tapeworm. If you're lucky enough to have a job in the legal capitalist economy, you go out and work. If you're black, you work like a dog. Then you go buy food. Most of the time you buy the food in your own community, which means it's the worst food you can buy. Then you cook the food, chew the food and swallow it.

The tapeworm doesn't do anything. It just hooks on to your intestines. No matter how much you eat, you never get bigger. You just eat and eat and eat, but you're still withering away and don't understand why. The tapeworm gets bigger and bigger and bigger.

That's the relationship that Europe has imposed on us and the rest of the world. It is parasitic, like a tapeworm.

You can't get rid of this tapeworm by simply educating yourself—especially when you go to a tapeworm school to get your education. You can't vote the tapeworm out of you. The tapeworm will never leave of its own free will, because if the tapeworm lets go of your intestines, it will die. It needs you in order to live and it hangs on for dear life.

You have to take the right kind of medicine to get rid of a tapeworm. Then you can end up flushing it down the toilet. That's what we have to deal with, a tapeworm that's got to be flushed down the toilet of history.

Primitive accumulation of capital: our enslavement and our stolen resources

Sisters and Brothers, Comrades, this process of brigandage and piracy created the world that we live in. It isn't that they did everything only to Africa, is it? Look at where we are. We are standing on the land of the Indigenous people—who have almost been wiped out. We don't know how many millions of people were killed.

The Europeans came to the Americas. There were instances when the Indigenous people in this hemisphere, the so-called Indians, were forced to literally live in the gold and silver mines. They were sometimes in water up to their chest, bringing out gold and silver even as they died.

The gold and silver was brought to Europe and built factories there. There were so many resources stolen from the Africans, the Asians and the peoples of Latin America that it empowered a new European class. This new merchant class—the entrepreneurs— acquired more power than the old ruling class—the kings, the nobility. The entrepreneurs were able to overthrow the nobility of Europe and even made a war from North America that they called a "war of independence," the so-called American Revolution.

This whole process was called "primitive accumulation" by Karl Marx. He characterized it as an accumulation of capital that didn't require capitalist production for its starting point, but on the contrary was the starting point of capitalist production.

The ones who started capitalism had to have some loot from somewhere. It didn't rain from the sky. If people who are in this room are religious, you know there was no basis for God to give it to these creatures. It had to come from someplace, didn't it?

That is the question that Marx asked. He said, "We are therefore trapped in a vicious circle, unless we presuppose that there was an accumulation of capital that was not a consequence of capitalist production, but its starting point." What is the starting point? He said it was "the interment of the Indians in the mines of the Americas." It was "turning of Africa into a warren for the commercial hunting of black skins."

We're not just talking about Africa and what they did to the Indigenous population here. We are also talking about the fact that the British fought a war in 1841-42 against the people of China, to turn China into a nation of junkies. They called it the Opium War.[3] That was also a part of the primitive accumulation of capital that began with the enslavement of the African.

The French held Viet Nam as a drug colony for a hundred years.[4] There were more than three thousand legal opium dens in Viet Nam under the French. The French got most of their colonial booty from the drug trade. This is another example of the primitive accumulation of capital that we are talking about.

It is severe, Sisters and Brothers. This is something that we need to understand if we want to get a real grip on the question of political economy and our own oppression.

What is the national drink of the British? Tea. Where does tea come from? Sri Lanka and India. What is the national food of the Italians? Spaghetti or pasta. Where does it come from? China.

What do they claim is the national drink of this country? Coffee. Where does it come from? Brazil and West Africa.

Do you know that in Hershey, Pennsylvania they have ten years' worth of the world's supply of cocoa? Cocoa beans do not grow in Pennsylvania. They come from West Africa. Yet because of this parasitic relationship that we have with U.S. imperialism, in West Africa they can't even use cocoa beans. They end up buying Hershey Bars from Mr. Hershey in Pennsylvania.

That's the relationship that we are talking about. In this country when people eat food, they eat it off of plates that they call "china." Then when they've stuffed themselves so much with the fruit of the labor and the resources of the peoples of the world, they go back to Mr. Hershey to get an Ex-Lax in order to relieve themselves.

That's the world economy that we live with, Sisters and Brothers. Today in Africa, three percent or less of the trade is within Africa itself. Ninety-seven percent or more of what they call trade "with" Africa has the resources leaving Africa, going to Europe, going to North America and increasingly to Japan. That's the relationship. It is a parasitic relationship and we have to overturn it. If we don't overturn that relationship, we will die. It is that simple.

We are already dying. The question of life for Africans on the planet Earth is increasingly problematic. They are even making predictions that in the next century there will actually be a decline in the population of Africa due to AIDS[5] alone. That's the extent of the contradiction that we are confronted with.

No way out short of revolution

When we say we are Africans, we are talking about understanding that our struggle is *one struggle, as one people,* worldwide. We have to overturn this rotten relationship that we have with parasitic white power. Otherwise there is no future for us.

We've been told that our problem is that we just don't know how to do good job interviews. We hear this terrible, terrible slander about "self-destruction" which is especially directed at what they call African youth.

We are led to believe that the contradictions we are confronted with are no longer the consequence of African people being oppressed and exploited, but are something self-inflicted. They say we suffer from some kind of pathology.

"Babies having babies," they say. That is a biological impossibility. You don't have to go to Howard University to understand that babies do not have babies. It is something that you're not even supposed to think about. You're just supposed to have a gut reaction to it.

They say we're suffering from a pathology in our community that they sometimes describe as the "permanent underclass." They say this pathology results in African people not having the "work ethic," as they put it.

You and I are to believe today that they brought us here enslaved and we didn't have the "work ethic"! Maybe they thought that four hundred years later the Lakers were going to need some basketball players.

No, they brought us here precisely because of our work. If the truth be told, the white man doesn't even know the meaning of work. It is the African, historically in the modern world, who has defined what human labor is on the planet Earth.

This terrible slander and war are being waged especially against young African people.

In order to carry out their lives, young people are always looking toward the future. "What am I going to do tomorrow? What am I going to be?" Older people are generally looking backwards, reminiscing on how things used to be. It is the youth who are forward looking. That's almost a matter of biology. Generally that is where revolution is centered—in the youth.

Sisters and Brothers, I know that much of what I have to say is different from what we've been hearing in the last period in this country, and that is no accident. I'm a revolutionary. I don't believe there's any way out of this for black people—for Africans—short of revolution.

I didn't just come to this conclusion easily, because all human beings want to solve problems the easy way. I'm a human being too. I started off wanting to solve this problem the easy way. I got involved in demonstrations and other forms of protest, sure that the white man downtown just didn't know what was going on. I thought as soon as we let them know what was happening, they would come down and straighten things out.

I didn't know anything about history. I didn't know we had been doing this for four hundred years. No one had told me, "Son, neither praying nor preaching, nor singing nor dancing, nor anything else has helped us in all that time."

Now if our situation had just started last month, we could have said, "Maybe we can talk our way out of this." But four hundred years! You don't have to be a brain surgeon to recognize that four hundred years is too damn long to owe anybody anything!

Origins of the Black Revolution of the Sixties

We need to understand this last period of struggle in order to move forward. It's this last period of struggle that's been the sticking point for our movement and for our consciousness.

First, I'd like to say there was a revolution in this country, the Black Revolution of the Sixties. It was a revolution as serious as anything that has ever happened anywhere on the planet Earth. There was a Black Revolution in this country in the '60s that was defeated militarily.

In the African People's Socialist Party we call the Black Revolution of the Sixties the "dress rehearsal" for the real thing. You know what a dress rehearsal is, don't you? Everybody puts on their outfits, what they're going to wear when the real deal goes down. They go out and practice. It was a revolution that was a dress rehearsal for what is about to unfold right now, before our very eyes.

Some people denounce the Black Revolution of the Sixties. Some people repudiate it, including people who were key figures of the movement at the time. That's the highest expression of opportunism.

Black Revolution happened. That black revolution was at the center of all struggle, all social progress that happened in this country.

It was not peculiar to Washington, D.C., although it happened here too. Revolution was the main trend in the entire world. Africans were not the only ones struggling against imperialist white power in the 1960s. You remember the Tupamaros[6] in Uruguay and the courageous Vietnamese who chased Uncle Sam out of Viet Nam by the skin of his teeth? The Sandinistas[7] were a part of this process. Cuba led it off in the 1950s.

The struggle that was led by Mangaliso Sobukwe[8] in what they call South Africa was opened up in the 1960s with the campaign that resulted in the Sharpeville Massacre and the founding of the Pan Africanist Congress of Azania. The '60s were ripe with revolutionary struggle everywhere, and it was happening here in this country.

We need to understand why the Black Revolution of the Sixties happened, because some people say it was a consequence of good speeches made by Dr. Martin Luther King or other leaders. They say Hubert Humphrey,[11] Lyndon Baines Johnson and John Fitzgerald Kennedy were wonderful white men who had decided to assume responsibility for the white man's burden and to free us all.

The answer to the question of what happened in the 1960s is not to be found in individual leaders, good speeches and heroics. It is found by examining what was happening in the real world.

Preceding the Black Revolution of the Sixties by two decades was the second imperialist war. They call it World War II and say it was fought for democracy because they were fighting Hitler. Lynching was the national pastime in this country in the 1940s, but they were talking about fighting some fascist or Nazis in Germany and other places.

That is a joke, isn't it? Did you know that King Leopold of Belgium[9] killed from twelve to twenty million African people just in the Congo alone? Did you know that something like a hundred million African people died *just on the trip* from Africa to here?

Did you know that despite all of that, despite the near-genocide of an entire nation of Indigenous people, the word "genocide" did not even appear in the English language until the 1940s? In the 1940s there was an instance of white people doing to white people what white people had historically been doing to Africans and other people everywhere on the planet Earth. *That* was serious business.

When the Jews were Germans they did not protest what Germany was doing in Southwest Africa, now called Namibia. If they had protested what Germany was doing to Africa, maybe the Jews wouldn't have gone into the ovens in Germany. That's the real deal. Some people don't like us to say that, but that's how it happened. The Jews were good Germans when Germany was slaughtering Africans.

Did you know Leopold of Belgium used to cut off our hands, cut off our ears, cut off parts of our mouths in the Congo? There were literally mountains of hands, but there was no word "genocide." It didn't exist.

When you say that genocide is being committed against black people today, they look at you and chuckle, "Not genocide. Don't you think that's a bit strong?" They say that because the concept of genocide for anybody other than white people is unthinkable. Hitler's crime was not that he killed six million people, but that he killed six million *white* people, something that was never ever supposed to happen. The Jews act as a cover for reaction because they hold up "the" holocaust as the worst thing that's ever happened in human history, which is nonsense on its face.

The second imperialist war was a war to redivide the world. It was a war to redivide us: to redivide Africa, Asia and Latin America. Some of the European powers, for whatever reason, felt they hadn't gotten a big enough piece of the pie. They talk about Hitler being so bad, but Churchill[10] made Hitler look like a boy scout. Churchill presided over the British empire on which "the sun never set." Hitler was just trying to catch up.

The imperialists were struggling to redivide the world. That's why the war was fought. There were no good guys in that war. They were all thugs fighting to redivide the world.

U.S. emerges as leader of world capitalist production

As a consequence of that war, Europe was devastated. The only known use of atomic weapons in history was by the U.S. against Japan, during that war. The economic infrastructures of Europe and Japan were destroyed. That left the United States the most powerful country on the planet.

That meant that now not only was the United States untouched by the war itself, the U.S. also had access to colonies that had previously been controlled by Europe and Japan. Now as opposed to the British having sole control of Nigeria, the United States was in there as well. As opposed to the French having sole control in Cameroon, the United States was in there as well. All over the world the United States was in places where previously only European and Japanese imperialism had been located.

With all these raw materials coming into the United States, the U.S. was developing a tremendous productive capacity. One problem it was confronted with was where to get the labor power to transform raw materials into finished products. In the past they had gotten this labor power from Eastern Europe—that's where the word "honkey" came from.

I know you thought you made it up, but the word "honkey" was coined in this country around the period of the first imperialist war, when Europeans, in particular Hungarians, were brought over here and given jobs. Other white people were in competition for these jobs, so they came up with the term "honkey." I'm sorry, white folks.

The U.S. couldn't go to Eastern Europe to get the labor after the second imperialist war, because as an outcome of the second imperialist war, Eastern Europe was a part of the Soviet Bloc. Where were they going to get the workers from? Way down upon the Swanee River. Black workers were going to come from down South. That was the period when most of your parents left the South, during the '40s and the '50s. They moved up here to get jobs.

In order for the imperialists to have access to the black workers in the South, they had to change the relations of production in this country. In the North, they had what they called "capital intensive" capitalist production. This is production based on factories, machines and so on. In the South, production was "labor intensive," based on back-breaking labor by black people, digging ditches, laying ties, picking cotton, etc.

The question became how to get access to those black workers. The relations of production in this country were then codified by law in a way contrary to what the United States needed. Black people were prohibited from having certain kinds of jobs and from having the education that would make us capable of functioning in those jobs. We were prohibited from having the social mobility to leave the South.

In some instances you couldn't even leave town. They had us tied down to debt on the plantations. If you tried to leave, they put you in jail and then on the chain gang. Once you were on the chain gang, they rented you back to the joker who you were working for in the first place. This was the system of "convict leasing."

Those were the kinds of relations of production that existed in this country. This had to be busted up in order to get the labor force they needed. They had to make it possible for Africans to get into school. As everybody knows (notwithstanding all the nonsense they spout in the philosophy department here) education in every society is designed to make the people capable of producing. Education is also designed to provide an ideological underpinning for a given society.

That's why, a long time ago, my Daddy used to accuse me of being an educated fool. That's why you have white, white nationalists, and you have black, white nationalists! Education is designed to reproduce the philosophy and the ideology of the ruling class so that it continues to exist.

That's why they don't want Black Student Unions. That's why Kiamsha and the Pan African Student Union on this campus are having so many problems. They don't want us to break free of the process that the education imposes on us.

Alliance of black middle class and liberal white ruling class

During the period following the second imperialist war, people like Hubert Humphrey and a bunch of other so-called liberals started springing up. Liberalism is a response to an economic reality. Politics aren't anything but concentrated economics. They were liberals because they only wanted a limited revolution in this country, one that would only challenge the things that kept black people from working in factories. They wanted us to be able to leave the South to go and be exploited in the factories in the North.

That's what it was about. An alliance was forged in the 1950s between this liberal sector of the white ruling class— whose liberalism was defined by its need for a limited revolution in order to transform the relations of production—and the liberal sector of the black petty bourgeoisie, the black middle class, if you will.

They might not have had a meeting where they said, "Boss, I want to form an alliance," but it came down in the real world. The black petty bourgeoisie required change too. It wanted change that would allow it to integrate into the white capitalist system. That's why they raised the question of integration.

You know the question of integration didn't come from the poor oppressed masses. How could it have? A cracker was lynching or whupping you every time he could. Nigger-knocking was the national pastime, and the black middle class was walking around saying, "I want to be close to white people."

The black petty bourgeoisie was self-alienated. He hated himself. He was always running from himself. As soon as he could, he moved away from himself to get next to the white man. He had no confidence in the ability of African people to free ourselves and saw the only change and only progress as coming through the white man.

Malcolm X talked about it. He told you that it was the liberals who funded the Civil Rights Movement.

This alliance is also the basis for the Civil Rights Movement holding up philosophical nonviolence. People say, "No, there was philosophical nonviolence because Martin Luther King was a Christian." The Ku Klux Klan was Christian! I mean that literally.

It's funny, but it's a literal truth. So were all the white people, particularly in the South—Bible-thumping Christians.

Their Christianity didn't keep them from killing us. Our Christianity was supposed to offer us up to be killed.

They say the Civil Rights Movement was nonviolent "because Martin Luther King read books by Gandhi." The books Martin Luther King read by Gandhi were printed by white people who read the same books and they never talked about nonviolence!

The black Civil Rights Movement was based on nonviolence because it represented an alliance between the liberal sector of the black petty bourgeoisie and the liberal sector of the white ruling class. The white ruling class liberals who funded the black Civil Rights Movement were not about to fund a movement that might end up buying an Uzi or even a "Saturday night special." That's why it was based on philosophical nonviolence, to an extremely ridiculous degree.

I participated in the movement. When I say they taught nonviolence, I mean it. You couldn't go on a demonstration before first going to a class that taught you how to get beaten—as if we weren't already experts at getting beaten. They literally hit you and poured stuff on you to make sure that you weren't going to hit the white man back when he attacked you.

This was an alliance based on a need of the black petty bourgeoisie to integrate into the capitalist system. It was an alliance based on the reality that in many counties and cities throughout the South, the African was in the majority, and the black petty bourgeoisie was well-educated, generally speaking. They were undertakers. They were the high school principals. They were lawyers, doctors and the rest of it. Then there were these old backwoods, tobacco-chewing, redneck hillbillies who were the sheriffs, who ran the county and the city.

Those Negroes knew that if they had a chance, they could run that county, that city and that police department much better than that hillbilly.

They fought for you to have the right to vote so they could have the right to get elected. That happened in the real world. Can I prove it? Look around you. There are from seven to ten thousand black elected officials in this country today and African people are worse off in 1991 than we were in 1961. Not one of those black elected officials will say, "Feed, clothe and house my people." Everyone's got an excuse.

It's important to understand this because we get taught this old flim-flammery that passes itself off as history—fairy tales, Mother Goose stories.

This alliance came down in order to make a limited revolution happen, but they couldn't anticipate certain things. They couldn't anticipate that there was going to be an Ella Baker.[12] They couldn't anticipate old sharecropping Fannie Lou Hamer down in Mississippi. They couldn't anticipate Willie Ricks,[13] that poor boy in Chattanooga, Tennessee who turned out to be one of the best organizers that the world has ever seen. By 1964, and even earlier, things began to go wrong.

The black petty bourgeoisie was leading this movement, but it was never an easy leadership. They couldn't just say, "All right, I'm leading you to slaughter."

African working class rises up

Coming out of Harlem, New York, in this period was a magnificent giant who was critiquing this thing, saying all the time, "What kind of revolution is that when you're walking around singing 'We Shall Overcome'?" He said, "In a revolution, you don't do no singing because you're too busy swinging." He said that a revolution based on loving your enemy, a revolution to sit down on the toilet next to white folk, that's no revolution. Revolution is based on land. Revolution is based on bloodshed. There's never been a revolution without land and bloodshed. That's what Malcolm X kept saying—challenging everything, shaking up everything.

In 1964 the Student Nonviolent Coordinating Committee (SNCC) organized what they called Freedom Summer down in Mississippi. SNCC was an organization which in my view has yet to receive proper recognition for its historical significance. SNCC bridged the gap between the Civil Rights Movement proper and the revolutionary nationalism that was being espoused by Malcolm X. In fact, Malcolm met with them. He even set up study groups. He went down to Selma, Alabama, and he had Fannie Lou Hamer speak at rallies in Harlem.

SNCC organized the Mississippi Freedom Summer in 1964, among other things, in order to bring a whole lot of white folk down to Mississippi where so many black folk were getting killed by white people. Nobody was paying attention to that, so SNCC said, "Let's bring a lot of white folk from the North down to Mississippi, because that's going to bring the press with them. When these white folk start getting killed, then we'll have national and international attention on what's happening to our people."

The other thing that the Mississippi Freedom Summer was designed to do was to build the Mississippi Freedom Democratic Party, which organized black people to go to Atlantic City, New Jersey to the national convention of the Democratic party. There they challenged the Mississippi lynch mob Democrats for their right to represent the black people and all the people of Mississippi.

They had gotten an agreement from the liberals that the convention would seat the black folk and then throw out those lynch mob crackers. But when they got to Atlantic City, Lyndon Baines Johnson didn't do it.

Johnson is still held up by liberal Negroes as the great good guy president. Malcolm X said that the only difference between Johnson and any Mississippi white person was that a cracker in Mississippi spoke with a Mississippi accent and Johnson spoke with a Texas accent.

When the Africans got to Atlantic City, Johnson told them, "You must be out of your mind if you think I'm going to get rid of these white people and seat you all." He sent Hubert Humphrey, who sent his protege, Walter Mondale—who Jesse Jackal told you to vote for a few years ago. Mondale told Fannie Lou Hamer and the black people who had risked their lives to come to Atlantic City that he wasn't going to give them the Mississippi seats. At best they would get two nonvoting seats.

Fannie Lou Hamer replied, "We didn't come all this way for no two seats when everybody is tired." She turned around and led the Mississippi Freedom Democratic Party and black people, many of us, out of the Democratic party. That represented the beginning of the tremendous split that was coming down between the black movement in this country and the liberal sector of the white ruling class.

That split got aggravated even more because the Student Nonviolent Coordinating Committee left Atlantic City and went into Lowndes County, Alabama, where they built the Lowndes County Freedom Organization.

They were in Alabama, which was a lynch mob state—sort of like the state of New York, if you will. They said that we need to help black people have courage and so we need to have symbols that represent courage. They said that since the symbol of the Alabama Democratic party is a white rooster, we need a symbol that would put fear into the heart of that rooster and into everything else white in Alabama. They said, "Our symbol will be a black panther out of Africa." They built the Lowndes County

Freedom Organization that came to be known as the Black Panther Party.

After they built the Black Panther Party in the Lowndes County, Alabama, the first generation of Africans who had grown up as urban workers in Oakland, California, began to hear the message. In 1966, they said, "We will call ourselves the Black Panther Party." They put on blue turtle neck shirts and black leather jackets and picked up shotguns. They said, "Real political power comes from the barrel of the gun." That represented the final split between black people and the liberal sector of the white ruling class in this country.

Struggle for power, not against racism

Earlier in 1966, the Student Nonviolent Coordinating Committee had raised up the call for "Black Power," a slogan and demand that put us more closely in alignment with all the people of the world who were fighting against colonialism. It was an anti-colonial demand. It helped us to clear out some of the cobwebs in our head, some of which are still in the process of being cleared out.

We were just learning how silly it was for them to have us running around fighting against racism. "Racism" is based on the centrality of white people. It's a bit of self-aggrandizement by white people that says that you're supposed to just fight to integrate with them, which is nonsense.

Racism is the ideology of imperialism. Racism is the ideas in the brains of white people. What we had to fight for was power, so that no matter what was in the brains of white people, they couldn't mess with us. "Black power! Black power!" That was an anti-colonial demand.

No place on the planet do they demand that people fight against racism except for us. They didn't say to the Vietnamese, "You have got to fight against racism." They didn't say to the

Nicaraguans, "You have got to fight against racism." The only people they tell to fight against racism are Africans, both here and in Africa.

In other words, fight to make your enemy like you. Isn't that what they say? What's the solution to your problem? "Integrate." Look how illogical that is. If the solution is integration, the assumption is that there used to be a time when everybody was all together. Then somebody came and separated us from white people. So we can make it all better if we just integrate again.

That's nonsense! Our struggle is for power. They have us fighting to be accepted by a lyncher, by a slave master. If you are fighting to be accepted, you can't even hit your enemy back. They don't have to have the police. They can slap you upside the head and do anything they want. You can't do anything because if you hit him back, he won't like you and you won't be accepted.

You hear me? It's nothing but treachery. They have a mode of logic at work in our community that is a vicious terrible trap, treating us like we are not even human. Even a dog would bite somebody who continuously attacked it, but we couldn't do that because they taught us we were supposed to be fighting against racism.

They also saw the Black Power Movement develop and they assassinated Malcolm X because he had become the ideological vanguard of the movement.

The U.S. government murdered Malcolm. Anybody who believes the United States government didn't murder Malcolm X just got here from another planet.

In Birmingham, Alabama in 1963, African people rose up and started fighting back. This was evidence that we were breaking away from the control of the black petty bourgeoisie. In Jacksonville, Florida, Africans started physically fighting back.

In Watts in Los Angeles, California in 1965, under the slogan "Burn, baby, burn," African people burnt the joint down.

They sent in Sick Gregory—you call him Dick Gregory[14]—to try to get the black folk to go home and be nonviolent, and the people shot him.

The government dragged Dick Gregory out of Watts and sent in Martin Luther King, Jr. He told black folk that you have to be nonviolent and the people booed him off the platform. Black folk were tired of turning the other cheek. They said, "The next time I turn another cheek, it's going to be in the process of executing a left hook."

The Black Panther Party sprang up and the movement began to get away from their control.

Counterinsurgency against African people in the U.S.

By 1967, the federal government consolidated its war of terror against our people and our movement into a program called the Counterintelligence Program or COINTELPRO. It was under the leadership of the FBI. It was the creation of a man named William Sullivan.

COINTELPRO was quite clear in its goals. Its number one goal was to "prevent the rise of a black messiah" who could electrify the masses of African people. It said Malcolm could have been the messiah if he hadn't already been killed. You can get copies of the COINTELPRO papers, probably right here at the library.

They said Dr. Martin Luther King could be such a force should he ever abandon his obedience to the white liberal philosophy of nonviolence. Not long after that, in 1967, Martin Luther King made a speech at Riverside Church in New York City where he publicly questioned his ability to continue to adhere to the philosophy of nonviolence. He said, "I have problems talking to black people about nonviolence when young black men and women are coming to me saying, 'Dr. King, how can you tell us to be nonviolent, as violent as America is being in Viet Nam?'"[15]

In 1968, the sanitation workers in Memphis, Tennessee, went out on strike. Usually the black preachers and the black petty bourgeoisie could simply come out and tell the workers what to do, when to march and how to march. Now it was black workers who were saying, "Martin, come down to Memphis to walk with the black workers." As a consequence of this and other actions, along with the serious contradictions which were boiling over inside this country as African people achieved revolutionary consciousness, Martin Luther King violated the alliance that was established between the liberal white ruling class and the liberal sector of the black petty bourgeoisie.

He was executed for it on April 4, 1968. Africans all over this country and in many places around the world rose up. It was so serious we burned Washington, D.C. down. They put tanks around the White People's House here because they thought we were better organized than we were.

The movement continued to try to move forward, but a vicious war had been initiated. That war—COINTELPRO—resulted in black people being murdered all over this country. We do not know how many were killed. We know they killed more than thirty members of the Black Panther Party alone.

We know that John Mitchell, who was the attorney general of the United States, had declared that the Black Panther Party would be destroyed before the end of 1969. In that year alone, twenty-seven members of the Black Panther Party were murdered and seven hundred members were arrested in this country.

The Black Panther Party had a newspaper that came out every week. It had a distribution of a quarter of a million, so we could keep on top of what was going on. The bourgeois media would tell us what was happening with the Black Panther Party every time they killed a Panther or arrested one.

We don't know how many others were killed or arrested. Revolutionary organizations, small organizations, community organizations were formed all over this country, and many of their members are still locked up.

We do know about some of them. Sundiata Acoli[16] is a giant; he had graduated into what was supposed to be the black petty bourgeoisie but committed revolutionary suicide, class suicide. He left the aspirations of the black petty bourgeoisie and joined the working class. He became a member of the Black Panther Party and then the Black Liberation Army, and he fought to free black people.

He's been locked up now for as long as Nelson Mandela was locked up in what they call South Africa. You don't see any of these white or black liberals walking around saying, "Free Sundiata Acoli! Free Geronimo Pratt! Free Albert Nuh Washington! Free Anthony Bottom! Free all those folk who've been locked up for fighting for black freedom!"[17]

They locked up a lot of us. By 1969, the war against our movement was going full-fledged.

I want you to reflect on this, Sisters and Brothers, because twenty-two years ago yesterday, the final blow against the movement occurred. On December 4, 1969, the FBI, after having first drugged Fred Hampton[18] to make sure that he was helpless in his bed, initiated a predawn raid. They knocked on the door and somebody said, "Who's there?" "Tommy." "Tommy who?" "Tommy gun."

They shot their way in. The first round killed Mark Clark[19] who was sitting at the door on security with a shotgun across his lap. In his death throes he pulled the trigger and a round from his shotgun went off into the ceiling. That was the only round that was fired by the Black Panther Party. The police rushed in shooting.

Fred Hampton lay in bed with his eighteen-year-old wife who was eight and a half months pregnant. She talks about how she could feel the bed vibrating from the rounds which were being fired into it. She talks about how most of the rounds that came were directed at the side of the bed where Fred slept.

After the firing stopped they came and dragged Fred's wife out of the bed by her hair—eight and a half months pregnant in the December Chicago winter. They stuck a gun to her swollen belly and said, "What do you know? We got a broad here." Then they took her out of the room. She heard voices coming from the bedroom saying, "He'll barely make it." Then she heard two shots and somebody said, "He's good and dead now."

That was the murder of Fred Hampton, who at twenty-one years of age had organized the largest chapter of the Black Panther Party in the country, initiated the Free Breakfast for School Children Program and set up the Free Sickle Cell Anemia Testing Program for the Black Panther Party. He was one of the few Panther leaders who at that point was not in prison or chased into exile. They destroyed the Black Panther Party with the assassination of Fred Hampton and for all practical purposes they broke the back of the Black Revolution of the Sixties.

Drug economy imposed on African community

After the defeat of the Black Revolution, they wanted to make sure that African people would never, never rise up again. They imposed on our community not a drug problem, Sisters and Brothers. A drug *economy* has been imposed on our community.

The same white ruling class that will not give a job to an African in the legal capitalist economy has imposed an illegal capitalist economy on our community. Now if somebody's paying the slumlord, they're paying him with dope money. Much of the money that sends our children to school is dope money.

They permeate our community with a drug economy. It destabilizes the community, so that Africans are no longer acting like Africans, but acting like white people. Historically we think and act collectively. You're always thinking about the other fellow. That's your problem.

When there is a drug problem in the community, the African doesn't care about anybody—not about his neighbor, his sisters, brothers, cousin, his mama—nobody but another hit. This drug economy serves to prevent us from achieving revolutionary consciousness.

To have revolutionary consciousness you have to have the long view. You've got to be able to think and predict what you want to be doing five or ten years from now, well beyond the next fifteen minutes when you've got to have another hit.

Finally, the drugs provide the political justification for an ongoing terroristic military attack against the black community and the abrogation and nullification of every national democratic right that we fought and died for in this country in the 1950s.

All over this country right now they have transformed housing projects into concentration camps, similar to what they did in Viet Nam and Occupied Zimbabwe, which they called "Rhodesia." Housing projects are surrounded with barbed wire fences. In many instances you have to carry passes to go into a housing project to see your grandmama.

In Chicago, in some projects you even have to go through eye scans to get in. In some of the high rises, it's not good enough just to have a pass to get in. You have to have a pass to go from floor to floor.

In Washington, D.C., they carried out a public coup. They took away state power from the thugs you all elected. They negated the black people's vote and sent in all these other thugs, all these new military organizations.

They have highly militarized organizations in African communities all over this country. In a little city called St. Petersburg, Florida, they call this the "Green Team," this romantic name. They wear ski masks, military outfits, camouflage and they carry automatic weapons. In Clearwater, Florida, they call them the "Ninjas." They wear black and hoods over their faces and carry automatic weapons. In Baltimore, it's the "Quick Response Team." In Oakland it's the "Drug Task Force."

In places like Oakland, California they kick the people's doors down and make men and women undergo body cavity searches in the name of looking for drugs. This is designed to humiliate and destroy the morale of the population, to keep you always questioning your own authenticity as a human being.

This war is happening all over the country and it is being justified in the name of the so-called "war on drugs" or "war against gangs."

White power in black face

Another part of this counterinsurgency was the initiation by Richard Milhous Nixon of "black capitalism." It was a part of creating a buffer between the African masses and the white ruling class. It functions also as an ideological transmission line of ruling class white nationalist values into our community.

In so many instances across this country the black petty bourgeoisie functions as a neocolonial traitor sector. We say neocolonialism; some people call it Negro colonialism. It is white power in black face. It is the same tactic they have used against oppressed peoples all over the world.

The struggle against neocolonialism is the final struggle that we are involved in. It is the struggle that the people in Iran were involved in when they overthrew the Shah who was put in power in 1954 by the CIA—by Kermit Roosevelt in particular, the son of Franklin D. Roosevelt whom you all love so much, the great liberal. It was neocolonialism that Fidel Castro overthrew in Cuba when he got rid of Batista, that old Uncle Tom Cuban sellout lick-spittle *gusano* worm that Uncle Sam had put in power.

It is the final struggle. As Kwame Nkrumah[20] said, neocolonialism is the last stage of imperialism. When neocolonialism is destroyed, the last thing standing between us and white power has been removed and then we get down to the real deal.

This neocolonial power acts as a cover for imperialism. Marion Barry, the former mayor of Washington D.C., was a thug. Marion Barry had forty-six thousand black people arrested in a two-year period in the so-called war against drugs. Only fifteen hundred of the forty-six thousand ever went to court. His replacement Sharon Pratt Dixon is a thug. She's going to lock up your children—fourteen-year-olds—as felons.

We have a problem, Sisters and Brothers. The brothers and sisters in the projects are hungry, starving and without leadership. The leadership has been killed.

Negroes are talking about how they are scared of the brothers and the rest of it, but the brothers are starving. They are without leadership or anything else, and we're supposed to say they are the scum. I want to tell you, those Negroes downtown are the scum. The mayors are the scum in the community. Those who have sold out black people are the scum.

I'll say it over and over and over again. Those are the thugs in their evening clothes, in their fine wear and their chauffeured limousines. They have deserted our community and turned us over to the foul embrace of a CIA-president and U.S. white power. They have no faith in the masses. It's not just because Wilson Goode[21] dropped a bomb on the black community. It's because the neocolonialists don't say, "Black people are starving." You know they're starving. I know they're starving. Those scum have better education than we do, so they know black people are starving. But they never say, "Feed and clothe and house my people."

Black politicians say they represent progress, but they don't represent progress. They represent a revolution that has been hijacked.

There you are: there's a whole war against the black community that functions as a part of a counterinsurgency to make sure that we shall never rise up again. But the Black Revolution still lives!

When they shot up the house in Chicago on December 4, 1969 and killed Fred Hampton, it was designed to terrorize not only the remaining members of the Black Panther Party in the city of Chicago, but all black folk, all over this country. They wanted to let you know what they'll do to you if you ever think about revolution.

They started off attacking the leadership and the organizations. Once they had done that, they attacked the masses of people to make sure revolution doesn't happen again. Now we are building the National People's Democratic Uhuru Movement (NPDUM)[22] to fight for and defend our national democratic rights.

Organize to stop the war against the African community

Sisters and Brothers, we held the founding convention of the National People's Democratic Uhuru Movement in Chicago, Illinois, on April 6 of this year, the anniversary of the assassination of Li'l Bobby Hutton.

People forget about Li'l Bobby Hutton. Martin Luther King was killed on April 4, 1968. Two days later Bobby Hutton, a seventeen-year-old Black Panther, was mowed down by police in Oakland, California.

NPDUM is a mass organization based on democratic rights, just like the Civil Rights Movement was based on democratic rights. NPDUM is open to anybody of any nationality just like the Civil Rights Movement was.

There are differences, however. Unlike the democratic struggle of the 1950s and '60s that held up integration as the highest expression of democracy, NPDUM holds up self-determination as the highest expression of democracy.

We built the National People's Democratic Uhuru Movement under the leadership of the African People's Socialist Party, a revolutionary organization. All mass organizations and movements are under the leadership of some sector of society whether they know it or not. This one comes from a revolutionary party that has the intention of destroying U.S. imperialism forever.

We see this counterinsurgency as the main stumbling block standing between us and a full-fledged revolutionary movement. In order for the revolution to move forward, we have to get beyond this counterinsurgency that is wreaking havoc in our communities.

Sisters and Brothers, I know people in our communities are saying we need more police. The people are scared because they aren't organized. I want to tell you that there is no tradition of democracy in this country for black people, and that it would be a terrible thing to respond to our situation in that fashion. That is just like saying, "Take away my democratic rights."

Sisters and Brothers, people were lynched just to have the right to vote and walk down the streets. Now a Ku Klux Klan member is running for president[23] with the same platform as James Earl Carter, Ronald Wilson Reagan and George Herbert Walker Bush. The Republican who was just elected governor of Mississippi got elected in part because he promised to challenge and overturn the Voting Rights Bill that gave you the right to vote.

These are the times that we live in. We cannot allow them to take away our right to democracy. We need the democratic space in order to make the revolution.

You see television programs like "Cops," where police come and kick your door down. These prostitutes who call themselves news reporters are taking pictures, watching black people being knocked to the ground and guns stuck to our heads without regard for warrants, rights or anything else.

We can't go for that. We have to fight back. We have to build a militant movement.

We must defeat the counterinsurgency so that we can have the democratic space to make this Revolution. We built the National People's Democratic Uhuru Movement and we call on you to join it.

You've got to take a stand because we have to go beyond this point of simply talking about things. We have to organize black people! For the children of Africa, you must join the Revolution led by the Party of the African working class.

Uhuru!

1 Followers of Karl Marx, 1818–1893, the German philosopher, political economist and revolutionary, author of the *Communist Manifesto, Capital* and many other theoretical works.

2 The Olmec were a highly advanced civilization of African people living in Mexico as early as 1300 BC. The earliest civilization in Meso-America, the Olmec left massive stone heads with distinctly African features, along with calendars, mathematical documents, hieroglyphic writing and other art and artifacts.

3 In the early nineteenth century, Britain, the biggest drug cartel in history, began forcing tons of opium on the Chinese people, creating massive addiction among the population and extracting enormous wealth for the British. The Chinese resisted this imposition of drugs in what is called the Opium Wars of 1840–42 and 1856–60 when the British navy, built off the trade in African people, overpowered China.

4 One third of France's colonial revenues came from the opium trade imposed on the French colony of Viet Nam, where the French in 1918 had 1,512 dens and 3,098 retail shops for the sale of opium.

5 Acquired Immune Deficiency Syndrome, a virus affecting up to a hundred million people on the Continent of Africa alone. Many believe the AIDS virus was created by the U.S. government.

6 The Tupamaros National Liberation Army was active in Uruguay in the 1960s.

7 The Sandinista National Liberation Front led the revolutionary struggle to overturn the U.S.-backed regime of General Anastasio Somoza in Nicaragua, winning victory in 1979.

8 Robert Mangaliso Sobukwe, 1924–1978, helped found and lead the Pan Africanist Congress of Azania that led the anti-colonial struggle in South Africa. He died in prison.

9 Leopold was king of Belgium from 1865 to 1909. He was the sole owner of the Congo Free State, a private project undertaken to extract rubber and ivory which relied on slavery and was responsible for the slaughter of millions of Africans.

10 Winston Churchill, British prime minister 1940-45.

11 Hubert Humphrey was the vice president under the presidency of Lyndon Baines Johnson, 1964–1968, and the 1968 Democratic party candidate

12 Ella Baker was a key leader of the Civil Rights Movement and a founder of SNCC (Student Nonviolent Coordinating Committee).

13 Fannie Lou Hamer and Willie Ricks were outstanding members of SNCC. Ricks coined the demand "Black Power!"

14 Dick Gregory was an African comedian and Civil Rights activist of that time.

15 The actual words of Dr. Martin Luther King's "Beyond Viet Nam" speech given at Riverside Church in New York City on April 4, 1967 are:
"As I have walked among the desperate, rejected, and angry young men, I have told them that Molotov cocktails and rifles would not solve their problems. I have tried to offer them my deepest compassion while maintaining my conviction that social change comes most meaningfully through nonviolent action. But they asked, and rightly so, 'What about Viet Nam?' They asked if our own nation wasn't using massive doses of violence to solve its problems, to bring about the changes it wanted. Their questions hit home, and I knew that I could never again raise my voice against the violence of the oppressed in the ghettos without having first spoken clearly to the greatest purveyor of violence in the world today: my own government."

16 Sundiata Acoli was a Black Panther Party member who was arrested on the New Jersey turnpike in 1973 along with Assata Shakur. He is serving a sentence of life plus thirty years.

17 Geronimo Pratt is a former Black Panther Party member who was released from prison after twenty-seven years as a political prisoner, in 1997. Anthony Jalil Bottom is a former Black Panther who has served over twenty-five years as a political prisoner. Political prisoner Albert Nuh Washington died in prison on April 28, 2002.

18 Fred Hampton was the brilliant young Chairman of the Illinois chapter of the Black Panther Party who was killed by the FBI and Chicago police department on December 4, 1969.

19 Mark Clark, Black Panther Leader from Peoria, Illinois was twenty-two when he was assassinated in Chicago along with Fred Hampton by FBI and police on December 4, 1969.

20 Kwame Nkrumah, 1909–1972, was the first president of independent Ghana from 1957 until a U.S.-backed coup overthrew his government in 1966. Nkrumah was the outstanding leader of a movement for one united and liberated Africa "under an All-African socialist government."

21 Wilson Goode was the black mayor of Philadelphia, PA who had a bomb dropped on the home of members of the MOVE organization on May 13, 1985, killing five adults and six children and burning down sixty-one homes in the surrounding African community.

22 Now called the International People's Democratic Uhuru Movement (InPDUM).

23 Ku Klux Klan member David Duke ran for U.S. president in 1988.

Los pueblos unidos
Long live the unity of the African and Mexican-Indigenous peoples!

Chairman Omali gave the following solidarity statement from the African People's Socialist Party to the National Raza Unity Conference organized by the National Chicano Moratorium Committee. The Conference was held at San Diego City College on Sunday August 11, 1996, the same day that the 1996 Republican National Convention was taking place in San Diego.

The African People's Socialist Party has had a deep working relationship with the San Diego-based Unión del Barrio, one of the founding members of the Chicano Moratorium Committee, since the 1980s.

Uhuru Compañeros y Compañeras!

To the conveners of this important conference I would like to express a deep and profound appreciation for being able to share this meeting with you.

From the Central Committee of the African People's Socialist Party, I'm able to say that we believe that this meeting happening here today is the most important gathering taking place in this country right now. Possibly it is one of the most important gatherings happening in the world today.

I do not say this lightly, because we understand that U.S. imperialism is responsible for the suffering and poverty of all the peoples everywhere on the planet Earth. If we are doing something here today to challenge the ability of imperialism to starve and brutalize the people, then here—in the belly of the

55

beast—is the most important meeting happening in the world. [Applause]

Compañeros y Compañeras, it is very easy for us in the African People's Socialist Party to unite with this conference. We offer our solidarity because, from our perspective, the foundation of U.S. imperialism is the exploitation and the oppression of our peoples.

Until the seventeenth century there was no such thing as "Europe" or the "European." There was no such thing as the "white man." Europe and Europeans originate from an area that was nothing more than a land of warring tribes and kingdoms, eventually becoming the power that Europe now represents. Europe consolidated its power by uniting its people as a part of the process of genocide, colonization, rape and plunder of the planet!

Compañeras y Compañeros, we recognize that this land is the land of the Indigenous people, of the Indio-Mexicano people![1] [Applause] We recognize that there could be no U.S. imperialism without the theft of this land, without the domination of Indio-Mexicano people. We understand that the political economy of the world—not only of America—has its origin in the theft of the land of the Indio-Mexicano people here, the enslavement of Africans—the so-called slave trade—and the domination of the other peoples around the world.

Therefore, we can state that we have absolute solidarity with this meeting in opposition to the Republican party convention. More than that, we stand with you in opposition to the Democratic party. [Applause] More than that, we stand with you in opposition to U.S. imperialism and white power. Here and throughout the world, we recognize that U.S. imperialism must be defeated! [Applause]

I understand there was another meeting yesterday where people, including a whole lot of African people, expressed their concern that the Republican party doesn't advocate multicultur-alism! [Laughter] Of course, people in this room understand that the whole concept of multiculturalism is a defensive fallback by white power, an attempt at a concession. Imperialism clearly rec-ognizes that the Mexican and the African people are coming to take back our land and to take back our resources. [Applause]

I'm told that these liberal organizations that met yesterday want to put together some demands and take them to the Repub-lican party, as well as to the Democratic party. While in general there is nothing wrong with taking demands to the Republicans and the Democrats, we support your conference today, precisely, because we understand that our fate does not lie with either the Democratic or the Republican parties, but with the oppressed peoples of the world. Therefore, our responsibility is to organize our people. [Applause]

Compañeros y Compañeras, we stand here in solidarity with you because we know that you understand—just as we have come to understand—that imperialism has many manifesta-tions. The struggle we have with the schools, with Proposition 187,[2] with the various attacks at the border, are simply profound manifestations of the loss of self-determination by our peoples. We know that our solution does not lie in simply solving the problem at the border or in simply getting Prop. 187 repealed, although we should struggle against those things. In the final analysis, however, there shall be no peace until we have self-determination—until we are self-governing people once again. [Roaring applause]

We know that we are living in a crucial time in history. What a magnificent time to be alive! Look all around you. Here you have U.S. president Clinton, an Arkansas cracker...[Applause] That's all he is. He's an Arkansas cracker with a Tennessee cracker as the vice president! Here they are obviously attacking our peoples, and you know Africans and Mexicans are supposed to be Democrats, right? Yet, it was Clinton who, among other things, said he was going to put 100,000 new policemen in this country. And where were they going to be? In the colonies of the African communities and the Mexicano barrios!

It was Clinton who pushed forth the "Crime Bill" that threatens our very existence and the freedom of our people. The Crime Bill threatens the African community, because by the year 2000, the majority of men of childbearing age in the African community will be in prison, or tied to the prison system in some way or another.

It was Clinton who put forth the notion that, after two years, women should be kicked off what they call "welfare." Of course you and I understand the slander when they talk about us being on welfare. The truth of the matter is that white power, and white people have lived off the welfare of the Mexicans and the Africans for the last five hundred years. [Roaring applause]

So here you have Clinton and the Democratic party making these terrible attacks on the rights and the life capacity of our people on the one hand, and then of course you have the Republican party doing the same thing. So, here you have every politician in the country running their campaigns against the Mexicans and the Africans. The basic policy of the Clinton government has been an anti-Mexican, anti-African policy. The Republicans swept into power in the congress in the 1994 midterm elections simply because they outdid the Democrats in their anti-Mexican and anti-African capacity. [Applause]

How did the Republicans get in power? There was no coup in Washington D.C. The fact of the matter is that the Republican congress is in power because white people voted them in power, because they were anti-black, anti-Mexican and against all the oppressed peoples of the world. That is the truth of the matter. [Applause]

But, Compañeros y Compañeras, we from the African

People's Socialist Party can stand here in solidarity with you, with the certainty that our time has come. All you have to do is look around the world. It is clear that a page has been turned in human history. Imperialism is in a profound crisis.

For the first time in more than fifty years you see white people killing and shooting other white people in what they call Eastern Europe, where more than two hundred fifty thousand people have killed each other. You don't see the bodies in the newspapers. They don't show pictures of the swollen dead bodies lying on the ground in the newspapers or on television, like you would see if it were Somalia or Rwanda.

They show us pictures of death and suffering from Somalia and Rwanda and Mexico and places like that because they want to demoralize us, and let the white people feel superior. They don't show us all the dead people in Eastern Europe because they don't want to demoralize the white people. They don't want to give us the idea that white people can die just like anybody else! [Roaring applause]

How does this crisis of imperialism manifest itself? It manifests itself in Europe just like it manifests itself here in North America. They can't frighten us. It is they who are afraid. That's why they want tanks at the border between Mexico and the U.S. You don't have a confident ruling class; you have some terrified wimps who are concerned with what's going to come out of the barrios and out of the colonies. [Applause]

No more Africans from Haiti, no more Mexicans coming across an artificial border! There have been too many of us already. They know that sooner or later our consciousness will catch up with the objective reality that we are living. They know that ultimately we will rise up and destroy imperialism once and for all. [Loud cheers and applause]

Compañeras y Compañeros, again, I really want to express a deep appreciation for being able to be here. You know, we've gotten pretty good at being able to criticize imperialism. We can tell you everything that's wrong with imperialism. Today, we have to begin to help the masses visualize the future.

Our future is not to be found inside the Democratic or Republican parties. Our future is not to be found integrating into America. The future for our people involves the total destruction of an imperialist white power that can only live by sucking the blood of our people. Our future will be found in a totally liberated Aztlán and México, and a totally liberated Africa and African people throughout the world.

I have a deep and profound appreciation for this meeting. Listen, Compas, we come from a small organization and in many ways, the views that I hold today are minority views. They haven't always been minority views. Next week they won't be minority views. If not next week then next month, if not next month then next year, because clearly the masses of African people shall wake up and we shall win!

One of the things imperialism tries to do to us all the time is crush our confidence and the capacity for our own leadership. They constantly attack our ability to even see ourselves as a free people. We haven't been free for so long that we no longer know what it is to be free. Sometimes we're afraid of the idea. Do you know what I'm saying? [Applause]

This is a profoundly important meeting. My observations are that something very serious is happening in the Mexican community here. If imperialism were wise, it would be quaking in its boots, because oppressed peoples will come to power. This meeting is part of the path to liberation.

All Power to the people!
Chicano power to the Chicano people!
Uhuru! [Cheers and a standing ovation]

1 From the Principles of Unity of Unión del Barrio: "As Indigenous people, we recognize and uphold the right to self-determination of all Indigenous nations of the Americas. We (Mexicanos and other Indigenous people) are collectively the survivors of the genocidal onslaught of European colonization. We are bound by a common history, culture, struggle, and destiny. Central to our struggle is the principled unification of our forces as Indigenous people to end all manifestations of colonization, create a true unity of all Indigenous nations and peoples, and return the land to its rightful owners. We understand that liberation of Mexicanos must, and will, be tied to the liberation of all Indigenous people." Hence the term Indio-Mexicano.

2 Proposition 187 was a white nationalist California ballot initiative, officially called the "Illegal Aliens Measure," that won the vote in 1994. It denied health care, social services and education to the so-called undocumented Mexican workers crossing the illegitimate U.S. border to gain access to their own stolen land and resources.

The legacy of Che Guevara
Two, three, many Viet Nams!

In this speech, Chairman Omali Yeshitela addressed the Sunday African community meeting at the Uhuru House in St. Petersburg, Florida on October 4, 1997. This presentation salutes the thirtieth anniversary of the assassination of Guevara by CIA forces in Bolivia on October 9, 1967. It expresses the unity of African people with the struggling peoples throughout the Americas.

I think it's really important for us to understand Che Guevara.

While all of us understand that we are part of the African Revolution, the reality is that we are also a part of the Revolution of the Americas. Throughout the Americas there are oppressed people. Latin America, South America, Central America, the U.S. and the area called Canada are referred to by most people as the "Americas."

As African people in the U.S., we are part of the Revolution of the Americas. We are part of the revolutionary process that hungry, poor, oppressed and brutalized people—the hated, despised and spat-upon people—all over the world are trying to make. That is particularly true here in what is called the Americas.

There are places in Latin America that have been historically and contemptuously referred to as "banana dictatorships" by political pundits in this country. Most of these countries were controlled by United Fruit Company or some other U.S. corporation that saw them only as plantations where they had cheap labor that could produce fruit.

The economy of every country in Latin America was always an "export economy." You know what we mean by an export economy? That means that everything you produce is for somebody somewhere else. It's not for you. It's exported.

The people can't produce anything for themselves. They produce what the imperialists—white power—want them to produce. They produce what United Fruit Company wants them to produce—bananas and other fruit. They can't produce collard greens and lima beans. They can't produce products for themselves—automobiles or anything like that.

How do they get the lima beans and the collard greens and automobiles that they want? They are forced to pay exorbitant prices to buy them from the U.S.

In order to do that they have to have what is called "hard currency." That means money from an imperialist power such as the U.S. It means the dollar. How do they get the dollars to buy collard greens and automobiles that they want? They have to sell bananas to Uncle Sam at a depressed price.

Any time a leader comes along who says he wants to take control of his or her own country to produce for the people who live in the country, to free the country from United Fruit and the United States Marines, you know what happens? The CIA or some other instrument of U.S. foreign policy comes in, assassinates the leaders and overthrows the government. Then, there they are growing bananas all over again. That's why these countries are referred to as "banana republics."

For the U.S., Cuba was just a place for sugar cane and cheap labor to make sugar. The sugar was owned by U.S. corporations.

Certain kinds of gambling and prostitution were illegal here in the United States, but to make it convenient, they allowed the Mafia and several corporations to turn Cuba into a brothel for wealthy Americans. White people could leave here, go to Cuba and buy Cuban women. They could use the country as a place for gambling and all the vices that people find so hateful. That's what they went to Cuba to do.

Che symbolizes true revolutionary spirit

The Cuban Revolution disrupted all of that.[1] That's why the U.S. imperialists hate Cuba. Cuba became an example for all the world's poor people who said, "If Cuba can do it, we can do it."

Nobody symbolized the struggle of poor people against a powerful Yankee empire to the north more than Che Guevara. Che was a revolutionary, an extraordinary revolutionary, a leader in Cuba's revolution who fought in other countries as well.

Why is everybody suddenly interested in Che Guevara? The bourgeoisie is making a Che Guevara beer. There are books out on Che. There are t-shirts and posters. Che is everywhere. People are asking, "Why all of a sudden is everybody into Che?"

People love Che because he represented principle. Che stood above all the people who sell their souls to imperialism. He represented the ability of the poor and the oppressed people all over the world to fight against imperialism.

He was noncompromising, a man of principle. Even the bourgeoisie and middle class Americans have to look up to him. When I say "Americans," you know I'm talking about white people.

They can't look to Clinton,[2] who is ducking an indictment and has a reputation that nobody would brag about. Nobody would want their child to grow up and be what William Jefferson Clinton seems to be about.

They don't have anybody to look up to. Che Guevara is the one. They hated him when he was alive, but he was so significant that even the people who captured him held him in awe. Some of the people who participated in capturing Che Guevara have written books about him.

Che was asthmatic. He was a very interesting soldier, a soldier for the people, a soldier for the poor and oppressed. Che said, among other things, "At the risk of sounding ridiculous, revolutionaries are motivated by great feelings of love." This exemplifies Che and exemplifies revolution as well. Who would go up against the death that everybody knows U.S. imperialism can bring? Why would you do that? You have to have a great capacity for love for the people.

Che also said, "It's not a matter of well-wishing, but sharing the very same fate whether in victory or in death." He was probably talking to liberals and white leftists, because they are always wishing us well and "good luck."

When you look for an ally you look for somebody who's going to share the fate that you have to share. We are always skeptical of people who say they are going to be our friends. They are our friends from way over there, but they are never willing to share the fate of the oppressed. In fact, in the '60s when the struggle came down, most of the white "revolutionaries" cut their hair and got jobs in their uncle's pharmacy or their cousin's stock brokerage firm or something to that effect.

Che Guevara was a tremendous human being. He raised up the concept of the "New Man," one who could be committed to a life based on principle, a life struggling against injustices.

When Fidel Castro and the Cuban delegation came to the U.S. to speak before the United Nations, they made a conscious political decision to stay in Harlem. It was a statement of solidarity with African people.

You should know that Che Guevara armed forces to try to help us make the revolution in Africa. Che was with Kabila[3] in the struggle in Congo. Che characterized Kabila as a café revolutionary. Kabila is the person who just came to power in what used to be called Zaire and is now called the Republic of the Congo.

There is a reactionary Cuban, Felix Rodriguez, who brags about wearing Che's watch on his arm. Rodriguez was working for the CIA when they killed Che. He said that he's the one who killed him. Today he still wears Che's watch.

It is my desire to live long enough to see the revolutionary process happen rapidly enough that we will be able to take that watch off his arm, even if it means taking off his arm.

When they murdered Che, he was a fearful thing for them. They cut his hands off so that they could ship them back to check his fingerprints and make sure it was him. They didn't want to leave anything unchecked because the legend of Che Guevara was similar to that of Nat Turner.[4]

Nat Turner was captured and murdered in the Tidewater area of Virginia. White people all over the South were having heart attacks from their fear of Nat Turner. Even after Nat Turner had been killed, there could be a rumor that Nat Turner was in town and a white slave owner would fall dead on the spot.

The same thing was true with Che Guevara. The legend of Che Guevara haunted the whole of Latin America, so they wanted to make sure that he was dead. They cut off his hands and they said they sent them to the regime in Bolivia. Of course they said Bolivia, but I bet they sent those hands to the CIA.

Their fear was such that they buried Che's body and would not tell anybody where it was. They didn't want it to become a place where oppressed peoples from around the world would come and create a monument, similar to what the site of the murder of TyRon Lewis[5] can become for them. It's only this year that they finally told where Che Guevara's body was hidden. His body was exhumed and taken back to Cuba where he was properly buried.

He was a tremendous revolutionary who influenced all of us. All revolutionaries of that era were influenced by Che Guevara.

Che represents genuine solidarity

In the '60s, we had fierce battles with the white left. Almost all the white left stepped over the Black Revolution to get to the anti-war movement. They were unable to unite with African people in our struggle.

In 1969 the white left organized no response to the FBI murder of Fred Hampton, the twenty-one year old chairman of the Illinois chapter of the Black Panther Party. They didn't organize around what was happening to us in our communities.

Many of the same people who were with an organization called Students for a Democratic Society (SDS) had worked with the Student NonViolent Coordinating Committee (SNCC) before it became an all African organization.[6] The white people "loved" black people so much that they had to be in our organization. They had to be working in the African communities.

Our movement decided that having white people in our organizations and our communities did not serve us well. The movement thought that it would be better for these white people to go back to white communities and make struggle there since most of our problems came from the white community. They refused to do that. They didn't love us that much anymore. That's when they discovered Viet Nam.

Suddenly, there was a whole movement of white people opposed to the Vietnamese War. Most of the white left struggled to "bring the boys home" from Viet Nam. They wanted peace. They would say things like, "No more Viet Nams." Viet Nam wasn't a bad thing. It was a good thing. The Vietnamese were oppressed people who rose up and defeated white power—kicked its ass! They wiped the U.S. out, pushed it out of their country.

As opposed to the white left raising the slogan of "No more Viet Nams," or "Bring the boys home," Che said, "We need two, three, many Viet Nams!" We need Viet Nams everywhere. That's precisely what our position is and that's the significance, in part, of Che Guevara.

Che was a genuine internationalist, a genuine revolutionary, and he made the ultimate sacrifice in the struggle to free oppressed peoples around the world.

Che was a revolutionary. He wasn't a social worker. He died in the jungles of Bolivia trying to lead an armed force which would make revolution that would not only overthrow the Bolivian dictatorship, but would help to create a revolutionary conflagration throughout Latin America. He was a tremendous force.

Uhuru!

1   Fidel Castro led the Cuban Revolution that overturned the U.S.-backed colonial dictatorship of Fulgencio Batista in 1959.

2   William Jefferson Clinton was U.S. president from 1993 to 2001.

3   Laurent Kabila was a youth leader under Patrice Lumumba's revolutionary government in the Congo in the early 1960s. After the overthrow of Lumumba's government and his assassination, Kabila became associated with the armed struggle waged in the name of Lumumba against the neocolonial Mobutu regime. Kabila later became the neocolonialist president of the Congo following the ousting of Mobutu in 1997. Kabila was assassinated in Kinshasa, the capital of Congo in 2001.

4   In 1831 Nat Turner, an African preacher, led a powerful uprising of enslaved Africans in Virginia against the white slave owners. Turner and his forces killed fifty-five white people on several plantations before the rebellion was defeated by armed white citizens and state militia forces. Turner escaped and hid out for six weeks before he was jailed, tried and hanged along with sixteen other African people. The Nat Turner rebellions struck terror in the hearts of Southern plantation owners.

5   Eighteen-year-old TyRon Lewis was killed on October 24, 1996 by St. Petersburg, Florida police. Lewis was shot with his hands up, unarmed in his car during a traffic stop. The murder of this young African sparked a major African community rebellion that night and again three weeks later in response to the police attack on the Uhuru House after the grand jury exonerated the killer cops. Lewis' killing was the center of years of mass organizing by the Uhuru Movement for economic and social justice for the African community.

6   In 1966 SNCC voted to dismiss all white members of the organization and called on them to go back into the white communities to organize support for the struggle of the African community.

City of African resistance
St. Petersburg goes Uhuru

This presentation was given in Philadelphia on November 16, 1997. It is an excellent summation of the mass work of the Party in St. Petersburg following the October 24, 1996 police murder of eighteen-year-old TyRon Lewis, which sparked rebellions in the African community.

On November 13, three weeks after Lewis was murdered, a grand jury in St. Petersburg exonerated the killer cops. On that day more than three hundred militarized police attacked the regularly scheduled meeting of the National People's Democratic Uhuru Movement held at the Uhuru House. The police shot the city's entire supply of tear gas into the hall where more than a hundred people of all ages were gathered. In response, African workers again took to the streets, shooting down a helicopter and forcing the police to retreat.

Following the police murder and the rebellions, the African People's Socialist Party worked tirelessly to unite the entire African community around the interests of the African working class. Years of intense mass struggle ensued, during which the Party, and Chairman Omali himself, emerged as the undisputed representatives of the African community of St. Petersburg. Yeshitela successfully forced the city government and ruling class to acknowledge, for the first time in history, the demands by the community to end the brutal police containment policy and to implement genuine economic development that would uplift the entire African working class.

This speech was first published in a slightly different form in the Special Supplement to The Burning Spear *dated November 1997–February 1998.*

Uhuru!

In order to talk about the struggle that has been waged by African workers in St. Petersburg, Florida, I need to establish the overall political context. For a long time it was understood by people around the world that African people inside this country and wherever we are located are oppressed and exploited. With the relative success of our worldwide liberation movements of the 1950s and 1960s, it was recognized that oppressed peoples, at least in theory, had a right to be free. This was accepted because of the serious struggles waged by oppressed peoples all over the planet.

The viciousness of imperialist white power was being exposed on a daily basis for the whole world to see, and a lot of people worldwide were sympathetic to the struggle of black people in this country. No matter what else they thought about it, white people in the U.S. had to recognize that black people were oppressed and exploited. To some degree white people were able to understand that the United States government had something to do with that oppression.

In the 1960s we saw a revolutionary movement develop among African people in this country. As this movement rose up, the United States government fought against it with a fury. They assassinated our leaders all around this country and jailed movement activists in a very brutal way.

Some of this was televised quite publicly so the whole world could know about it. The assassination of Martin Luther King Jr. was public. The assassination of Malcolm X was in front of an audience. There was the brutal murder of Fred Hampton. All around the country, cops were shooting Panthers in staged shootouts, and the leadership of the black revolutionary movement in this country was crushed. When I say leadership, I'm talking specifically about the leadership of African working and poor people, who led an activist, independent movement in this country.

The U.S. government crushed down our Black Revolution of the Sixties, wiped it out. It killed people all over this country—just murdered and slaughtered people, and threw people in dungeons and prisons.

The Black Revolution was central to all revolutionary and progressive activity in this country. When they crushed our movement, they effectively crushed the leadership for everything else that attempted to be progressive or revolutionary.

The U.S. government waged a counterinsurgency against our movement. As part of that counterinsurgency, politicians were raised up as the new leaders of the black community. Some political forces became significant only because progressive and revolutionary forces were killed.

When our movement was crushed, the U.S. government waged a campaign against black working and poor people, and by extension against the whole African community. A campaign of slander and demonization was initiated. As a consequence, today no one remembers that Africans are oppressed and exploited. Now, African workers are targeted as the problem. We are the "criminals." White people are scared of us.

It's so illogical when you think about this. African people have only had the vote for the last thirty years. Thirty years ago white people would actually lynch you for trying to vote in this country. Today, it is assumed that black people are a terrible threat that everybody's supposed to fear. It is the most ridiculous, obscene kind of thing.

African working class without a voice

In the absence of the independent revolutionary organizations that we had in the 1960s, nobody speaks about and articulates the interests of the masses of African working and poor people. We only get statements from the politicians and from liberal and petty bourgeois, middle class organizations that lead the charge *against* the black community.

Now you've got Africans occupying positions of authority to maintain the system of oppression of the African community. They killed off our revolutionary movement. They killed off our revolutionary leaders. Then they raised up black leaders to function for white power.

So the masses of African people are now demonized. You've got drugs and other things imposed on the community. They have demonized the community, called everybody who's in the community a "criminal," saying that we bring the conditions on ourselves. We are now the "permanent underclass."

In the past, people recognized that the Black Panther Party had a constituency. It was a legitimate constituency of people with legitimate needs and aspirations that were summed up in their Ten Point Program. They might not have liked the Panthers, but they could not deny that the Panthers had a constituency in the African working class communities.

But now they've destroyed the people's organizations and characterized the people as the problem. They don't have to listen to black folks. They can let whole communities be wiped out. The devastation in the African community is not explained today as being a consequence of oppression by white people or the government. "They brought it on themselves." Nobody speaks for African workers anymore. "If an organization is talking this old radical talk, it's because they're extremists and they don't have any social base." So they just dismiss it.

This affects whole federal and local budgets. You don't have to spend that money on the needs of the African community now. You can put it in places to shore up white power. You don't have to worry about infant mortality or anything else that's happening to black people. You can create economic institutions to feed white people by putting African people in prisons. You don't have to pay attention to poverty or homelessness, because there's no spokesperson for our community. Nobody speaks for the African community.

That makes it easy for the U.S. government to kill people in the streets and not have to explain it. There is a long list of people who've been killed by the police. If these were white people, they would be armed to the teeth and shooting police.

Nobody has to pay any attention to the African community. Just lock them up and put them in jail if they don't act right. Put police on the school grounds to lock up the children. This is the situation.

Any revolutionary organization on the scene has been characterized as some dinosaur left over from the 1960s, completely out of tune with things as they are—an extremist, marginal manifestation without any social base. That's how things are in this country today, generally speaking. That's part of what makes the struggle in St. Petersburg significant.

Police killing used to justify greater repression

On October 24, 1996 the police in St. Petersburg, Florida shot eighteen-year-old TyRon Lewis three blocks from the Uhuru House. It was not supposed to be a problem because he was a black male, and the black male has been defined as menacing. Young African men now are supposed to be menacing. They can't walk down the street without being menacing.

So they can kill TyRon Lewis in broad daylight. If there's a brief uprising as a result, they can handle that. That's alright, they can crush it.

In fact, the rebellion justifies a greater kind of repression. They kill TyRon Lewis, and then that justifies bringing in Weed and Seed.[1] They say, "O.K. We're going to bring in some economic development." What's the form of the economic development? It's a $300,000 Weed and Seed program.

First of all, $300,000 is less money than the mayor paid for his house, and they're going to bring it for the whole black community. That's an insult.

Secondly, Weed and Seed is a police program. It is a designer program that allows the cops to use the most anti-democratic attacks on the people, and to do it within defined borders where it's just black people who are getting the brunt of it. They can use preventive detention, wire tapping and federalized penalties against black people in an area defined as the Weed and Seed areas. So, you've got one law for white people, while black people are under a special federal law whose sentences are three times greater than those given to white people.

So this is what they do: they put the rebellion down and then create a police cordon around the community to make sure that after having put it down, there's more repression than there was before they killed the boy.

Now it's not just the St. Petersburg police department in the community. They have sent in the FBI, the Drug Enforcement Administration, the Bureau of Alcohol, Tobacco and Firearms, the Florida Department of Law Enforcement, the state attorney's office. All of these forces have been brought into this target area where African people live.

Problem solved, from their perspective. TyRon Lewis is dead. Everyone in the white world knows he's supposed to die. If you don't believe it, all you have to do is look at the letters to the editor in the newspaper, and listen to the most popular talk radio programs in the city.

All they talked about was why TyRon Lewis should have died. "He should have gotten out of the car. Bob, what do you do when the cops tell you to get out of the car? You just get out of the car. Isn't that what you do, Bob? You just get out of the car. If he had nothing to hide, he should have gotten out of the car, Bob."

This is the kind of thing that poses as an explanation for why Africans get executed. Now there's the death penalty for not getting out of your car. It's not in any law books that I have ever heard of that if you don't get out of your car, you die. But it's alright if it's an African person.

A couple of months ago a white guy in St. Petersburg had a gun and was shooting up in the air. The police came, he pointed the gun at the police and they killed him.

You should have heard the outrage from the white community about killing this guy. He was armed, pointing and shooting guns at the cops. Nobody's disputing that. The white community was outraged. You should have seen the letters to the editor. "They could have shot him in the leg."

So TyRon Lewis was supposed to die. The rebellion was alright because they came in and crushed it down. This is the kind of thing that happens all over the country when the police kill an African.

Uhuru Movement intervened in the name of African workers

But the difference in St. Petersburg was that there was a revolutionary organization on the ground. We intervened in the process and helped the people understand what it meant that TyRon Lewis had been killed.

As a consequence, there was a profound struggle that jumped off. This was crucial. First, the African working class, which had been pushed out of political life by the terror of the government with the defeat of the Black Revolution of the Sixties, thrust itself with a fury back into political life.

Secondly, the rebellion in response to TyRon Lewis' murder was not aimless. It was focused. In Los Angeles, there was a rebellion after the beating of Rodney King, but there were no aims, no goals. It just exploded. Afterwards different people had opinions, but there was no leadership on the ground. There was no revolutionary leadership that had a direct connection to the people who made the rebellion. Miami had rebellions in 1980, '87 and '89, but nothing benefiting the African working class community was achieved as a consequence of them.

In St. Petersburg, the masses thrust themselves into history and political life. There was a political center there. The state attorney and the media immediately started saying, "Get the Uhuru Movement. They are the ones who started the rebellion. Get 'em, get 'em." They slandered TyRon Lewis and they decided they had to move on us.

The people thrust themselves into political life, but also there was political leadership for them on the spot. That was a crucial development not only for St. Petersburg, but also for the movement in this country. That's why they came at us.

They set it up with the media to define us in a fashion that would allow them to come and put people in prison. Every time they tried to prove that Uhuru was responsible for the rebellion, they showed pictures of Sobukwe, an APSP organizer, standing up on the car making speeches. So Sobukwe was definitely going to jail. He was heading straight into the chain gang. According to them, that's how it was supposed to be.

Then, the African People's Socialist Party built a coalition, the African American Leadership Coalition. We didn't start out to build the coalition, actually. We just started out working for self-protection, self-defense.

The local chapter of the Southern Christian Leadership Conference (SCLC) held a meeting, planning to run down to city hall and ask for some of the money that was coming into the city as a result of the rebellion. We heard about the meeting and went to it. The media was sitting in the hallway waiting for the SCLC to come out and tell them what the plan was.

I went into the meeting and told them that they were just asking for money. They were not saying anything about the conditions of the people, so we struggled that they had to include the people's demands.

We said that you've got to call for the prosecution of the cops who killed this brother. Call for reparations and the release from jail of everybody who was arrested during the rebellion. We called for them to demand, "Hands off the Uhuru Movement."

Most of the middle class Africans in the meeting united with those demands, except the SCLC guy. He didn't want to do it. He wanted to do everything but that. But we forced him to say that he was united.

The people saw us on television. They saw all these diverse forces sitting down together, and black people were really moved by that. They said, "Finally the community is united." The people put pressure from below which helped this guy from the SCLC get on the right track. It also helped him because he figured this was the only way he could get the money. Plus he almost admitted to the white folks in my presence that with him being in this coalition, "We got Omali under control."

That was fine. I have no ego in that way—I'll be "under control." Now all the preachers were involved in the coalition. So for the State to come get us, they had to come through the preachers. That complicated things for white power, because if I'm just this marginal force and the Uhuru Movement has no base in the community, then why were all these people standing there with us?

Community defends Uhuru Movement on November 13

On November 13, 1996, the day the grand jury exonerated the two cops who had killed TyRon Lewis, we in the Uhuru Movement were seeing signs that the police were getting ready to move on us in a serious way. We were in a meeting trying to strengthen the coalition. We called on them to come to our regularly scheduled National People's Democratic Uhuru Movement (NPDUM) meeting that night. One of the preachers said, "Our position should be that an attack on one is an attack on all." The coalition called a press conference right away, and though the unity was somewhat shaky, they said, "An attack on one is an attack on all!"

Later that same day the State attacked the Uhuru House in a very serious way. The *St. Petersburg Times* was printing editorials really castigating the preachers, chastising them for being in a coalition with Omali Yeshitela. They needed me isolated, they needed Uhuru isolated, but they couldn't do it! They were saying to the preachers, "You shouldn't be part of this coalition because Omali Yeshitela refuses to renounce violence." That was the stuff coming from the media. But we were able to hold onto the relationship with the forces in the coalition.

When they attacked us on November 13, it was a crucial moment. This was more important than the rebellion of October 24, the night of the police murder of TyRon Lewis. October 24s have happened all around this country. It's not that they kill us that's so significant; *it's what we do in response to the killing that's significant.* They needed the Uhuru Movement out of the way. That's why they moved on us and slandered us.

On November 13, they came to get rid of us so they could go back to business as usual, especially since they had all these plans for a baseball team that they are dropping down in the middle of the African community. So they brought in everything, believe me. You really had to be there.

On November 13, some three hundred members of a variety of local, county and state police organizations attacked the Uhuru House with a barrage of tear gas. They attacked black babies and children, women and men. There were more than a hundred people there for the regularly scheduled meeting that night. Hundreds more were outside.

The ferocity of the attack resulted in several fires being set by tear gas canisters and depletion of all the tear gas in the city police armory.

The obvious intent of the attack was to kill the Uhuru leadership. However, the heroic masses of the community—their faces covered with bandanas—rose up, rock, bottle and gun in hand, and repelled the invaders. They shot down a helicopter and wounded two policemen. They saved the lives of the people in the Uhuru House and defended the integrity of the community.

The Uhuru Movement was incredible during all this. All our forces stood tall! On the outside of the building, the work that we had done for so long in the community was paying off. The people came to the defense of the movement. They actually defeated this armed force that was outside and pushed them back!

In explaining what happened to our building the media said there were gunshots aimed at the police which came from the vicinity of the Uhuru House. We were to learn later that the state attorney's office had put out a statement from the grand jury absolving the cops of any responsibility for killing TyRon Lewis.

The statement said the cops were justified in killing TyRon Lewis, but blamed the Uhuru Movement for causing all these problems. It was clear that the statement was supposed to have been justification for the destruction of our movement, including the physical destruction of the people in that building.

Their plan was to attack our building, kill our leadership, then put an article in the paper explaining that the cops were innocent but we were guilty. So the grand jury that was supposed to be dealing with the cops that killed TyRon Lewis actually indicted us! The plan was: the cops walk, we're dead, and the explanation from the grand jury is we were the ones who started everything in the first place.

But none of it worked, because we survived the whole thing thanks to the heroism of that community! The attack on November 13 was supposed to solve the problem for them. When it didn't work, we began to see contradictions emerge inside the city council, which is made up of representatives of the ruling class. City council members began fighting with each other, arguing, having open debates. Heavy criticism was leveled at the chief of police because he didn't finish us off.

Three days later they staged a little unity march which talked about "black and white unite." They were going to march chanting "u-ni-ty, u-ni-ty." The march began on Ninth Street and Eighteenth Avenue heading towards downtown. The Uhuru House is on Thirteenth Street and Eighteenth Avenue. We decided that we would join that march from the back. When the march took off it was mostly white people. When the black petty bourgeois sellouts didn't see us, they joined the march as well.

After the march had taken off, we ran to catch up with it. There were about thirty of us in uniforms and combat boots. Everyone in the march was chanting "unity" and holding hands. As we ran down the street in uniform towards the march, the people in the community began cheering. African people standing on the side lines were cheering, "There they are!" An article in the *St. Petersburg Times* described how this dual march was going on with the people in the front chanting "unity, unity," while we were in uniform running and chanting, "Black people united will never be defeated!"

The Uhuru Movement and I had been so demonized by the city and the media. But when the mayor got up to speak at the rally downtown at the end of the march, people started immediately heckling him. So the mayor didn't stay up there very long. He beat it off the platform before the booing could reach a crescendo. But when I came up to speak, the people welcomed me like a hero. It was tremendous. The prestige of our movement just went up so much because they had tried to kill us and yet we walked out of there. The prestige of the movement just skyrocketed. Now the mayor was heckled off the platform in downtown white St. Petersburg and I was welcomed as a hero!

Subsequent to that, Henry Cisneros from the U.S. Department of Housing and Urban Development (HUD) came to town to investigate the situation. Clinton[2] had sent him because he didn't want contagion; he didn't want St. Petersburg to be happening everywhere else. Cisneros saw right away that they couldn't do anything they wanted to do without coming to terms with the Uhuru Movement! He asked for a private meeting with me before he met with the city council. As a consequence of the meeting he created the Citizens Advisory Commission that would oversee the theoretical money, the phantom $20 million the federal government was supposed to send in to deal with the situation in St. Petersburg.

Cisneros told the city council "I've been all over but this is the worst place I've ever been" in terms of the treatment of African people. He was saying, "I've never seen anything like this. The police are just incredible," etc., etc. The city council was so subjective; they had personalized what happened so much that they couldn't see what was in their best interest. Cisneros was able to tell them that they were going to have to deal with Omali Yeshitela and the Uhuru Movement.

Cisneros created the Citizens Advisory Commission. I said I didn't want any part of it and he said, "I really wish you'd be part of it." So we thought about it and agreed that it would be a good idea.

Uhuru Movement stands consistently firm

So here's what happened. We started out clearly being an organization of the African working class and poor people. That's where our work is based. Then with the rebellions we went into this coalition and were working among the petty bourgeoisie. Finally with the Citizens Advisory Commission, we find ourselves actually participating with representatives of the ruling class and elements of the State organization. The State, the government and the ruling class have a problem because they don't have anybody who can lead them out of this mess they're in. So we're working on three different levels now.

Our stand was consistently firm, fighting for the interests of the African working class. In response one of the worst middle class forces—the guy from the SCLC—split off because he couldn't get what he wanted. He called a press conference to try to destroy the coalition and certainly to isolate me. That didn't work.

We moved the coalition to call a black community convention which would unite the whole black community on a single agenda for the first time ever. Thus we moved forward and left this guy behind.

It's been our work in this coalition to create a strategic thrust for everybody to move all in the same direction. This is why people haven't easily been able to sell each other out. The SCLC guy attacked us because he wanted to go for the sell out, but we kept things moving in a certain direction, making it hard to do. Soon the middle class sector started seeing that we were winning a place for them. We moved to create a strategic trajectory for the whole community based on the question of economic development and the interests of African workers. That is the issue for everybody. The ruling class talks about "crime," we demand economic development. It's the only solution.

So we're working. We have criticized Weed and Seed. We went to 10,000 houses with a flyer summing up Weed and Seed. We go to the Weed and Seed meetings. Every time they put a microphone in front of my face, I criticize the city for trying to use police containment as a substitute for economic development. It is unacceptable and it will not work.

We defend the memory of TyRon Lewis even as they slander him and his family. We call on his mother to stand up at public meetings with the city, and we force the city to recognize her.

I pushed for an emergency summit on economic development which was held in August, 1997. We called the whole community out and wrote a paper on what we mean by economic development.

On August 23, the Uhuru Movement held a march with hundreds of people holding posters and banners calling for economic development and social justice. We created a strategic trajectory for the whole community. Now other folks have started chiming in, calling for "economic development." First the Citizens Advisory Commission said their thrust was going to be economic development. Then the mayor started talking about economic development. Everybody wants to talk about economic development now.

On November 4, there was a town hall meeting on economic development at a community center a block from the Uhuru House. Bankers were there. The Chamber of Commerce was there. The mayor and the people who head up the city's economic development program were there. Right now we have a commitment for something like a total of $6 million in economic development for the African community.

The thing that makes it significant is what we've been able to do. Usually they make a deal with somebody and call that economic development. Usually Reverend Chickenbone or somebody can get a deal to train one hundred fifty people for jobs that don't exist, and that's what they call economic development. They were always able to circumvent any kind of struggle because most of the black businesses are so hungry and poor they have not been able to fight for economic development for the community. They can only fight for themselves. So the government would give this little guy some money, and boom, the movement would be destroyed because he got what he wanted.

But we've been clear from the very beginning: we don't want some money. We're not looking for a job. The only thing we want is economic development for the African community! We have been able to make them produce something real—or act like they're going to produce something real—as opposed to the kinds of deals they're used to making.

The mayor told me they want to start a "business incubator" to help people by providing technical information about how to run and operate businesses, or to give them information that would make the banks more likely to give them loans. The mayor said this would be on Central Avenue in downtown St. Petersburg so it can be for everyone. I said that this has to be in the African community. So he said, "O.K. We can do that."

The November 4 town hall meeting on economic development was so very crucial, and we isolated some of the more self-serving sectors of the petty bourgeoisie. First of all, we demanded that the session be public. We insisted that these guys come out and make commitments not to some individual Negroes, but to the community.

Secondly, we demanded a public process. We are demanding a process that will enable the people to go where the resources are without having to go through some individual Negroes. We want to remove the middle person, who is likely to get all the resources and make the people vassals.

Uhuru Movement leads struggle against Weed and Seed

In October 1997, around the first anniversary of the killing, I was on a live television show with the mayor and the new chief of police who's a Negro. At the end of this little anniversary discussion we were having, they asked if anybody there had any last things they wanted to say and sum up. The chief of police said,

"Well, I just want to say that we've been looking out for trouble spots in the community, and people have been telling me that one problem area is Weed and Seed. Therefore it's clear that we're going to have to rethink Weed and Seed."

It's been a struggle for position, and currently the Uhuru Movement commands the high ground.

Now we still have a lot of work to do. At any juncture that they decide the price is too high, we'll see them move in other kinds of ways, including raising up whatever Negro leadership they want, or they may increment the people to death to make them feel they've overcome their own crisis.

We've done a tremendous amount of work. When somebody wants to talk about economic development or political direction in the white community, they no longer find a preacher with whom to have the discussion. Have you ever noticed that it's just in the African community that they find a preacher to talk about economic development? They don't find somebody who's involved in business or political philosophy, they find a preacher.

The people are really getting a lot of political education. Almost every week we're holding events and helping people to understand not only the political issues but also economic development. It's a crucial kind of political education. On Wednesdays, the National People's Democratic Uhuru Movement meeting is held and everybody from the movement comes. On Sundays, the African People's Socialist Party mass meeting occurs. At these meetings we lay out our strategy for the people.

One important element in the work in St. Pete has been the existence of the solidarity movement.[3] The existence of the solidarity movement has been a problem for them. We've been able to create the Northside Residents Opposed to Weed and Seed, which is an organization composed of white folks.

There was a televised meeting, called by the League of Women Voters, at which the mayor spoke. During the question and answer period the mayor called on this safe little old white woman sitting in the audience. She jumped up and jammed up the mayor about Weed and Seed. "Why are you putting this undemocratic Weed and Seed in the African community? It's not going to solve any problems."

It's been really important to work that front. It's important also because the Uhuru Movement is THE movement now. Uhuru has a white presence that's really important because we can reshape the political terrain in the city of St. Petersburg. All that liberal garbage that's functioned to attack us in the past can now be neutralized.

Currently, our most crucial work is block organizing. We've got a map of the city and we're dividing the city up into twenty sections now. For every section we want to have a section leader right out of that community. For this we're trying to win people who are Uhuru supporters. We want them to commit to just doing Uhuru work in the neighborhood where they stay. The solidarity forces are currently dividing up the white community into sections as well.

On every block we want to put a block captain. We will organize the entire city in that fashion so that no matter where the government attempts to go, no matter what kind of thing they want to do down the road, we will have put down Uhuru houses throughout the city. Every house becomes an Uhuru house. That way, we'll be able to maintain the high ground that we have now.

New style of mass work

The work of this past year has been difficult in that for the last thirty years or more our movement's basic work has been criticism of the system. This is the first time we have ever been in place to actually make and implement policy! It is not the solution overall, but we have an opportunity here to actually change the conditions of existence for the masses of people and put the struggle on a higher level.

During this recent process we have said things that have confused some people. We have, for example, defined the situation in St. Petersburg as a win/win situation for everybody. We've told the capitalists who want to get something like the baseball team, "You can have what you want, but the thing is we've got to get what we want. We have to have economic development."

Some people have asked, "What do you mean the capitalists can have what they want?" Well, revolution isn't happening right now. They're going to get it any damn way. The problem is not that the capitalists are going to get what they want. The problem is that we have to win everybody to understand that we've got to get what African workers want.

What happens is this: you raise the relative position of the masses of African workers in relationship to the position of the capitalists. The people cannot get strong except at the expense of the bourgeoisie. I don't care what the capitalists think. The thing is to win everybody to agree that the masses have to be raised up. That's the thing. Win maximum opinion about that.

The capitalists are dragging their feet. I'm criticizing the banks and others. I'm criticizing the owning classes because they're not doing what they're supposed to do, and its part of the deal. Win masses of people to agree that they are supposed to have economic development and they'll be looking funny at the banks and owning classes for not holding up their part. That's the kind of thing that we've been able to do.

The other thing that is so crucial is that today nobody is trying to demonize the black community in St. Petersburg any more! You might hear some whacko on talk radio, but generally speaking that does not happen. Generally speaking, they can't dismiss the African working class as ignorant, inarticulate and pathological. In fact, it is quite articulate. The reality is that when the Uhuru Movement opens its mouth, it is the masses of poor people who are speaking. That is the concession that we've won that I think is crucial to the development of our movement here and throughout the country.

St. Petersburg goes Uhuru

This has been a powerful struggle. The *St. Petersburg Times* ran an article that talked about, "Uhuru leader met with the mayor. Uhuru leader met with the head of the Police Benevolent Association. Uhuru leader has written articles in the *St. Petersburg Times*. Uhuru leader goes mainstream."

But I said, wait a minute. I never said I wouldn't meet with the mayor—the mayor said he wouldn't meet with me. It wasn't us chasing the police and shooting tear gas at them—it was them shooting tear gas at us. Last November, the CEO of the *St. Petersburg Times* posted a memo on every bulletin board in every department of the newspaper offices that characterized Omali Yeshitela and Curtsinger, who was a thuggish, Ku Klux Klan-type police chief, as the same.

So if the mayor calls and has a meeting with me, if the police chief meets with me, and I have an article in the *St. Petersburg Times*, it seems to me the logic is not that I have gone mainstream, *but that they have gone Uhuru!*

It is so important that African workers cannot be trashed in the same way they used to be. They have to say that the people have the right to economic development. White folks are sending me letters saying they agree with me. White folks are telling the solidarity movement that Omali Yeshitela is the best black leader we've ever seen, and this kind of thing.

Right now we control the high ground. There's a lot that we still have to learn. We're just beginning to understand how funding happens. We've never been that concerned about these issues, but the city of St. Petersburg gets $15 million from HUD every year in the form of Community Development Block Grant (CDBG)[4] funds.

We don't know anything about a Community Development Block Grant, never cared anything about that kind of thing. But now we're in the situation where we can decide what's going to happen with it, or have a lot to do with those kinds of decisions. We can move it in directions that enhance our stature with the people and actually contribute to changing conditions for the masses of African people. So that's where we are in St. Pete.

Uhuru!

1 Weed and Seed is a federal police program that targets the most impoverished areas of African and oppressed communities. In the target area crimes are prosecuted on a federal, rather than local level, with correspondingly higher sentences, thereby setting up Jim Crow law. A variety of federal and state police agencies band together to enforce martial law and containment policies, allowing extra-constitutional acts by the State such as wiretappings, preventive detentions and other tactics. The "seed" aspect, which supposedly brings resources into the target area, never benefits the African community.

2 Then-U.S. president William Jefferson Clinton.

3 The African People's Solidarity Committee (APSC) is an organization of white people working under the leadership of the African People's Socialist Party. APSC organizes in white communities building support for the movement for the liberation of African people.

4 CDBG funds are granted to cities based on their statistics of poverty, yet the funds never benefit the African working class.

The wolf and the double-edged blade

U.S. war against the African community

This speech is an address to the Black Power Organizing Conference in Philadelphia on May 31, 1998. It is one of the Chairman's best, most comprehensive summations of the current conditions that African workers face all over the U.S. and the world. It defines the war imposed on the African community as a counterinsurgency waged by the U.S. government. An excerpt from this presentation was used as the piece "Wolves" by the rap group dead prez on their album "let's get free."

Uhuru!

I would like to say some things briefly about the African People's Socialist Party, which is the organization that I chair. We are a revolutionary organization. By that, I mean that we are convinced that this country, this system, does not have the ability to do justice for African people. If we are ever going to know justice, freedom and democracy for African people, we must have a revolution. It's that simple, but I know that's a difficult issue for a lot of folk.

Nevertheless, it is the truth. It's important to talk about that because we can continue to have discussions that make us feel good, but which won't take us anywhere. We have to have an analysis of the reality that confronts us as a people. We have to use that analysis to change our circumstances and bring about what we want for ourselves and our children in the future.

We are a revolutionary organization. We believe that if one wants to know what it will take for us to become free, all one has to do is to look at history and see what it took for us to become enslaved. If we find any place in our history that we voted ourselves into slavery, then I say, "Let's vote ourselves out of slavery." If we can find any place in history when we sang our way into slavery, then let's sing our way out of it. But that's not the case, Sisters and Brothers. The reality is that we're going to have to cut, shoot, and bomb our way out of the circumstances that we find confront us.

There's a lot of work that we have to do before we are ready for that phase of struggle, but our objective is total, absolute liberation for our people. You can't have it any other way. There is no way that you can talk about sharing the power over your life with somebody else and then think you've got a right to complain about what that person does to you. Either you want the power or you don't.

We are a revolutionary organization that was founded in 1972 at the back of the attack and defeat of the Black Revolution of the Sixties. The Black Revolution of the Sixties was one of the most consequential things that ever occurred in this country. It is something that we have to struggle to understand.

Everyone who becomes involved in the process of changing the world, changes him or herself as well. In the 1960s, people who one day were simply uneducated share croppers went out to try to change the world and were transformed. People like Fannie Lou Hamer, Willie Ricks[1] and other known and unsung heroes stood up and built a tremendous movement. They discovered their own interests, which were separate and distinct from those of either the liberal sector of the white ruling class or the African petty bourgeoisie.

By 1964, when the first Civil Rights Bill was enacted, and 1965 when the Voting Rights Act was passed, the movement should have been over, effectively. The basic democratic rights that the Civil Rights Movement and the African middle class had been struggling for had been achieved. But the masses of African workers and poor people were able to determine that, yes, the preachers and the lawyers got what they want, but what *we* want and need is "Black Power!"

We came to understand that the issue was not about making the oppressor like us, or struggling against his racism. The issue was not running around trying to educate the oppressor to stop doing something bad to us. The issue was to get the power over our lives so that no matter what the oppressor thinks about us, he can't do anything to hurt us. In fact, if you wanted to, you could do a job on him. That's what became clear to us.

The movement achieved that amount of clarity. It was a movement that took its ideological leadership from Malcolm X. Some people like to attribute the significance of Malcolm X and his words to Elijah Muhammad.[2] I do not. In fact Elijah kicked Malcolm out of the Nation of Islam precisely because he did not represent what Elijah represented. There was a tremendous split in the movement at that time between folk who believed in revolution and those who didn't. You never heard anybody from the Nation of Islam before or since Malcolm X talk about revolution.

That was the thing that drew the line. Somebody was talking about revolution, and Malcolm was that person. He became the ideological father, if you will, of our movement, even today. In fact, Malcolm was killed by the imperialists precisely because of where he was trying to take the movement. Malcolm was assassinated in 1965, but it was too late. By 1966 the movement was talking about power over our own lives.

Greatest threat to U.S. internal security

In 1966, the demand for Black Power came out of Mississippi, exposing the real nature of the struggle that we were waging. The demand made it clear that what we want is power over our own lives. At the juncture when the movement determined that the issue was power, our movement became like the other revolutionary struggles of oppressed people that were happening everywhere in the world. Our movement emerged as an anti-colonial movement at the moment the issue became one of power. When African workers said "Black Power," they united with struggles like the ones being led by Che Guevara throughout Latin America and Africa.

By 1967, we saw the rise of the Black Panther Party, which took the struggle even further. The Black Panther Party was immediately and explicitly informed and influenced by Malcolm X, who told us that since it's legal to have a shotgun, every African should have one in his or her house. He also said that we should form rifle clubs all over this country. Huey P. Newton heard Malcolm X and formed the Black Panther Party. He said that it was the influence of Malcolm X, and the Student Nonviolent Coordinating Committee (SNCC), which was influenced by Malcolm X also, that gave rise to the Black Panther Party and what it represented.

With the emergence of the Panther Party we saw tremendous anxiety in this country. So much so that J. Edgar Hoover, who was then the executive director of the FBI (Federal Bureau of Investigation), which is one of the secret political police agencies in this country, characterized the Black Panther Party as the "greatest threat to the internal security of the United States since the Civil War."

Not Gaddafi, not Saddam Hussein, not the Russians, but ordinary African working class folk, most of whom lived in housing projects and had to use public transportation to get from one part of the city to the other. That's a statement about where power can be found. It is in the masses of African workers and poor people, who, given organization and ideological clarity, can achieve anything. That's the thing that Hoover and the FBI recognized. Unfortunately, not too many of our leaders today recognize that.

The FBI and various military intelligence organizations were involved in crushing our revolutionary movement. We know that the Black Revolution, once unleashed, gave rise to virtually every other progressive entity that sprung up in this country. It was the Black Revolution that took white women out of the kitchen and the homosexuals out of the closet. It was the Black Revolution that energized the movements of other oppressed peoples, including the Indigenous peoples in this country. It was a powerful and profound movement that shook this country to its very foundation.

After the federal government assassinated Martin Luther King,[3] rebellions by African people surged throughout this country. I shall never forget the sight of tanks circling the White House. The government made the assumption that Africans had achieved enough organization that we might actually be able to seize the White House. The U.S. government knows where the power is. This is why the government put in place a program to cut down and undermine the Black Revolution and assassinate our leaders. They created what we refer to as a "counterinsurgency."

Counterinsurgency is a military term for a type of warfare that is used against an oppressed people who are fighting for their liberation. Counterinsurgency uses every form of attack: psychological warfare, actual armed struggle, economic warfare. The primary strategic aims of counterinsurgency are resource and population control—to control the resources and the population to make sure that they never rise up again.

The name of the government's counterinsurgency against the Black Revolution was "COINTELPRO," short for Counterintelligence Program. COINTELPRO was the program used to assassinate and imprison our leaders and destroy our organizations. The architect of COINTELPRO for the FBI was William Sullivan.

Sullivan was the man who orchestrated the murder of Fred Hampton,[4] the beloved twenty-one-year-old Chairman of the Illinois chapter of the Black Panther Party. Sullivan led assaults on our movement, including the attack on the Black Panther Party in Philadelphia where the Party members were stripped naked in front of the press. This was psychological warfare designed to make you demoralized and feel that you couldn't win.

Immediately after the defeat of the Black Revolution, then-president Richard Milhous Nixon rewarded Sullivan for destroying our movement by sending him to a post in Southeast Asia. He was supposed to make war against drugs. He was sent to the area of Southeast Asia known as the "Golden Triangle," where most of the world's heroin was grown.

Sullivan was sent to Southeast Asia to fight a war against drugs that we didn't even know existed. Shortly after he got to Southeast Asia, Sullivan recruited people like G. Gordon Liddy, E. Howard Hunt and Richard Secord, who was involved in the drug scandal with Oliver North.[5] They became a part of an organization that he created, the Office of Drug Abuse Law Enforcement (ODALE) that later became the Drug Enforcement Administration (DEA). This agency was the origin of the heroin epidemic that hit our communities as soon as the Panthers and other organizations were taken off the streets. This was during the time when the United States government was involved in a counterinsurgency war against the heroic and courageous people of Viet Nam.

On the one hand, they were making war on the people of Viet Nam. On the other hand, they were making war against African people here. Inside this country the counterinsurgency took the form of heroin—pumped into our communities by the U.S.

government. Heroin was everywhere. There was not a city that was too small or too rural—if African people were there, heroin would be there. This was around 1971 and 1972, the year of the founding of the African People's Socialist Party. That was the year when, as far as they were concerned, the Black Revolution and revolutionary trend in the world was supposed to be all over.

Then in 1979, four years after the defeat of the U.S. by the Vietnamese people, we saw the Sandinistas[6] ride into power in Managua, Nicaragua. They overthrew the Somoza regime that had been put in place by the United States government.

Crack as chemical warfare

When the Sandinistas took over Nicaragua, the strategic counterinsurgency efforts of the United States government shifted from Southeast Asia to Latin America. And guess what? It just so happens that most of the world's cocaine grows in Latin America. All of a sudden, African people supposedly lost our taste for heroin. Suddenly, we got involved in cocaine. Not just cocaine but a cocaine derivative called "crack." It was something that someone went into a laboratory and created, so that it would be cheap enough for massive distribution throughout the African community.

So there was a counterinsurgency war being initiated against the Nicaraguan people and the Nicaraguan Revolution, and another war being initiated against African people here. Now that the Black Revolution had been destroyed, the counterinsurgency was being waged against the entire African population to try to make sure that we stayed demoralized and powerless and would never again build the Black Revolution. This counterinsurgency takes the form of crack cocaine—chemical warfare! This is what the United States government has done to African people.

In August, 1996, Gary Webb,[7] a white guy working for the *San Jose Mercury News*, kicked off a series of newspaper articles revealing the FBI involvement in creating the crack cocaine epidemic in our communities. This came out of San Jose, California. It just so happens that San Jose is about forty-five minutes away from Oakland, where we waged struggles from the early 1980s up until now exposing the fact that the United States Government has imposed drugs in our communities.

In fact, in 1989, after the assassination of Huey P. Newton, we raised this slogan, "Who killed Huey? Don't tell no lie, it's the government, the government, the FBI." They wanted to tie Huey to the drug question, but we raised the slogan, "The White House is the crack house, and Uncle Sam is the pusherman."

Gary Webb got fired from his newspaper job for writing those articles and came under serious attack from various other sources. Webb exposed 160 pages of actual documentation from court records and interviews with people who were involved with putting the drugs in our community. He talked about young Ricky Ross, a 19-year-old high school drop out. Ross had been a high school tennis star who quit school because he couldn't read. A CIA agent found Ricky, who had never seen cocaine in his life, and made him participate in distributing crack cocaine throughout this country.

Era of defeat

We talk about the CIA but you know that it was the American government that put crack cocaine in our communities. The CIA *is* the American government. The FBI was not just J. Edgar Hoover, it was the American government attacking the Black Revolution of the Sixties. In this instance, the government used the CIA to crush the morale of our community so that revolution would never rear its head in this country again. And so, a movement was crushed down. As a consequence of this chemical warfare, we don't know how many people are locked up in prisons or dead.

For years after the assault on the Black Power Movement, the African community lived in an era that we characterize as an era of defeat. You couldn't even talk to the masses about revolution, because the last memory that people had of revolution was of tanks in the streets and militants being assassinated. They had killed our leaders in very exemplary ways. The way they killed King—they shot him in the mouth. They brutally and publicly killed Malcolm and Fred Hampton.

They didn't have to kill any of those folk in that way. They could have fixed it so it looked like they had a heart attack. They could have made it look as if they slipped in the bathtub and cracked their skull or had a car accident. They didn't do that, because J. Edgar Hoover wanted to make it clear to young Africans: if you become a revolutionary, you'll be a dead revolutionary. These assassinations were designed to demoralize the community and to create a sense of the invincibility of white power—a sense that you can't fight them without dying.

During this period, we would talk to African people all of the time. We would say "Let's get organized. Let's do something!" They would say, "Well, it doesn't make sense to get organized because every time we get a leader they kill him." That was the sentiment in our community. In many instances, people were terrified. You would sit in a meeting like this, with children present, and have the door kicked in by FBI agents and other cops who ran in with their guns drawn. This was common in the late sixties. The FBI would attack a building and destroy the materials. They would take your newspapers and put them in the middle of the room and set them on fire, or piss on them or other kinds of things. It was terror.

This was what we had to overcome. They put the crack cocaine in our community, and it demoralized the African workers and poor people who are the heart of the revolution. Then we saw all of these so-called Negro leaders attack the community, saying that the community was the problem, that we needed to "atone." The government wasn't the problem, they said, it was the people who were the problem. So, our Party had to struggle against this concept that was out there, even among the African working class itself.

What we found was that the people who were out there pushing crack cocaine often thought that it was their idea that they were doing this. But it wasn't their idea. What the imperialists, the capitalists, white power had done was taken away all of the other options for survival for the African working class. They were saying that if you want to live, this is what you can do to live.

The wolf gets blamed for trying to live

I'm not a hunter, but I'm told that in places like in the Arctic, where Indigenous people sometimes might hunt a wolf, they'll take a double-edged blade and they'll put blood on the blade. They'll melt the ice and stick the handle in the ice, so that only the blade is protruding and that a wolf will smell the blood. He wants to eat, and he'll come and lick the blade, trying to eat. What happens is when the wolf licks the blade, of course he cuts his tongue, and he bleeds, and he thinks he's really having a good meal. He drinks, and he licks, and he licks and, of course, he's drinking his own blood, and he kills himself. That's what the imperialists did to us with the crack cocaine.

You've got these young brothers out there thinking that they're getting something that they're going to make a living with. They're getting something so they can buy a car: "The white people have cars, why can't I have a car?" They're getting something so they can get a piece of gold: "White people have gold, why can't I have gold?" They're getting something so they can buy a house: "White people have houses, why can't I have a house?"

They actually think that it's something that's bringing resources to them, but they're killing themselves, just like the wolf who's licking the blade. They're slowly dying without knowing it. That's what's happening to the community. Are you with me on that? That's exactly and precisely what happens to the community. Instead of blaming the hunter who put the damn handle of the blade in the ice for the wolf, what happens is the wolf gets blamed for trying to live. That's what happens in our community.

You don't blame the victim, you blame the oppressor! Imperialism—white power—is the enemy. It was the enemy when it first came to Africa, snatched up the first Africans and brought us here against our will—*is* the enemy today. That's the thing that we have to understand. There can't be any compromise on that.

I know your television got stolen by someone on crack—mine got stolen too! But we can't limit the discussion and the understanding to some immediate personal contradiction that we have with somebody who's been victimized by imperialism! I know you've got a sister or an aunt or a cousin or somebody who ripped you off because they're on that stuff, but we can't limit our understanding based on our own personal relationship to it, because imperialism is making war against all of us. Your cousin got hooked first, and he becomes an instrument of imperialism when he does what he does to us in our community.

The community is demoralized. This is one of the most effective tactics of the counterinsurgency, because the victim actually believes that he is responsible for what's going on. Then the victim becomes increasingly demoralized by his own behavior, because he knows that something's wrong with what he's doing.

Another thing that happens is that the drug addiction creates the political justification for militarizing our community, for taking away every right you think you've won. You think you've got some rights. You think that you've got freedom of speech or assembly. But they use the existence of the crack that they put in your community as a justification for taking away your rights from you.

Thirty-four years ago in this country, any African who would try to register to join the Democratic party, would be taken out and lynched. He would have his sexual organs cut off and stuffed in his mouth. This is America I'm talking about! An African couldn't drive from one part of the country to the other and stop at a service station to go to the bathroom without facing death. Today, they want to convince you and I that suddenly the African population is the criminal population. Now it's white people that are supposedly terrified of us. This is a consequence of the success of the counterinsurgency.

They destroy our leaders, destroy our organizations, disperse the members of the organizations, and then turn reality upside down. The media are a part of the counterinsurgency and they redefine the historical relationship that we've always had. Many of our own folk, in particular the so-called black leaders, unite with the definition that they have created for us.

Neocolonialism: white power in black face

The counterinsurgency is not just the drugs. The counterinsurgency also takes the form of neocolonialism, which some people refer to as "Negro-colonialism." Neocolonialism is white power in a black face, and it's used everywhere in the world. Under direct colonialism, it was clear who was running things because the white man was in control of every aspect of our lives. "Neo" means "new," and neocolonialism comes about only when the masses become so politically astute that they will no longer accept obvious domination by foreigners.

Then it becomes necessary for them to use what they call indirect rule, or neocolonialism. Neocolonialism is white power in a black face, in a brown face, in a yellow face. Neocolonialism is white power in disguise, white power masquerading as something else, white power in a dashiki. The most significant way that they utilize neocolonialism in this country is through the electoral process.

Look at Philadelphia as an example. It was under the boot of this terrorist thug—Mayor Rizzo—who left the planet Earth before we got organized well enough to help his exit. He bragged that he had a police department so vicious that it could defeat the Cuban army. The masses of African people rose up to try to get organized to get rid of this thug. This was the basis of a huge movement that existed in Philadelphia—the Black United Front. A black Democratic party hack named Wilson Goode, who never made a single move to help African people, came to the forefront of this movement. In all the years that he was in the Democratic party, he never stood up for African people. He never stood up to Rizzo. He never said, "Feed, clothe, and house my people." The African community got behind Wilson Goode, and elected him as the mayor. People worked like hell and did some fierce political work in this city.

In Philadelphia, there was a remnant of our movement that didn't get wiped out—at least visibly. They were called MOVE. They wore dreadlocks and called themselves "Africa." They were a real problem for the city of Philadelphia, and the city decided to get rid of them permanently. When Rizzo attacked and tried to get rid of MOVE, the African community pushed him back. In 1985, Wilson Goode gave the order to fire bomb the MOVE house.[8] He bragged about it. I saw him on television, saying, "Yes, I gave the order, and I'd do it again!" He had a bomb dropped on those African people! Why didn't he drop a bomb on Rizzo?

When Wilson Goode bombed MOVE, it confused so many people. African people were in a state of denial, because they had done a lot of work for this guy. They made excuses for him. What would have happened if Rizzo had dropped that bomb? Not only would Philadelphia have been on fire, but every city in this country with a black population would have been burning. They could get away with it because of Wilson Goode. That's neocolonialism. It's there to confuse the masses of the people.

Today there are an estimated ten thousand black elected officials in this country, and four times as many Negroes who have been appointed to some kind of administrative capacity in government. Yet, the material conditions of African people in this country in 1998 are worse than they were in 1968. Not one of the forty or fifty thousand Negroes who have some modicum of power, have said "Feed, clothe, and house my people."

Neocolonialism became an effective cover for white power. "It can't be racism because y'all got a black police chief," they say. "It can't be racism because the mayor is black." And we agree with them. It's not racism. It is colonialism, domination by a foreign and alien power over another people.

A colonial power will use anybody. The British used the Kenyan rifle people[9]—black people in Kenya. They recruited them from all over Africa, all over the British empire, to put down revolution and resistance by African people. But everybody was clear that it was colonialism that they were fighting against, and that's a key thing that we need to understand. If you get into this racism trap, you can't understand why it is that Goode dropped the bomb. You can't explain why black people have been in white people's armies to kill other black people. But it is colonialism. It is the political power that we have to fight. We have to have the power.

The issue is not whether white people like you. The issue is whether you have the power so that whether they like you or not, they can't hurt you. When you have power, though, you find out a lot of people will like you who didn't like you before. If you really want somebody to like you, get some power, and see how many friends you will have overnight! I'm telling you that's what the struggle is about. It's about power.

This is why neocolonialism became an important aspect of the counterinsurgency. It was the attack on the Black Revolution of the Sixties. Then it was drugs. And then it was this neocolonialism—this white power in black face that dominates our community everywhere.

Rebuild the Black Revolution

Since the founding of the African People's Socialist Party in 1972, the task of our movement has been to try to rebuild the revolution. We have worked to bring the masses of African people back into political life, because that is the essential character of a revolutionary period.

You know you have a revolutionary period when the masses have been swept up into political life like we saw during the era of the Black Panther Party. That's when young African men and women set up free breakfast programs, established the free sickle cell anemia testing programs and security teams to monitor the police in our community. They built revolutionary consciousness among the masses of the people, bringing to them the understanding, as Huey P. Newton said, that "real political power comes from the barrel of the gun."

In a revolutionary period you have a mass of people who are thrown into political action, seeking to determine our own political future, seeking our own power—Black Power, nappy-haired power, thick-nosed power, big-lip power, boom-box-on-my-shoulder power. We set the terms for what we're talking about, not the oppressor. That's the struggle. Power is the thing that we have to have and that we've been fighting for.

Today we are moving into a new era. We can no long characterize this period that we live in as one of defeat and demoralization. Clearly, today we live in a period of resistance and crisis—crisis for the system and resistance among more and more oppressed peoples around the world.

You can see this crisis in a number of ways. The bombing of the Oklahoma City courthouse was a crisis for the system. A white boy blew up the whole federal building and killed 168 people. That's a crisis.

It's a crisis that the system cannot even define what is happening. It's a crisis that the entire congress of the United States would pass a resolution against Nation of Islam leader Khalid Muhammad because he made a statement about white people and Jews, but that same congress can't make a single statement about a white militia after they kill 168 people. A white boy did it. A crisis that was evident in the fact that they were ready to blame it on an Arab or black people or anybody not white. But when they found out that a white boy had done it, they couldn't even begin to talk about it. That's a profound crisis.

This is a crisis that makes me say that maybe we should take the guns out of the hands of young black people, and put them in the hands of young white people! It's crisis when white boys go to school nowadays and kill everybody in the joint. It's a part of the crisis when even white folk have concluded that the system can't solve their problems, and growing numbers of white people are armed to the teeth all over this country.

There was a time when all over this country those white people were armed, but they were organized to kill African people. They would never blow up a federal building or kill white people unless the white people were so-called nigger-lovers. They'd never try to attack the government, but now they're armed to the teeth to blow up the Feds. That is the crisis that exists inside this country.

We also see resistance growing. We saw resistance in the Million Man March.[10] I want to make it clear that I'm in total disagreement with what I think was the most reactionary, backwards call associated with the Million Man March, where somehow a million black people were supposed to go to

Washington D.C. to "atone for our sins." Washington D.C. is the headquarters of the crimes against the peoples of the world. It is the headquarters of the crimes against African people, and they say *I* should atone for my sins! What they should have done is to call for Clinton to come out with his hands up! You understand?

When two million African people showed up in Washington, D.C., it was clearly an indication that the people wanted to resist. When you saw thousands of people come out to the Million Women's March, it was clearly a sign that people are looking for ways to resist. They haven't found those ways yet, but they are looking for resistance.

We have to take advantage of this era of crisis and resistance. The problem is that this resistance has to be given shape and form. The problem is that it's not enough for the oppressor to be in a state of crisis. Sometimes, crisis makes this guy more desperate and more reactionary than at other times.

I'm told that now in Philadelphia, if you're homeless they put you in jail, and if you can't pay the fine, then they take away your right to have a house. They're imposing the most vicious kind of oppressive laws all around this country. The prisons are full, stuffed with African people everywhere. This is a consequence of crisis. Now, we have a responsibility to become organized. We have to build revolutionary organizations. We have to participate in efforts like the National People's Democratic Uhuru Movement[11] that is essentially fighting to push back the State to give us the democratic space that we need to pursue the revolutionary interests and aspirations of the masses of the people here and around the world.

Thank you very much. Uhuru!

---

1 Fannie Lou Hamer and Willie (Mukassa) Ricks were leaders and heroes of the Student Nonviolent Coordinating Committee (SNCC), a critical organization that bridged the transition from the Civil Rights Movement of the 1950s to the Black Power Movement of the '60s. Hamer, who died in 1977,

led a contingent of African workers to the Democratic party national convention in 1964, demanding that the SNCC-organized Mississippi Freedom Democratic Party be recognized by the convention. When the Democrats granted them only two seats, Hamer stated, "We didn't come all this way for no two seats!" Ricks, as a fiery young orator, first made the famous demand, "Black Power," which reverberated around the world.

2 Elijah Muhammad was the leader of the Nation of Islam during the time that Malcolm X was a member.

3 Martin Luther King was killed on April 4, 1968.

4 Fred Hampton was the Chairman of the Illinois chapter of the Black Panther Party and a brilliant rising young leader of the Black Panther Party who founded a free clinic and free breakfast for school children program in Chicago. Chairman Fred was only twenty-one years old when he was assassinated by Chicago police and the FBI on December 4, 1969.

5 Liddy, Hunt and Secord were well-known figures in the Watergate scandal of the 1970s. Along with Oliver North, Liddy and Hunt also played key roles in the Iran-Contra scandal in the 1980s in which sectors of the U.S. government were funding and leading a paramilitary force known as the Contras. The Contras waged a counterinsurgent war against the people of Nicaragua under the revolutionary Sandinista government. This war was funded by sales of drugs brought into the U.S. by the CIA. The drugs particularly targeted the African community.

6 Sandinistas was the popular name for the Frente Sandinista de Liberacion Nacional (FSLN), which led the revolutionary movement for the liberation of Nicaragua.

7 Gary Webb was the author of *Dark Alliance*, the 1996 series in the *San Jose Mercury News* that was later published as a book. Webb committed suicide in California in December 2004.

8 The MOVE house on Osage Avenue in Philadelphia was bombed on May 13, 1985. Six adults and five children were killed. Sixty-one houses in the surrounding African community were destroyed in the conflagration.

9 Africans from Kenya, Tanzania and Uganda were recruited by the British colonizers to fight in the Homeguards and the King's African Rifles, military counterinsurgent forces used against the Mau Mau liberation movement of the Kikuyu people in Kenya in the 1950s.

10 The Million Man March, led by the Nation of Islam, took place on Oct. 16, 1995 in Washington, D.C.

11 Now the International People's Democratic Uhuru Movement (InPDUM), founded by the African People's Socialist Party in 1991 to defend the democratic rights of the African community.

Tiger Bay Club presentation

White rulers can no longer disregard African workers

Chairman Omali was invited by the St. Petersburg Tiger Bay Club to speak to their monthly lunch meeting on July 9, 1998. Tiger Bay is a St. Petersburg political discussion group whose membership is made up largely of local white ruling class politicians and businessmen.

The invitation to speak to the club came during the period of massive publicity for the Chairman and the Uhuru Movement following the October 24, 1996 police killing of eighteen-year-old TyRon Lewis. The police killing sparked a rebellion that night, followed by a second rebellion on November 13 after a force of three hundred police attacked the Uhuru House. (See "City of African resistance" on page 69 for an in depth summation of this period.)

As the voice of the mass demand for genuine economic development for the African community and an end to the brutal policies of police containment, Chairman Omali became the recognized representative of the African community.

In this presentation the Chairman confronts the white ruling class of St. Petersburg from a position of real power and leverage on the part of the African working class.

A little more than thirty years ago Africans were often murdered in this country for simply attempting to register to join the Democratic party. We could not stop to use a service station toilet on the highway or any other public facility without fear of arrest, beatings or even worse.

Indeed, the conditions of existence for African people

became a major foreign policy problem for the U.S. government. The entire world knew of America primarily because of its brutal treatment of African people.

Yet today, a mere thirty-four years after the formal granting of civil rights and thirty-three years after formally winning the right to vote, Africans in the U.S., especially the working class and impoverished youth, are characterized as vicious predators, an inarticulate and pathologically criminal community.

A little more than thirty years ago, incessant struggle for democracy by our people resulted in the primary public policy debate in the U.S. revolving around issues of black liberation. Today the public policy debate, while still involving African people, revolves around the most effective means of police containment in our increasingly impoverished community.

This turn of affairs did not come about overnight. It came as a consequence of a process that saw thousands of young African militants arrested and killed throughout this country during the 1960s.

It came as a consequence of the political murders of Minister Malcolm X and Dr. Martin Luther King. It came as a result of the brutal assault by the FBI on politically independent African organizational formations with which the owning classes of America and the U.S. government had ideological and political differences.

With our leadership imprisoned and assassinated throughout the U.S. and so many of our organizations destroyed with their membership dispersed, African people within the U.S. began to experience a great assault on the basic democratic gains we had won during the sixties.

A community that was now ideologically and politically defenseless watched in horror as most of the basic civil rights, assumed to have been won during the Civil Rights Movement, were taken away, one after the other, often in the name of fighting against crime.

The America that has never even formally acknowledged the immorality of African slavery, Jim Crow and lynch mob justice, has cynically absolved itself of any responsibility for the conditions of existence of my people.

Instead, it has declared these conditions, which are symptoms of economic exploitation and political oppression, to be the result of pathology, of self-inflicted emiseration. America claims our conditions are the natural due of a people whose collective moral foundation proves inadequate to the rigors of civilized existence.

The owning classes use for their purposes the acquiescence of a pliant, generally hand-picked black leadership that has always defined its goals within the acceptable parameters of the white establishment and their representatives. This allows the establishment to simply refuse to acknowledge the interests of the majority of the African community, which is employed and unemployed workers.

The politically and ideologically independent representatives of the African working class—those who continue to survive—have been characterized as marginal and extremist. Their views have been exiled from the arena of public political discourse.

The reason I am here before you today is because the masses of African workers and poor in St. Petersburg thrust themselves back into history on October 24 and November 13, 1996, after the police assassination of eighteen-year-old TyRon Lewis and the attack on the Uhuru House, our office.

Although the city of St. Petersburg is typical in its policy of police containment of African people, it has its own history and its own interests which inform its actions.

Its history is one of a city that was founded as a center for white tourism, and its political economy is based on this fact.

The African population of St. Petersburg was brought here for the purpose of providing a cheap labor force for this tourist industry. Our significance as a cheap labor force grew to include the nursing home industry that was an offshoot of tourism.

From the beginning there was a built-in tension to this relationship. On the one hand our cheap labor was seen as essential to a profitable tourist industry, while on the other hand there was the irrational fear that our black presence was a threat to this same tourism. The resolution to this quandary has been police containment of the African community.

This policy of police containment achieved a new and urgent significance with the introduction of the idea of a baseball team for St. Petersburg. Like many of the decisions concerning economic development for the City of St. Petersburg, the determination to boost the city's economy with the acquisition of a baseball team came at great expense to our community.

In this case the price was the black community of the Gas Plant area. We had already experienced community destruction with the razing of Methodist Town and all its black businesses.[1]

Africans had also lost neighborhoods and businesses when an interstate was brought through the city, ripping apart the African community. And now, the Gas Plant area would go, again in the name of economic development.

The stadium for the baseball team rests like a giant tomb on the corpse of what was once a dynamic African community. It is partially surrounded by another African community and various institutions historically associated with Africans.

This is the reality that resulted in the attempt by the city to create an African-free, sanitized zone around the stadium. This reality led to struggles on the part of African people for the democratic right to use the public parks in the proximity of the stadium.

It was this reality that resulted in the broad daylight police execution of TyRon Lewis[2] on October 24, 1996. James Knight of the St. Petersburg Police Department was the triggerman who killed TyRon Lewis, and in our opinion, Knight was one who thoroughly enjoyed his work.

It was this reality that informed us in the Uhuru Movement to say that the real issue was not Knight, nor even the cops whose cartoons[3] mocked the death of Lewis, but the policy of police containment that established the conditions within which they functioned.

However, I want to be clear that this description of a reality and politic based on historical conditions and economic factors should not be mistaken as an assumption on my part that we are on an historically predetermined course that demands permanent confrontation. This is not my belief.

Indeed, I am convinced that the possibilities for progressive change in St. Petersburg are greater than anywhere in this country. They are greater precisely because the primary contending social forces are quite conscious of what their material interests are, and both are therefore in a position to base their political relationship on these interests.

The public police execution of TyRon Lewis ignited a popular rebellion that made it politically impossible to continue to ignore the African working class masses. The popular, physical defense of the Uhuru leadership, which came under police attack at our office on November 13, 1996, was also a declaration by the people of the significance of the Uhuru Movement as an actual, that is to say, real, on the ground, representative of the most dynamic sector of the African community.

This is what Henry Cisneros[4] saw during his brief visit to St. Petersburg in the aftermath of the police shooting and community rebellions.

This is what helped mayor David Fisher[5] to retreat from the rash and politically immature declaration that he would never meet with Omali Yeshitela.

The reality is that it was the perceived threat to tourism and an anticipated billion dollar baseball industry that led to the shooting of TyRon Lewis. This was another attempt at unilaterally-determined economic development that would come at the expense of the African community as in the past.

However, this same perceived threat to the tourist and baseball industries led to recognition of the need to accept the fact that the African community also has interests and aspirations that have to be considered. Thus the stage has been set for an honest relationship based on democracy, mutual respect and the possibility of replacing the failed policy of police containment of the African community with a policy of economic development that is the only path to social justice.

The possibility for profound change is here in St. Petersburg. However, it will take a bold leadership with more courage than has been demonstrated up to now. It will take a leadership that is willing to end the political inertia responsible for the trajectory of the past, a leadership willing to accept the lessons learned from the shooting and rebellions of 1996.

These lessons were real. Their value must inform us now, even as the memory of the burning buildings and teargas-inflamed nostrils continue to fade.

We can no longer continue to do things and base relationships on political habits that do not recognize the value of black labor or which disregard the integrity of African opinions, aspirations and material interests.

We must see a leadership from the city and the city's financial institutions that gives as much practical commitment to economic development for the African community as it does to the economic activity associated with the baseball team.

The financial institutions must end the economic quarantine of the African community. They must provide an infusion of massive amounts of capital to be used for self-employment and improvement and expansion of existing businesses, along with the initiation of new, economically consequential enterprises, all of which will contribute to the creation of community commerce and economic development.

This is a different cry from the traditional call for jobs, which generally has little or nothing to do with economic development.

This is a different cry from the traditional call for the location of expatriate corporations and businesses within our community, because such corporate businesses are essentially nothing more than a means of capital extraction that often stifles the development of community enterprise and can actually lead to economic underdevelopment.

No, my friends, when we speak of community commerce and economic development, we speak of a community engaged in economic activity, the consequences of which—whether as worker or entrepreneur—will be the actual development of our own community.

And finally, we must admit to the failure of the disingenuous policy of police containment. It is at best a poor substitute for economic development. At worst, it is simply colonial occupation. It has never worked anywhere in the world in the past and it will not work in the African community today, nor should it.

The Jim Crow program of Weed and Seed,[6] which allows for the occupation of the most oppressed, economically devastated sector of the population by an array of oppressive federal, state and local police organizations should be denounced by all freedom loving people everywhere. Certainly we in the Uhuru Movement will continue to denounce it.

In closing I would like to say that African people are good.

We have played a central and very critical role in the development of the culture and economy of this country and this city. Our demand today is that we be allowed to do the same for ourselves.

To this end we are committed to relentless struggle. We welcome all who will to join with us.

Uhuru!

1 The Gas Plant and Methodist Town were two once-thriving African neighborhoods of St. Petersburg. Both were destroyed by development plans in the city and bolstered economic conditions for the white citizens at the expense of the African community.

2 Eighteen-year-old TyRon Lewis was killed on October 24, 1996 by St. Petersburg police. Lewis was shot with his hands up, unarmed in his car during a traffic stop in front of a crowd in the busiest intersection in the African community. The murder of this young African sparked a major African community rebellion that night and again three weeks later, when the police attacked the Uhuru House after the grand jury exonerated the killer cops. For the next several years, the murder of Lewis was central to the Uhuru Movement's mass organizing strategy calling for economic development and social justice for the African community.

3 After TyRon Lewis was killed by St. Petersburg police it was exposed that the police had circulated throughout the department anti-African cartoons ridiculing Lewis' murder.

4 Henry Cisneros, the U.S. secretary of housing and urban development (HUD) under the Clinton administration, was sent to St. Petersburg by Clinton to investigate the situation following the African community rebellions after the police murder of TyRon Lewis and the attack on the Uhuru House in 1996.

5 Mayor of St. Petersburg in 1996 at the time of the police murder and African community rebellions.

6 Weed and Seed is a federal police program that targets the most impoverished areas of African and oppressed communities. In the target area, crimes are prosecuted on a federal, rather than local level, with correspondingly higher sentences, thereby setting up Jim Crow law. Weed and Seed uses extra-constitutional means, including wiretaps, preventive detention and enhanced sentencing. A variety of federal and state police agencies band together to enforce martial law and containment policies, conducting sweeps and setting up a network of snitches and informants. The "seed" aspect, which supposedly brings resources into the target area, never benefits the African community.

Liberate Africa
and all her children
Build the African Socialist International

Chairman Omali delivered this presentation in London, during the August 1999 preliminary conference to build the African Socialist International (ASI). This piece is especially important because it shows the history of the work done by the African People's Socialist Party to finalize the ASI as an organizational tool to unite African people for the liberation of Africa. After decades of work throughout the U.S. and on an international level, the ASI meeting in June 2005 will build an Interim Committee with the responsibility of organizing the founding Congress of the ASI. Under the title "On the African Socialist International," this presentation appeared in the May 1999–April 2000 edition of The Burning Spear *newspaper.*

Uhuru! I would like to express my deep appreciation to Comrade Luwezi[1] for the tremendous amount of work that he did to put together this preliminary conference to build the African Socialist International (ASI). The level of discussion that we've had over the past few days has been profound. The process of achieving unity required the kind of discussion and struggles that have transpired this weekend. One brother made the point that there is nothing wrong with struggle. Certainly, ideological and political struggles are essential if we are going to move forward.

I would like to give some history of the effort by the African People's Socialist Party to build the African Socialist International. It is something that began at least twenty years ago. The vision of the ASI was pushed further at our Party's First Congress in 1981, nine years after our Party's 1972 founding. Initially, when we talked about trying to pull together the African Socialist International, our efforts were compromised in part by our own organizational ineptitude.

Our early efforts were frustrated additionally because, at that time, many Africans were conscious of the struggles to overturn direct white power colonialism in places like Rhodesia and South Africa. The majority of African people, however, did not yet understand the question of neocolonialism.

African people were not capable of being enthusiastic about pulling together an all-African International organization such as the one we in the African People's Socialist Party envisioned. Africans everywhere were intoxicated by the national liberation struggles that were waged during the 1960s in Africa, many of which had just won independence in the 1970s. Prior to this, Africans in places like the United States had come to hate our identity with Africa because it was so associated with oppression, exploitation and various forms of slander by our slave masters and oppressors.

When the national liberation movements sprang up throughout Africa in the 1960s, African people were enthusiastic to see that. Most of us were unprepared for the fact that neocolonialism would dismantle, in fact smash, the hope promised by these liberation movements. The reality was the African national liberation movements failed to solve the problems of the broad masses of African people. Instead of solutions, we have seen corruption and oppression from neocolonial regimes, which sit on the backs of the people. These are puppet states, which are limited, among other things, by colonially-established borders, as well as by the class aspirations and interests of the puppet leaders.

In the African People's Socialist Party we are convinced that the struggle for African freedom has reached its limitations within the borders defined for us by imperialism. That is true whether those borders are in Africa itself or whether they are in places like England, the United States or the Caribbean. These imposed borders serve effectively to keep African people separate from each other. They serve as an effective means of extracting wealth and value from Africa and African people.

Thus even today in 1999, the latest figures I have seen indicate that only seven percent of all trade in Africa occurs among Africans ourselves. This means that the vast majority of the "formal" trade, as they characterize it, is the theft of value and resources from Africa by Europe, North America and increasingly Japan.

For the longest period in North America, the struggle of African people has been a struggle essentially for rights under colonial domination, rights within a colonial system. Sometimes this has represented itself as some kind of revolutionary struggle. Yet it made an assumption of a privileged fate for African people within the United States that was separate from, and at the expense of, African people in Africa and throughout the world.

In Africa we have seen an attempt at separate solutions for the forty-eight or so sub-Saharan African territories. Of course, this has only resulted in the reinforcement of neocolonialism and the continued extraction of value from Africa. Any progressive or revolutionary development in Africa is inevitably attacked viciously by European and American imperialism.

The reality that we have to face is that Africans in Europe and the United States are too often merely spectators of these attacks, ignorant of our interests and our strategic relationship to the liberation of Africa itself.

While many progressives, militants and revolutionaries continue to debate the historical basis for unity among African people, the Organization of African Unity (OAU)[2] does nothing more than consolidate imperialist borders that separate us and serve to extract value.

Neocolonial agents of imperialism are acting even now as the advanced guard of imperialism. They host economic summits designed to open up Africa for further transference of her resources to be shared by a Pan-African coterie of thieves.

Today, the crisis of imperialism is reflected in the crisis of neocolonialism, which is deepening the misery of African people worldwide. Reports given at this meeting today will reflect this crisis and the growing emiseration of our people throughout the world. The reports will also reflect the fact that the African working class aligned with the poor peasantry represents the social force of the future, absolutely necessary for our advancement as free people into the next millennium.

The struggles for rights under imperialism which many of us are working for in Africa and abroad, while tactically significant, are no substitute for revolutionary transformation which requires the ascendancy of the African working class in alliance with the poor peasantry as the new ruling class. The current crisis of imperialism demands that we Africans come together to assume responsibility for our fate.

Hence the call to build the African Socialist International, a worldwide organization for African liberation fighting on many fronts around the world in strategic unity. The ASI must be based on revolutionary principles with the objective of liberating and unifying Africa and all her children who have been dispersed throughout the world. The ASI must be a party which has as its fundamental objective the elevation of African workers and toilers to their rightful role as leaders in society.

As we have said, this is a preliminary process. It is an initiative by the African People's Socialist Party. But we've tried to make it an initiative that involves the people in the process. Since August 14, I have spoken in venues throughout London and other cities in England. I have been trying to share our ideas with the masses of African people. I'm sure that we have made mistakes in the process, but the process allows for criticism of the mistakes. There is an element of transparency that we fought to make happen.

This two-day meeting is tied to our objective of trying to make a planning process—a plenary—happen here in London in April 2000. The plenary will be preceded by the distribution of political documents in December. That allows us at least four months of discussion and struggle so that we can forge unity at the April meeting.

In the interim, we would like to see a standing committee emerge here in London. The committee would act as a clearing-house to receive information from places around the world where African people are engaged in discussion and struggle regarding this paper. The clearing house would then disseminate that information.

The committee would also collect contacts so that we can maximize our outreach to the African community throughout the world. Everybody can participate in this. It's not a situation in which only some people's opinions are valid. The standing committee will raise money and resolve logistical questions.

The African People's Socialist Party has learned so much during this process. As we struggle to build the ASI, we test ourselves in the process and get to know each other better.

In this process we must address the immigration question. This is a crisis that is occurring throughout Europe, particularly here in England and in France. Africans are either being denied entrance, being kicked out or jailed.

African communities that are immediately affected by this crisis should not have to fight by themselves. If there are Congolese rotting in prisons in France, all of us ought to be concerned. If Africans from Ivory Coast are threatened with deportation because of the connivance of the British government and the neocolonial Ivorian government, all of us ought to be concerned. If Africans from Zimbabwe here in England are being threatened with deportation to that despotic neocolonial government of Zimbabwe, Africans everywhere ought to be concerned. We need the ability to move in a unified way.

What do we know about the struggle of the people of Ivory Coast other than what we have learned at these meetings this weekend? We have to be able to create public forums to discuss the various struggles of African people in various places. By creating these forums, the African community can be aware of these struggles and help to defend our people against imperialism as it is impacting on us, here and every place else. We can begin to communicate with each other right now. We have to take on these kinds of issues immediately. If we do that it can impact on the consciousness of everybody.

It is crucially important for us to work for the creation of African Internationalist consciousness all over the African world. It must be a fundamental task to win African Internationalist consciousness so that the masses of African people can no longer identify themselves as "black Brits," or "black Americans," or even "Tutsis" or "Rwandans." We are African people first!

We owe no loyalty to any of these neocolonial puppet state. and our neocolonial oppressors have no loyalty to us! They have no loyalty to the Nigerian State or the Zimbabwean people. So why should the masses of people, any of us anywhere, be stuck with those kinds of labels? The struggle for African Internationalist consciousness is something that we can take out of this room right now.

The problem is that we have to learn about something that is happening to African people by reading about it in the bourgeois media. Our only sources are Associated Press, United Press International or the British press. Nobody has direct access to information about our struggles. We need to inform the masses of African people directly. If there are individuals and organizations among us who have access to journals, newspapers and other forms of information distribution, we should utilize them. All of these journals should put out information on struggles that African people are involved in everywhere.

Sisters and Brothers, one reason that we in the African People's Socialist Party were compelled to work to build the ASI is because Africans in the United States—and I believe it is true of Africans everywhere—cannot see the future unless that future is Africa. When I say Africa, I no longer mean Ivory Coast or Ghana or the Gambia or Sudan. I mean Africa! We are convinced that there is no future for us within the borders that have been defined for us by imperialism.

In the United States, how many more civil rights movements can we have? How many more rights can we beg from imperialism inside the United States or England or anyplace else? The reality is that our future is directly tied to Africa. That is something that we have come to understand.

The need for political education keeps springing up in this discussion. This process of building the ASI contributes to our ability to have meaningful political education. In the United States and other places, we only know ourselves by how reality impacts on us.

But we have a collective history and a collective identity that we've been separated from by these imposed borders. This process contributes to our ability to create a real political education, not only about the greatness and magnificence of African history, but also about the future of a liberated Africa.

We need to create political education exchange programs. We need to exchange information about the problems we are trying to solve in the various locations where we exist. We need to discuss what political education should look like and how we train our cadres. I believe that as a part of that process, we can come up with a pretty good agenda. We can formulate a curriculum and transform our understandings.

Central to political education is practice—doing the political work. There used to be a saying in New York City: "Ain't nothing to it, but to do it." I believe that practice is primary. If we go to work, we learn, share and sum up our experiences through this process. Then we go to work again and we learn more. I think this becomes a primary means by which we achieve political education.

A brother raised the question of northern Africa. It is a very important question that seldom gets discussed. It is ignored in public, although it is talked about in private all over Africa.

We have to build a revolutionary movement that requires everybody in Africa to fight for African liberation. Otherwise, we will have an Arab imperialism that sits there with the wealth of the oil, dictating things that happen in Africa, as the Arab countries often do today.

The way it is now, it is convenient for folk to be Africans when it's time to help shape opinions in groups like the neocolonial Organization of African Unity. When it comes to Arab meetings, then they are Pan-Arabs.

I believe that the future of Africans requires us to fight for Africa. Everybody in Africa will fight for African liberation or they will have to find someplace else to live. In the final analysis, African Internationalist consciousness will be forged in the actual struggle to destroy and overturn imperialism on the continent of Africa. African Internationalist consciousness is going to be consolidated in the process of liberating Africa.

Thank you very much, Sisters and Brothers. I believe that if we move forward from this point on, the future surely belongs to us. If we free Africa, we free the world! This is our responsibility. This is the burden that history has placed upon the shoulders of African people all over the world.

Izwe Lethu i Afrika![3]

1 Luwezi Kinshasa is the Director of International Affairs for the African People's Socialist Party

2 The Organization of African Unity was formed in 1963 as an organization to unite all African countries. The founding of the OAU was greatly influenced by Kwame Nkrumah, the first president of liberated Ghana. In 2000 the OAU became the African Union (AU).

3 A call and response slogan first popularized by the Pan Africanist Congress of Azania. "Izwe lethu" means "the land is ours," "i Afrika" identifies the land.

The struggle in Zimbabwe

Land to the African peasants!
Power to the African workers!

The following is an excerpt from a speech made by Chairman Omali at the Marcus Garvey Library in London, England on April 25, 2000. It was first printed in The Burning Spear *issue of May-July 2000.*

African people are facing very serious conditions all over the world, but one of the most pressing struggles is in Zimbabwe. The situation there is more complicated than it appears.

During the 1970s, the African People's Socialist Party built the first solidarity movement in the United Sates for the Zimbabwe African National Union (ZANU),[1] which is now in power in Zimbabwe. We toured leading ZANU cadres throughout the United States on a regular basis. Those on tour would change rather frequently, however, because they would often desert and go over to the side of Ian Smith.[2] So ZANU would send another person and we would work with them.

The African People's Socialist Party set up ZANU's office in New York City and staffed the first person in that office. We did not do this casually. We did it in opposition to the Zimbabwe African People's Union (ZAPU), which was a contending force. We did it because of ZANU's commitment to the land and its commitment to "an all African solution." We did it because ZANU said that it recognized that the solution for African people could not be resolved in Zimbabwe, but that Zimbabwe was a part of the

125

effort to liberate all of Africa. We were able to unite with ZANU on that basis, and we worked very hard for that organization.

We disagreed with ZANU's acceptance of the Lancaster House Agreement, which was a settlement that ended the liberation struggle in Zimbabwe. We disagreed because the armed struggle had reached a point where ZANU could have won everything.[3]

We understood, though, that ZANU was under pressure. This pressure was coming not only from the United States and England directly. The imperialist powers were also exerting pressure on Tanzania, Zambia and the Frontline States where ZANU had bases.

These Frontline States actually threatened to kick ZANU's forces out of those countries unless they went to the table and made the deal. So, even though we disagreed and were critical of ZANU for making the deal, we understood the pressure ZANU was under when that happened.

In the Lancaster House Agreement, both England and the United States promised that they would compensate the white settlers who had stolen our land, paying the white farmers in Zimbabwe for the land they occupied. Personally, I didn't think they should be compensated for anything. I thought that allowing them to leave with their lives would be doing them a favor. They were brutal racists, colonialist thugs who perpetrated the worst kinds of crimes against our people. They were lucky to be left alive.

Over the years, we have come to have serious differences with ZANU because it turns out to be a petty bourgeois, neocolonial organization. Even as it has struggles with the white farmers on the one hand, it is in bed with imperialism in a deep way on the other hand.

Neocolonialism is the most significant enemy that African people around the world are confronted with. Neocolonialism is white power in black face. All over Africa and all over America we have white power in black face, and increasingly we see white power in black face here in England. It's a profound contradiction that we have to deal with. Our struggle is not simply to replace a white oppressor with a black oppressor.

We have problems with Zimbabwe President Robert Mugabe for a number of reasons, including the fact that in the twenty years since ZANU took power the land question has never been resolved.

When did Mugabe begin to deal with the land question? Not until the veterans of the liberation army—the people who actually fought against the thuggish Rhodesian government—began to hold demonstrations in 1997 against the government because their pension money had disappeared. ZANU leaders were getting fat.

Other kinds of economic crises were also creating dissatisfaction among the masses of people in Zimbabwe—the workers and peasants. Of course the peasants were dissatisfied because they had no land. Four thousand white people own seventy-five percent of the arable land in Zimbabwe today. Most of that land is not even used to grow anything. It's just lying fallow ever since ZANU came into power. So when the veterans began to demonstrate because of the disappearance of their pension money, Mugabe raised the land question to pacify the veterans.

During this period, France and the United States have been involved in a serious battle in Congo. The United Sates is challenging French hegemony over so-called francophone Africa. One expression of that is the war that has been taking place in Congo, killing many, many African people there. All kinds of forces are involved in Congo for various reasons, some of them for their own narrow, local interests. Mugabe owns an interest in diamond mines in Congo. He is sending the children of peasants and workers from Zimbabwe into Congo to make war in his own interest. This is the struggle that we have with Mugabe and with ZANU.

In 1997, when Mugabe threatened the white farmers by taking the land, the International Monetary Fund (IMF)[4] devalued Zimbabwe's currency, creating a profound economic crisis and making the people even more dissatisfied. Mugabe tried to hold on to power by attempting to change the constitution to allow him to stay in power beyond his term.

The effort to change the constitution was defeated soundly. It was defeated in part because the African masses were dissatisfied, but also because the white farmers participated in supporting, if not organizing, the Movement for Democratic Change (MDC). Its leader was just here in London meeting with the imperialist boss.

The Movement for Democratic Change funded and set up rallies on the white-owned plantations where many Africans work. The MDC spent money to defeat Mugabe at the polls. When they beat Mugabe, he raised the land question again and unleashed the war veterans in the struggle to take the land. This is part of the current crisis.

If the African People's Socialist Party were stronger and had the ability, our position in Zimbabwe would be to raise up the slogan, "Land to the peasants and power to the working class." We would sweep ZANU out of power. "Land to the peasants and power to the workers!" That's what we need, but we don't have organization on the ground in Zimbabwe.

The most positive thing we have seen there is the Zimbabwe Union of Democrats, an organization headed by a woman named Margaret Dongo. At the age of fifteen, Margaret Dongo was actually a guerrilla who fought for ZANU. Later she denounced ZANU's corruption and was kicked out of the party. She is the only independent force in parliament and has organized what seems to be a relatively honest progressive movement on the ground. Other than that we don't see any kind of revolutionary force in Zimbabwe.

The Movement for Democratic Change is a tool of the white farmers. There is no way you can support it. It is worse than ZANU. Some people may be confused about this. I have heard talk about "doing the right thing" by supporting this entity. Then there are others who support Mugabe and ZANU unconditionally because of the opposition coming down against him from the white farmers and the bourgeois media.

Our position is this: we unite with Mugabe and ZANU against imperialism and the white farmers; and we unite with the masses of peasants and workers in Zimbabwe against Mugabe! [Applause]

Ultimately the people have to have power and we have to express the aspirations of the people for true African independence. Right now Mugabe is manipulating that situation for his own interest. We have to struggle for a united and liberated Africa under the leadership of African workers and poor peasants.

Izwe Lethu i Afrika!

1 ZANU was the movement for the national liberation of Zimbabwe, formerly the British colony of Rhodesia. ZANU-PF is Zimbabwe African National Union Patriotic Front.

2 Ian Smith was the colonial ruler of Zimbabwe prior to its independence in 1979.

3 Culminating years of military struggle for national liberation, Robert Mugabe and ZANU entered into the Lancaster House Agreement with Britain and the U.S. in 1979. This settlement gave nominal power to ZANU while protecting the position of Zimbabwe's white settlers, who were allocated twenty seats in parliament. Land reform, specifically the redistribution of white-owned land to landless black peasants, was promised to African peasants but in fact officially delayed for ten years.

4 The International Monetary Fund is an agency of the United Nations, established in 1945. The IMF targets, in particular, countries that are former colonies by providing "loans" that tie these countries economically to imperialism. IMF policies deepen economic dependency, further impoverishing already ravished countries to nearly genocidal levels.

Black vote stolen!

The ruling class resolves every electoral crisis at the expense of African people

The following is Chairman Omali's insightful analysis of the stolen African vote in the 2000 presidential election by the Republican party and forces backing U.S. president George W. Bush. The Chairman astutely points out the ongoing historical attempt by all sectors of the white ruling class—Republicans and Democrats alike—to resolve elections and other crises at the expense of African people.

This presentation was made in St. Petersburg, Florida at the December 2000 meeting of the Central Committee of the African People's Solidarity Committee (APSC). The African People's Socialist Party formed the solidarity committee in 1976. Made up predominantly of white people who organize in the white communities, APSC works under the direct leadership of the Party's strategy to build white solidarity for the struggle for the liberation of Africa and African people. This presentation was first published in the August 2000-January 2001 issue of The Burning Spear *newspaper.*

In the 2000 presidential election, the Republican party developed a strategy to elect George Walker Bush that required the elimination of the African vote as a factor. Considering the fact that the vast majority of African people in this country who participate in political life do so almost solely through the electoral process, that is a very profound statement. A sector of the bourgeoisie decided to negate the participation and political life of African people in order to carry out its own interests. That's profound, but it's really not a new thing. The same strategy has been played out over and over again in U.S. history.

In 1968, Richard Milhous Nixon developed the so-called Southern strategy to win the presidency. This strategy was based on the negation of the African vote as a factor, concentrating on winning Southern whites to vote for the Republican party in the presidential election. The Southern whites voted for Nixon even though they remained loyal to the Democratic party on local and congressional levels, since the Democratic party controlled the Southern local power base. Nixon developed that strategy on an anti-African program and won.

James Earl Carter's election in 1976 was significant because as a Southern Democrat he was able to arouse the most reactionary assumptions of white people. The Carter administration was only able to make it through one term. Carter was easily unseated by the counter-revolutionary 1980 presidential campaign of Ronald Wilson Reagan who openly declared war against the rights of African people.

In 1992, William Jefferson Clinton ran a campaign that viciously attacked the African population in order to win over large sectors of the white population. These attacks on African people made it possible for the Democratic party to win a presidential election for the first time since the Carter administration.

A Southern Democrat and a very adroit politician, Clinton carried out the same kind of electoral strategy as Nixon's. While campaigning at Jesse Jackson's Rainbow Coalition meeting, he attacked Sista Souljah, a popular, militant rap artist. During his campaign, Clinton also executed Ricky Ray Rector, a mentally disabled African man in Arkansas where Clinton was governor.

While in the White House, Clinton attacked affirmative action and welfare and led the assault on African women and children in public housing with the "One strike, you're out" executive order.[1] Clinton did those kinds of things to win over the white vote. So the Republican party in this 2000 comeback attempt simply put forth its own expression of the same strategy of negating the African vote. Only this time it represents a crisis.

Tilden-Hayes Compromise a similar situation

I just want to comment on this stolen election by the Republicans by taking us back to 1876. This is something a lot of political organizations will not understand very well because there is a tendency to liquidate or underestimate the potential for anti-black repression in this country.

But let me tell you this: it's clear that in this country *any* form of political expression by African people is challenged. It doesn't matter if it is a revolutionary form of political expression, such as the Black Revolution of the Sixties where the U.S. government retaliated by assassinating our leaders, or whether it is in the electoral process itself. *Any* form of significant African political expression, especially independent political expression, comes under assault in this country.

In 1876, there was a situation similar to the current one in 2000. The election that year was a contest between Samuel Tilden, a Democrat who was the former governor of New York, and Rutherford B. Hayes, a Republican who was the former governor of Ohio. The Democratic party was deeply entrenched in the South. It was supported by the sector of the white ruling class that was deeply interested in development in the South.

This was some eleven years after the Civil War, which under the leadership of the Republican party ended chattel slavery in this country. That meant that the majority of African people in this country were sympathetic to the Republican party, the party of Abraham Lincoln.[2] Inside the Republican party was a faction that was characterized as the "radical Republicans" who were very much to the left of Lincoln.

At the end of the Civil War, as in any defeat, there was

military occupation of the South by federal troops. The rights of the Southern plantocracy had been taken away on many fronts, and African people actually rose to power in government. This era is called "Reconstruction."

This was not something that white people in the South, particularly the ruling class, took lightly. There was an ongoing campaign to undermine Reconstruction. In fact, this may have precipitated the assassination of Lincoln, who was replaced by his vice president, Andrew Johnson, who started to deconstruct Reconstruction in a very serious way. Johnson overturned the promise of "forty acres and a mule" to the formerly enslaved African masses and everything that was associated with it.

The ongoing struggle to undermine Reconstruction was a struggle to undermine the power of African people that had come at the expense of the Southerners or whites. It played a role in shaping the election of 1876. There were a lot of economic factors involved, as well. As I mentioned, Tilden had been the governor of New York and so he was not Southern-based, but there were economic interests in the South in which Northern capitalists were involved. Tilden actually won the majority of the vote, like Gore did in this election. Tilden won in part as a consequence of terrorizing the African voters throughout the South. Terror was used as a means of keeping people from the poles.

Three Southern Republican governors refused to accredit electors to their states because the Democratic victory had come through terrorizing African voters. This led to the creation of a congressional committee that gave the presidency to Hayes. In response, mobs of white people marched throughout the country yelling, "Tilden or blood!" There were even threats of another civil war.

Hayes assumed the presidency in the midst of this turmoil and crisis eleven years after the end of the Civil War. In order to be able to govern, he had to make a deal with the Democrats. So the contending sectors of the ruling class came to the table and made a deal.

The Tilden-Hayes Compromise was an agreement that the Republican party would remove the federal troops that were in the South protecting the lives of African people during the Reconstruction. The compromise negated all political power that had been attained by African people with the Reconstruction government.

The fundamental thing is that Hayes snatched the federal troops out of the South. With the federal troops gone, there was an escalation of terror and the emergence of the Ku Klux Klan[3] that murdered and lynched thousands of African people. This resulted in what the African community has characterized as the "Exodusters," based on the Exodus from the Bible, where thousands and thousands of African people left the South trying to find a place of safety and security. Sometimes we set up independent black cities. In fact, there was a move to try to turn Oklahoma into an all-African state. According to history books, the leader of that effort was mysteriously killed.

With the overthrow of Reconstruction in 1876, the apartheid system of Jim Crow was imposed. African people were taken out of the political process, their right to vote taken away. Lynch mob rule prevailed and was not formally overturned for almost a hundred years. Not until 1964 were Africans given what were supposed to be formal civil rights in this country and in 1965 the Voting Rights Act was finally passed. We had the right to vote for only a brief period after the Civil War and that was only regained in 1965.

For the totality of the existence of African people in this country, we've had only thirty-five or forty years that we were able to vote. So this current offensive against the participation of African people in the political life of the United States is a real question. It's not just a little question. It is not just an aside. It is not just a footnote to what has happened. It is the factor that has defined the existence of African people in this country.

The initial constitution adopted by the state of Florida after the Civil War was turned down because it denied Africans the right to vote. Although the constitution was amended to grant Africans the right to vote, laws were then created that would take the vote away from people who had been convicted of felonies. The laws, of course, were enacted to guarantee that African people were the most likely to become felons. The same thing was done throughout the South. There was a real assault on our basic right to participate in political life. It was a clear effort to keep Africans from expressing our political will and achieving any kind of power.

Bush and Gore complicit in attacks on African people

Now in the year 2000, there are 827,200 or more mostly African men who cannot vote in Florida because of this law that was passed after Reconstruction.[4] Three-quarters of a million Africans—one out of every seven African men in the state of Florida—are denied the right to vote because of a felony conviction. The 1965 Voting Rights Act was a guarantee from the federal government that African people would have the right to vote, the first time we could vote since we were disenfranchised in 1876 by the Tilden-Hayes Compromise.

It is of no little interest that Gore[5] does not want to be president enough to challenge the Republicans by saying that African people in the state of Florida have been disenfranchised. If he had defended the black vote, he would have deepened the struggle to a point where he could probably have become president. But Gore cannot raise the African vote as an issue. He can only talk in general terms about people's vote needing to mean something.

The Democrats Gore and Clinton are probably responsible more than any other administration in the last era for the number of Africans who cannot vote. Ninety-three percent of African people in Florida voted for Gore in this election, but Gore and Clinton have been locking up Democrats, putting them in prison more than anyone else. One out of every ten African men—and African men are Democrats—in this country is locked up in a prison! As soon as African men reach voting age they are locked up. Seventy percent of eighteen-year-old African men will be in prison by the time they are thirty-six years old.

The Democratic party cannot raise this criticism of the Republicans for stealing the African vote in Florida. If the half million Africans who cannot vote because they are felons were able to vote, Gore wouldn't be worried about being seven hundred votes behind in Florida, because ninety-three percent of Africans are Democrats. Gore won't even associate himself with the NAACP (National Association for the Advancement of Colored People) suit raising the issue of Florida's violation of the 1965 Voting Rights Act in this election.

Do not make the mistake of believing that African votes were only stolen in the state of Florida. It was a Republican strategy that was implemented everywhere. The only reason we know about it in the state of Florida is because this is the critical state that will determine the next president. It didn't get raised with the same concern in other places where this happened.

There is the added factor of Jeb Bush, governor of Florida and the brother of George W. Bush. Jeb Bush controls the apparatus throughout the state of Florida, and is able to make things happen perhaps more effectively and with a passion and self-interest that is greater than Republicans in other places. This election crisis is not an issue of Gore or Bush winning the presidency. It is an issue of the disenfranchisement of the masses of African people, not a small question, again, when you look at the fact that the majority of Africans who participate in political life do so through the electoral process. So, in many ways it's not different from killing off all the Black Panthers or destroying our organizations. I think it is really crucial for us to understand this and to help the world to understand it as well.

We have to defend the right of African people to exercise their vote without it being ripped off in broad daylight. This isn't something that happened in secret. International media have been here watching this and yet it hasn't become an issue for anybody yet.

Africans in Palm Beach County live in misery, oppression

Media from all over the world were in Palm Beach County supposedly investigating the stolen vote. You cannot see the towns of Belle Glade, South Bay and Pahokee without understanding the depth of the oppression and exploitation of African people there. In 1960, CBS did a documentary on Belle Glade called "Harvest of Shame." The U.S. Sugar Corporation is the primary economic force there and the African masses are tied to that sugar industry the same way we were tied to plantations a century ago. The exploitation of African people in Palm Beach County is so deep and so profound.

More than seventy percent of the people who are in the county jail in Belle Glade are Africans. The highest incidence of AIDS in the world is in Belle Glade. In 1989, a doctor there declared that unless the AIDS crisis there was turned around the African community would become extinct! They have an AIDS rate that is fifty-one times the national average and twelve times higher than in Congo-Kinshasa where white people say AIDS started. The population there does not fit the typical AIDS profile. Africans in Belle Glade are heterosexual and half of those who have AIDS are women. It is an extraordinary crisis.

In that area, Africans get their water from Lake Okeechobee, which is filled with carcinogens that come from the run-off from the sugar industry, from cow waste, and from white people's sewage discarded from West Palm Beach. At one point the Environmental Protection Agency had to pass out bottled water to the population because the water is so contaminated with carcinogens.

The fact is that this is going to be true after the elections, just as it was true before the election. And the system will be made to work again, just as it was made to work in 1876. But it came at the expense of the African masses.

Today, because of the stolen election, whoever gets into the White House will prevail as a consequence of a deal between the Republicans and Democrats in order to be able to govern. The strategy was to eliminate African political participation as a factor in determining the election.

This situation demonstrates to us the significance of the Uhuru Movement, because the fact is that African people must have our own independent organization. We were Republicans when the Republicans double-crossed us. We're Democrats now and clearly the Democrats have double-crossed us. This is becoming clearer and clearer everyday.

Build the African People's Socialist Party! Uhuru!

1   While president (1993-2001), Clinton ended "welfare as we know it," severely limiting the only social service that guaranteed monthly aid to poor families and single mothers. Under Clinton's "One strike, you're out" policy, public housing residents accused of a crime, along with anyone who lives with them, are evicted without consideration of their due process rights.

2   Abraham LIncoln was president from 1861 to 1865, during the U.S. Civil War. In 1863, he issued the Emancipation Proclamation legally "freeing" enslaved Africans in the South. Lincoln was assassinated in 1865.

3   The Ku Klux Klan is a white supremacist terrorist organization formed in Tennessee in 1866, after the Civil War. Known for wearing white sheets and cone-shaped hats, the KKK murders and terrorizes African people.

4   1998 statistics show that 1.4 million African men have been disenfranchised as a result of felony convictions, thirteen percent of the eligible African male voting population in the U.S.

5   Al Gore was the vice president under U.S. president William Jefferson Clinton and the Democratic party candidate in 2000.

The meaning of September 11th

No more peace on the plantation

This presentation was given on September 21, 2001, ten days after the events of September 11th, at the Sunday mass meeting at the Uhuru House in St. Petersburg, Florida. In response to the threats of imperialist aggression against oppressed peoples by the U.S. government following September 11th, the African People's Socialist Party immediately began building the Florida Alliance for Peace and Social Justice,[1] which held its first peace march at the end of September 2001.

Uhuru!

We live in a time when rational thought is extraordinarily important. It's important all the time, but right now it is more important than anytime I can remember in my life. I've never seen a time like the one we are confronted with right now. In fact, the future of the entire world is hanging in the balance.

Clearly, the future of the people in Afghanistan hangs in the balance. We can see that. The government is working very hard to make sure no information gets out that it doesn't have an opportunity to clean up first. We've heard stories of U.S. bombings in Afghanistan that they've called "accidents." Some people were "accidentally" killed. I don't know how you have accidental war deaths when the intent of the war is to kill and destroy. We've seen pictures of refugees, terrorized people who are forced to leave their homes and flee to Pakistan because of U.S. bombings.

It's relatively easy to see that the lives of those people hang in the balance. But the lives of your children hang in the balance as well. The lives of the people in the African community—the one that you live in right now—hang in the balance.

We are living at a time when the majority population in this country is experiencing mass hysteria. White people are now functioning in a lynch mob-type mode. That's not an accident. The flames of hatred and bigotry and war are being fanned. We've seen also that this notion of an independent media is a lie. They like to brag about the media in America being independent. They say that in America there is a free and independent press, while in other places the media say and do what the government dictates.

Look at what's happening right now. If you've never before understood that the media in this country are in bed with the ruling class, then all you have to do is look at what's been happening since September 11th. They make it very clear. It's just like *The Burning Spear,* which says on its heading that it is the political organ of the African People's Socialist Party, representing the African working class here and around the world. Everything that you see on television or read in the newspaper represents the viewpoint of the white ruling class of America.

That's why this government has mandated that the media cannot show or print excerpts of videotapes from Afghanistan—from Osama bin Laden[2] and people associated with his organization. They say the tapes might contain some secret, coded messages to terrorists around the world.

What they really want is to make sure that they have a monopoly on information. They want to make sure that no other view gets out but theirs. They don't want anybody to understand anything that Osama bin Laden and his organization have to say. They claim he said this or he said that. If that's what he said, show us!

Even the Taliban government has told the U.S., "If you want us to give him up, you have to give us evidence that he did it. Show us the evidence that he did it, and we'll turn him over."

But the U.S. government won't show any evidence. Tony Blair, the prime minister of Britain, said, "Well, I've seen the evidence," but Osama bin Laden is not in England. He's in Afghanistan!

Show the Afghans. Show the Taliban. They say they'll turn him over. But the U.S. won't show any evidence because they don't have any. For them, it doesn't matter that they have no evidence, just like evidence has never mattered when an African in this country has been accused of a crime and been thrown in prison. Evidence has never mattered!

Everyday there's a new effort being made to take away civil liberties and democratic rights that people had assumed they'd have. For Africans in this country this is extremely important. It is important for white people, too, but they're too stupid to realize this.

Every democratic right in America, every semblance or notion of democracy in this country came as a consequence of the struggle of black people—either when we were enslaved or subsequent to slavery. There is no democratic right that does not exist as a consequence of our struggle.

So if they take away the rights of the African people in this country, they take away the rights of everybody.

But the polls show that white people in America are more than willing to vote away their freedom if it means they can keep going to the mall and living on the resources that they have stolen from the rest of the peoples of the world. They'll vote away every damn freedom as long as they can continue to be comfortable at the expense of everybody else. That's the contradiction that confronts us.

I read an article in the newspaper the other day that said there have been secret courts in this country since 1978. Secret courts with secret judges! These courts hear information that put people on trial. They pass out warrants giving them the right to lock people up. This has been going on for more than twenty years.

The only reason they put that in the newspaper now is because they want to repeal more rights, and they've got the kind of hysteria going on in this country that will allow them to be able to do this and other things.

Peace with social justice

We've been working here in St. Petersburg to build a peace movement. But this peace movement is different from the one in the 1960s during the Viet Nam War. The war in Viet Nam was nothing like the war happening today. You will find that some of the white people in this country who were for peace when the war in Viet Nam was happening, are for war right now.

They were demanding peace back then, but now they are demanding war. They're demanding war now for the same reason they were demanding peace then: not because they loved peace and justice, not because they loved the people in Viet Nam and supported their right to national liberation. They opposed war because they did not want to go to Viet Nam alive and come back dead!

They did not want to die in Viet Nam. The Vietnamese were showing them that if you came to their country to try to take their freedom and independence, they would send you back in a body bag. It was white people they were sending back in body bags.

Back in the sixties you saw a huge movement of white people who had never heard of Viet Nam before. Suddenly, they knew everything about Viet Nam because they didn't want to be there. Thousands and thousands of them marched in the streets saying, "Hell no! We won't go!" This happened because the Vietnamese would have sent them back dead! So they were for peace back then.

Why are these same people for war now? They're for war now because the war has been brought to them right here in America—into the citadel. They've discovered that they can die in America just like they died in Viet Nam. They believe that since somebody from the Middle East can come here and kill them, they want to make war and kill people in the Middle East in order to have peace in America. The same white people who wanted peace back then want war today for the same reason: they want to stay alive. It's got nothing to do with principle! It's got to do with the material interests of white people.

We as African people have a responsibility to understand what *our* interests are.

Why would the African People's Socialist Party be building a peace movement then? We're building a peace movement based on the principles of peace and social justice. We don't believe that you can have genuine, meaningful peace without social justice. The white people in the South during slavery wanted peace all the time. What did peace mean? Peace meant that the African slaves were not rising up trying to kill the slave master and burning down the slave master's house. They wanted peace, but they didn't want social justice. They didn't want an end to slavery. They just wanted an end to the slaves trying to kill them and trying to be free!

We live in a world that's constructed in a certain way and we want to talk about that. It's constructed like a huge plantation with just a handful of slave masters dominating everything. Some people want peace but they do not want social justice. They want to keep the plantation peaceful and the slaves quiet.

We are building a movement because we have to have real peace. George Bush has declared war against the entire world! It is a war without an identifiable enemy! The white ruling class has made its intentions clear: "This doesn't have anything to do with bin Laden. When we kill bin Laden, when we destroy Afghanistan, we still aren't finished. We intend to keep on killing people anywhere we want to. Anybody who's opposed to our foreign policy is an enemy!" Bush himself said that "Either you are for us or you're against us. If you're against us, we're going to wage war against you."

The U.S. congress, with the exception of one lone African woman from Oakland, California named Barbara Lee, just voted to make war against the world in the way that Bush wants that war made. Before Bush, the Reagan administration, in which Bush's father was the vice-president, declared that national liberation struggles would be characterized as "terrorist." That's what is happening in the world. So this war that they are talking about making to end terrorism is a war without an enemy, without a set duration, without terms, without limits!

This war that they are talking about is a war to destroy anyone, any group in the world that is opposed to U.S. foreign policy. It is a war against anyone who opposes the structure of the world economy that keeps the vast majority of us oppressed and enslaved and allows the white people of the world to live at our expense. It is a war against anyone struggling for their national liberation and sovereignty.

This issue is crucially significant to us, and we need to understand it. Part of what September 11th represents is that the world economy is structured on a foundation of slavery and oppression. The whole world is locked into this process. The necessary condition for the success, for the wealth, for the well-being of white people in America, Europe and increasingly Japan, is the poverty and slavery of everybody else. If America and Europe are to remain successful and wealthy, as they are today, the rest of us—everybody else on earth—must live in poverty. This is because America and Europe's wealth comes as a consequence of conquests that have stolen our resources and locked us into this process where we are constantly and continuously being bled to feed America.

Now, when I say we feed America, I'm not talking about some abstract question. We live in a world in which half the people on earth live on less than two dollars a day! The people in Afghanistan are living on one slice of bread a day! They didn't volunteer for that! They don't live like that because white people in America are "smart and good," and everybody else is "ignorant and bad or evil."

The fact is we live in a system that has been put in place with the gun and the sword. What you see all over the earth—whether it's in Afghanistan or Pakistan or Palestine, whether it's in Trinidad or Jamaica or Haiti, whether it is in Sudan or Nigeria or the south side of St. Petersburg—what you see, objectively speaking, regardless of what's in the brains of the people who live in those places, are the attempts they make everyday to overturn the verdict of imperialism which dominates their lives.

There are all kinds of funny philosophies that people put out here for you. There are people now in the peace movement that demand that we be pacifists. They say we have to be for nonviolence. Hell, I don't believe they're for nonviolence. If they were, every time a police car moves out of the police station, they'd be doing civil disobedience, laying on the streets to keep them from getting to this community, as violent as the police are against African people.

Pacifism tries to neutralize our struggle for national liberation

These white pacifists are not for nonviolence! They just want to make sure *you* are nonviolent! This world that we live in is structured in such a fashion that there's this relationship between a parasite and its host. America is the parasite living off the blood of the oppressed peoples of the world. And the white peace movement wants to keep it that way.

America is what they call an empire. Empire is where the word imperialism comes from. An empire is a country that dominates all the other countries, or many of the other countries of the world. There was the Roman empire and other empires that existed in history. The British used to brag about controlling an empire upon which "the sun never set." In other words, in every place, in every time zone, Britain dominated other people's countries. America is an empire! They even call New York the "empire" state! It is the empire state and somebody brought war to the empire on September 11th. America is an empire! The American people and the American government have an imperial attitude.

As Africans we cannot get caught up in these silly philosophies like pacifism that are out there to try to neutralize us so that we can't fight for our freedom. We are against the war, but we are not pacifists. I am not a pacifist. If you come at me, I shall do my best to accommodate you. I don't want you to be a pacifist because the oppressed cannot afford to be passive.

It's not that we love violence. It's because we *hate* violence that we cannot afford to be pacifists. If you do not fight them back, they will never stop being violent against you. It's because I oppose violence that I would try to take your gun and do something to you with it to keep you from ever committing a violent act again. That's my commitment to nonviolence.

We make a distinction between revolutionary violence and reactionary violence. Reactionary violence is attacking countries, trying to annex them, put them in slavery, and keep them in slavery, put them in colonialism, and keep them in colonialism. That is reactionary violence and I oppose reactionary violence. The bombs being dropped on Afghanistan today represent reactionary violence.

Revolutionary violence is violence that is used to liberate the people to end annexation, to end colonialism, to end imperialism, to end oppression, to end suffering. Yes, I support revolutionary violence! I have to support revolutionary violence. Otherwise, I'd have to wish that Cuba becomes enslaved again. I'd have to wish that China and all the other peoples around the world who had to fight for their freedom become enslaved again.

I have to demand the right to freedom for all the oppressed peoples around the world. You have a government that is talking about nuclear terror or a so-called nuclear defense shield. What is that about? America says that some country or some people or somebody has done something wrong to it and should be bombed. They are bombing Afghanistan now. America says it has a right to make war against them because they committed an offense against America.

Is that equally true for the rest of the world? If a people or nation feels that America has wrongly attacked them, do they have the right to retaliate against America with violence in the same way that America is responding with violence against the people of Afghanistan right now? There's a philosophical problem here.

We must not just support freedom for ourselves. We must support freedom for everyone. We cannot support oppression. Our struggle is for the liberation of the peoples of the world as much as it is for freeing ourselves.

I won't tell anybody not to go to war as a soldier for Uncle Sam because I think it might be illegal for me to do that. But if you do go, you're out of your mind! I will not tell you not to go until I check the legality of the question. But in the meantime, I'll talk about you like a dog if you fight for U.S. imperialism against other oppressed peoples just like yourselves.

We must fight for the freedom and liberation of Africa and African people—in unity with the struggles for the freedom and liberation of all oppressed peoples on the planet. Down with U.S. imperialism!

Uhuru!

1   The Florida Alliance for Peace and Social Justice was a statewide peace organization formed in 2001 by the African People's Socialist Party with the active participation of other colonized forces along with white activists. The Florida Alliance was committed to peace through national liberation and social justice for oppressed peoples including those inside the U.S.

2   Osama bin Laden is a Saudi Arabian blamed by the U.S. for orchestrating the September 11th attacks on the World Trade Center and the Pentagon.

Tribute to Winky Wright

A political analysis of Africans in boxing

Ronald "Winky" Wright is a talented and popular boxing champion from St. Petersburg, Florida. A friend of the Uhuru Movement, he is enthusiastically loved by the African community.

On October 12, 2001, Winky won the International Boxing Federation's Junior Middleweight title. On October 25, the Chairman spoke at a community tribute to Winky sponsored by the African People's Education and Defense Fund. In this presentation, the Chairman upholds Winky's talents while at the same time acknowledging the potential of all young Africans facing life in the oppressed African communities today. The Chairman also gives a brief political history of African people in boxing.

In this piece the Chairman chastises the St. Petersburg Times *for not covering and supporting Winky's outstanding career. In 2004, Winky won the World Boxing Association's and World Boxing Commission's Junior Middleweight title against Sugar Shane Mosely. The* St. Petersburg Times *continues to refuse to cover Wright's stellar rise to the top of the sport of boxing.*

Uhuru!

This night is about Winky. It's about Winky because, in my view, Winky is a representative of all of these young African people in our communities, not only here, but around this country.

Boxing has always been a very political issue. It hasn't been that long that they would even allow an African to fight for a championship. They kept black people from fighting for championships until the turn of the century, when they let Jack Johnson, a great heavyweight champion, fight. He fought for the championship, and bested everyone. It was an interesting situation, because white people used to travel all around the country, hoping that somebody white would beat Jack Johnson. People would come out like lynch mobs. Johnson had gold in his mouth. He had what white people called a "yellow grin."

The media wrote terrible things about Johnson. They hated him too, because Jack Johnson had a predilection for white women. So, they chased him out of the country. He couldn't even fight in the U.S., so he'd fight in Canada, in Cuba and many other places. Finally, they put criminal charges on him in order to defeat him the only way they could.

Jack London,[1] one of the so-called great American literary heroes—they've got a square named for him in Oakland, California—wrote all of these books that they still teach to children in the schools. Jack London tricked Jim Jeffries,[2] although Jeffries didn't know he was being tricked. London told Jeffries, "Please, come back and fight Jack Johnson. Knock that yellow smile off his face! Come back, because you are the last of the great white hopes."

London pumped up Jim Jeffries, but Jeffries made a mistake just by getting in the ring with Jack Johnson. Johnson carried Jeffries for several rounds, calling him "Mr. Jim" in the ring. Johnson said, "Oh, Mr. Jim, I thought you could hit!" He said, "Mr. Jim, I'm going to hit you on the left side of your head right now," and then he'd hit him several times. Johnson was an incredible fighter. After that they chased him out of the country. Some of you may have seen some of these old pictures, where he's laying on his back on the canvas, shielding his eyes with his gloves to keep the sun from getting in. He threw a fight in Havana to lose his title. Only then was he allowed to come back to the country.[3]

It was a long time before they would ever allow another African to fight. It took maybe a quarter of a century until they let Joe Louis fight. This time they knew they had the right guy, because Joe Louis was tame. Of course, he became a champion—won all of these fights. Then the IRS took his money from him. They put him in the poor house. It was a long time again, because they'd rather have a black gangster than somebody who would take a stand. And Jack Johnson had taken a stand.

Finally, this brash kid out of Louisville, Kentucky, came up—Cassius Clay, named after a slave master. He changed his name to Muhammad Ali, because he didn't want to be named after a slave master anymore. And boxing has been messed up ever since, you know. They can't get it back!

Boxing has been a poor people's sport. We see boxing, and it's Africans, it's Mexicans, it's Puerto Ricans, its Asians, because we are stuck and mired in the worst kind of poverty. That's what makes Winky Wright our kind of guy, and makes him so significant. It's not just that he's talented, because there are all kinds of talent in this community, despite the fact that you read only the most slanderous things about young Africans. There are all kinds of talent in our community. The thing that's also significant about Winky Wright is that he lives in a community that they characterize as a "target area," right?

In this "target area," according to the government statistics, seventy percent of the people live in or near poverty. People in the target area are living in an extraordinary state of desperation. You can't have seventy percent living in that situation without having absolute desperation.

The government of the city of St. Petersburg has pulled together what they call the "Five Year Consolidated Plan." The Consolidated Plan is an application for a grant from the federal government, to get a lot of money for the city. This plan tells just how poor black people are, how much housing we need, how many jobs we need, in this city. The city lays this out and says, "Give us the money." The thing is that they get the money. They get the money! They get the money based on the statistics of our poverty! But the money never comes to the people who it's supposed to help.

So, not only is Winky Wright talented, he has the discipline necessary. He had the foundational honesty from his parents and grandparents. He has friends, like Eddie Boo, like Mtundu, and all the other people who go to the same bootleg barber. He'd had this experience on the ground—and it was able to sustain him. He clawed his way through the fact that he lived in a city that was hostile to black people.

On October 12 he became the World Champion. On October 13 you look for an article in the *St. Petersburg Times*. It's not on the front page—it couldn't have been on the front page of the A section. Alright, maybe it's on the front page of the B section. Not on the front page of the B section! Well, alright, it has to be on the front page of the Sports section. But it's not even on the front page of the Sports section! It's on page nine. That is hostility.

When Winky Wright beat Vargas[4] they took that title from him. I met with the editorial board of the *St. Petersburg Times*. This is the same *Times* that we've been fighting tooth and nail, to try to get the African Festival Market[5] so that we can create some businesses for folk in our community. I said to the editorial board, "In Winky Wright, there is a treasure. He should be a treasure for the whole city."

I told them if the city was not so backwards, people would support Winky. Look at Muhammad Ali when he was Cassius Clay. A handful of rich white bankers saw that he could fight. They said, let's invest in this guy. We'll make some money and he'll make some money. They promoted him. The city of Louisville promoted him. But not you! I said to the *St. Petersburg Times*, you've got to support him! The reason they were able to take the title from Winky when he fought Vargas is because nobody else knew him.

If the *St. Petersburg Times*, the media right here in this city, had put it out, and let the world know about Winky Wright, then it would have been harder for them to steal the fight from him the way they did.

I met with them then, and I said, "I know you're hostile to boxing," because you've got these snobs who say that boxing is violent. But is boxing more violent than football that is based on actual war? Football is based on war. It is a game of warfare, even including the camp girls following it. What do you call those people who jump up and down with the pompoms? You know, cheerleaders! Is boxing any more violent than football? Is it more violent than hockey? [Audience says, "No, no."]

And so, on Saturday, October 13, you look at the *St. Petersburg Times*, and on the front page you see the losing Bucs,[6] when we have a winner here! So, what we do is embrace him. That's our responsibility. We embrace him. I appreciate all of these black people here who love Winky Wright. I appreciate all of these white people here who love the black community enough to stand up with Winky Wright. When you stand with Winky, you stand with a community that has been nothing but oppressed, a community that cannot see the light of day, except through examples like the one that Winky Wright gives us. [Cheering from the audience.]

I'm glad that Winky is accessible. I'm glad that he is the kind of person that he is. I think that he can be an example that can be meaningful for uplifting the young people in this community. If we are honest, and if we do as we should, we will recognize that Winky is just like all of those other Africans out there in the community.

We know Winky, but the reality is in most ways, he is not

different from all of those other young black people out there who get so slandered every day you open the newspaper. It ought to be easy to see, because if Winky had shot somebody, he would have been on the front page. It means that the only time an African in this city can be on the front page is when they shoot somebody or some other thing.

Winky has talent, but he's not the only talent, right, Winky? Jeff Lacy[7] is going to be the next Middleweight Champion of the World. And there are other people who are boxers. Some of them can't stay at the gym, because they haven't had the kind of encouragement that they should be getting. There is all kinds of talent in this community, and these young people need an opportunity to grow, and thrive.

I want to thank Winky for being an example of tenacity. I thank all of you for coming out to hold him up, so that all of the others who are out there will understand that we can fight. We can win if we persevere, and there are friends who are out there for us. Winky, thank you, Brother. Thank you for persevering, thank you for being here. This community loves you, and the world, when it gets an opportunity, will love you as much. I'm hoping that you'll get that opportunity! [Applause]

---

1   Jack London, 1876–1916, was an Oakland, California-based adventure writer and known white supremacist.

2   Jim Jeffries, 1875–1953, was a white heavyweight billed as The Great White Hope who lost to Jack Johnson in 1910.

3   Jack Johnson was one of the toughest boxers who ever lived. In nearly a half century of boxing he was only knocked out three times. He lost the championship to Jess Willard in 1915 in a fight in Cuba. Rumors suggest that the thirty-seven year-old champion threw the fight as a concession to authorities in a bid to return to the U.S.

4   Winky fought Fernando "El Feroz" Vargas on December 4, 1999. Many believed that Wright had won the fight even though the judges awarded the victory to Vargas.

5   The African Festival Market began in 1999 in St. Petersburg as a project of the African People's Education and Defense Fund, which brought African

vendors together for a weekly Saturday market. Despite the fact that the city and the *St. Petersburg Times* refused to support or help fund the market, it nevertheless became a catalyst for several successful start-up businesses in the African community with a higher success rate than the city's own "business incubator."

6 Tampa Bay Buccaneers football team.

7 Jeff Lacy, another champion boxer from the African community of St. Petersburg, defended his IBF Super Middleweight title against Rubin Williams in March, 2005.

Pay us the value of our stolen black labor!

Reparations to the African community now

This speech was given on labor day, September 1, 2002 at the regular African community mass meeting held every Sunday at 4 p.m. at the Uhuru House in St. Petersburg, Florida. It tells the true story of the value of the stolen labor of African people. "Labor day" is celebrated in the U.S. on the first weekend of September.

Today, people are celebrating what they call "labor day" without the slightest idea of why they are celebrating. Folk just see it as a day off—as an excuse to light up the charcoals, to bust out the forty-ouncers, to just sort of get down. It's another example of how we, as African people, find ourselves trapped in situations that we don't understand, sometimes celebrating something that actually works against our interests as a people.

Labor day is supposed to be a holiday that celebrates the value of labor and of workers. I don't know the specific story about why this day was chosen or who the laborers are who came to epitomize the holiday. But I do know this: those workers were not the ones whose labor created the economy that benefits white people and the whole imperialist world at the expense of African folk.

The truth is that the value of labor everywhere will never, ever be fully appreciated under this system, because all human labor has been diminished by slavery, the capturing of African people and our enslavement as a whole people. It's impossible to talk about celebrating and appreciating labor without talking about reparations for all the stolen labor that created the wealth that benefits white people and others who benefit from imperialism.

How can anybody talk about the value of labor or laborers when this economy was built with stolen labor on stolen land? Until it is recognized that all the value of labor that we talk about in America has its origins in the stolen labor of African people, then this discussion about the appreciation of labor is phony.

It's a phony discussion unless you are celebrating the stolen labor of African people. How do you celebrate that? With reparations. You give reparations. You say, "We've finally come to our senses. We now understand the value of labor, and we are going to celebrate this recognition by paying reparations to all of those African people from whom we've stolen their labor." That's what has to happen.

Now, some people don't get it. Many white people who say that they struggle for the benefit of labor, for workers, don't get it. Many of these same white people would say that they are opposed to reparations. Some say, "We're opposed to reparations because that would have to be paid with my white taxpayer's dollars." Others say, "We're opposed to reparations because it will create an artificial division between Africans and white people"—between African workers and the so-called, imaginary white working class.

I want you to hear what I said. Even white workers and their representatives will find themselves opposed to reparations, and they do that in the name of labor, in the name of the unity of all workers. So here you are, with the value of all of your labor stolen, the value of your parents', grandparents' and great grandparents' labor stolen. This stolen labor created the value that makes it possible for white workers to live in homes where they have two-car garages with a station wagon and a boat, even right here in this little rinky-dink city of St. Petersburg. Yet white workers will say that you are trying to divide workers when you try to get payment for labor that has been stolen from African folk.

Production and reproduction of real life

What is the motivating force in human society? What is it that drives human society? We get all kinds of explanations for that, but the one that we get most times is from the church, because that is where most of what passes as explanation for reality is taught to oppressed African people. The preachers teach us that the reason we are here on earth is to serve God.

This is what African people hear from the lying, thieving, parasitic preachers. I'm sorry if that sounds subjective, but the objective reality is that a preacher is a parasite. A preacher is a parasite because he is, or she is someone who does not produce anything but lives off of those who do produce. That's what is called a parasite and that's what a preacher is. It's not slander. I'm not talking bad about preachers. It's just objective truth that someone who lives off other people's production is a parasite, and that's what preachers do.

So they tell us we are here to serve God. You know that when you think of God, you think of a white man. I can describe him for you. He's got a flowing white beard and sometimes unruly white hair. His hair is mostly unruly when he's upset, and this God is usually upset, isn't he? The reason you know he's upset is because you're catching hell all the time. And the explanation you get for why you're catching hell all the time is that God is displeased with you, right? They say if you get right with God, then all of your problems will be solved. Isn't that what we hear most of the time?

The truth is that the driving force in all human society is the production and reproduction of real life. That's the thing that makes society happen. What am I talking about when I say that? First of all, I'm talking about reproducing ourselves—as a species. I'm talking about this process of having babies.

I know when a brother invites a woman to his crib, he's not thinking about the production and reproduction of real life, but that is in fact the motive force. That is why you had her come over, or you got him to invite you over. It is because of this need, this urge, this driving force to recreate ourselves as human beings, as people. So that's one thing, because if you don't have people, you don't have anything else, do you? So the creation of real life itself is one of the things we're talking about.

The other thing that we're talking about is the actual process of producing what we need to survive—food, clothing, and shelter. As we move through society, our capacity to do this gets better all the time. We moved from a time and place in history where our ability to do this was extraordinarily uncertain, where we might have had to travel to make sure that there was something to eat. We hadn't mastered such things as growing our food. We had to rely on the success of hunters, who went out to try and capture antelope or other animals to eat, because we had not yet domesticated animals. At one juncture, survival was a risky process, depending on bows and arrows and axes, rocks and sticks for success.

At some point in this process of the struggle to produce and reproduce real life, we got better at it. We learned how to grow food in a single place, so it wasn't necessary for us to follow the seasons. We didn't have to wait for lightning to strike a tree so we could get fire; we learned how to make the fire ourselves. Now fire is something that we can control and from that we can do all kinds of things.

So, we have gone from an uncertain quest to kill a bear or an antelope to try to get something to eat, to now where we can buy food in stores with this exchange value that we call money. Now with money you can pick up a piece of bear if you want it, or a piece of cow or a box of quick oats and what have you. We've moved to this place not through some magical process as some people would suggest, but through the ongoing struggle to produce and reproduce real life. It's this need that we have, this drive that we bring to society to create and recreate real life, which puts us here.

This process is how we make history. Culture flows from this process. The songs we sing are part of this—songs that praise the sun that provides the energy that grows the food, or songs about the rain that help to grow the food. We learned dances and ceremonies and things like this. This is how culture evolves.

If we are very efficient in the production and reproduction of real life, then we find the leisure time for the development of these things that we might characterize as our humanity. We become artists or poets. One of our problems now is that we are in this desperate situation with our backs constantly against the wall, trying to scratch out an existence.

You see from the earliest times those societies which were efficient in this whole process of creating and recreating real life. We can still see the evidence they left of their arts and scientific achievements. This is what we see of the great African civilizations—the sculptures, the pyramids, the gigantic, magnificent edifices that have never been replicated anywhere else on earth.

You see this, and then you see African people, who are many generations separated from that time when we were able to produce and reproduce real life for ourselves so effectively. We still know how to sing and dance and have this thing that people recognize as spirituality, despite the fact that we are now in such desperate straits that all of our energies have to be used looking for food, clothing and shelter. Are you with me on that?

That's why you are who you are—Africans. That's why you're not killers and people who are willing at the drop of a hat to annihilate entire cities and villages and countries to get some bread or gold or other resources. In this whole process of social development, our psyches have reflected the fact that we were efficient at being able to produce those things that are necessary for our existence. We were born in Africa where all of those things came naturally.

Look at the world and see where all of the imperialists have their daggers pointed today. They are targeting those who have the natural wealth and the value. They are targeting their guns and their bombs and their threats of destruction at those very places where we've come from—the places where nature was so kind that it provided everything necessary for the production and reproduction of real life relatively easily.

You think I'm making that up? Look at white people, who left Europe, running like animals. They went every damn way. They went to the U.S., Australia, Canada, New Zealand, Africa, then Latin America, getting the hell out of Europe because Europe was hostile to life. It was hard to produce and reproduce real life there.

The Europeans went to those places where it was easy to produce and reproduce. When they got there, they captured resources. They killed people and they kept their lily white asses there as long as they could stay there. People are still fighting to get these white people the hell out of there and send them back to where they came from. Isn't that true? And the white people don't want to go because they've moved to a place where the production and reproduction of real life is simple. That's where all human beings want to be.

White left dismisses value of African labor

So, we talk about this thing called labor. Here is one of the traps that some of our white leftist or communist or Marxist friends find themselves in. They do understand that all value is created by labor. They know that value is not created by doctors, professors, economists, presidents, lawyers or any of those things. Only labor creates value.

Nothing has value until a human hand is placed on it and transforms it and makes it into something that it wasn't before. Trees don't have value as wood until human hands touch them. Human hands touch trees and they turn trees into tables. They turn trees into houses. It's the human hand that touched it, that transformed it, that gave value to what used to be just a tree.

It's the same thing with gems that people like to wear around their necks. If somebody doesn't dig it out and do the work to bring it to you, the gem would have no value to you laying there on the ground. Bauxite brought out of the mines and worked with, becomes aluminum. And another worker is attaching it to a car that workers put together. This is the thing that gives it value.

Our Marxist friends, our white left and liberal friends often recognize this thing about value. Therefore they are able to talk about labor and its significance on the one hand, but on the other hand, even as they talk about this labor, they dismiss the significance of the African labor and the demand for reparations that we might make.

This happens because the Marxists and our white liberals and friends come to the question late. They see a car being built in Detroit. They see the bauxite being worked on in Detroit that turns into aluminum. They see the tire that goes onto the car. They see all of the work that goes on right there in Detroit at the so-called point of production.

But they didn't see the ten million people who the Belgians killed in the Congo to get the rubber to make tires in Detroit. They had to get the rubber from somewhere before they could attach it to that car. They didn't see the Africans who worked in the mines in places like Guyana or Guinea in Africa who brought that bauxite up out of the ground and made it possible for someone else to work with it in Detroit. Do you understand what I'm saying? That was invisible to them. They've left out this incredibly significant part of the equation when they talk about the creation of value.

And so, we live in a world where people can talk about the value of labor, they can sing praises to labor but leave the African out, because we are invisible in their consciousness. Even Karl Marx had problems with this, and he did perhaps a better job than other white people in talking about the true value of labor. When Marx talked about the emergence of an economy centered around the selling of commodities based on the expropriation of stolen value, he said that "wage slavery in Europe required as a pedestal slavery pure and simple in the New World." Ours was the "slavery pure and simple." "Wage slavery" referred to the work that white people do.

But Marx ran into a non sequitur, because even having come to this understanding, he could not logically follow it through. Marx was not able to say, "therefore, in order to end capitalism or wage slavery, in Europe or any place, we have to kick the pedestal out from under it, and that pedestal is slavery pure and simple."

Instead of saying that African and colonized peoples who make up this pedestal would lead the revolutionary struggle, Marx mistakenly came to the conclusion that in order to overturn capitalism, which creates wage slavery, we have to somehow give power to the white workers, all of whom live, along with the white bourgeoisie, on the pedestal of slavery pure and simple.

So, we are invisible. But let me tell you this: the working class—this force that we talk about when we now talk about labor—is a new force in Europe. Prior to the attack on Africa and the theft of African labor, there was no white working class.

There were white people living in Europe, but they were not what we characterize as workers. They were peasants. The majority of them were tied to the land—like what they called sharecroppers when they were doing it to us here in the South. Most of what their labor produced went to the landlord and the peasants could only keep a part of it. They were tied to the land like slaves to the extent that if the landlord sold the land, the peasant stayed with the land and got a new landlord. They were taxed and had all kinds of difficulties. But there was no such thing as a working class.

The emergence of the working class was what emancipated white people from serfdom. They were no longer the people who Robin Hood was helping. Y'all remember Robin Hood—stealing from the rich and giving to the poor? The thing that Robin Hood couldn't do was elevate poor white folks from their status as peasants and make them workers who would get more value for their labor power, who could no longer be sold, who could no longer be handled in the way they were handled before. What was it that did that? It was slavery. It was the rape of Africa and the theft of our people and our resources.

It was also resources that Europe was stealing in places like Viet Nam and China. All of these resources were now coming to and transforming Europe. So, now you see in Europe and North America the emergence of this thing they call the Industrial Revolution. This was the process that transformed these white people from peasants to workers.

Why did white power need to get these people off the land?
Because as long as they were on the land, they had food to eat,
they could grow their own collard greens, and what have you.
White power needed a destitute white person. Why did they need
a destitute white person? They needed a white person who had to
sell his labor power in order to live, to exist. Nobody's going to
work in a factory where they might lose their life, their arms,
their eyesight, if they've got another way to feed themselves.

So, white peasants were transformed into workers as part of
this incredible development of industry happening in Europe.
Gold, silver and ivory were flowing into Europe. They needed
ivory to make piano keys and billiard balls. They killed damn
near every elephant in Africa, and damn near every African who
they forced to bring them the elephants and the ivory.

Suddenly, in Europe, white people who were previously
stuck on the land were now needed to make ships and to smelt
iron for chains, for nails and other things. They were needed to
make sails and to sew clothing and to store food. This is how the
working class began to emerge, to facilitate the process of
sending ship after ship out to capture African people in Africa.

Before, a single little hat maker or shoemaker could
produce enough to meet the requirements of the neighborhood.
Now they needed a whole bunch of shoes at the same time. They
needed shoes for all of the people who were going to be sailors.
They needed clothing for them, and chains for the slaves. They
needed new ships to be built. This is how the white working
class emerged.

With this emergence of the working class, white people were
better off than they were before. Life for them gets even better the
more they steal from peoples around the world. They got better
houses. They could go to school for the first time. They didn't
have to listen to the nobility anymore. They could move where
they wanted to move, live where they wanted to live. They could

even leave cold, wet, stinky England and go to someone else's country. They were emancipated, finally. But they were emancipated at the expense of Africans and other people.

Now, the European worker is in a situation where, indeed, he can produce and reproduce real life for himself. But the African can no longer produce and reproduce real life for himself. It doesn't mean that Africans are not producing real life, it just means it's not for ourselves. We are now producing and reproducing real life for Europe and the rest of white people in North America.

We want the value of our labor to come back to us. The average life span of an African man in the U.S. is nine years less than that of a white man. We're not producing and reproducing real life when you have that kind of situation. In Africa it's even worse. So, we need to jumpstart this process to demand real appreciation for labor, and we do that with reparations. Pay us for the value of our stolen labor.

Africa is our solution

The salvation of African people is in Africa. There is no solution for us outside of the liberation of Africa. I don't care how difficult that might sound, and how uncompromising that statement may seem to be, it's true. I know that it's a difficult thing for some people to even deal with this notion that our freedom is tied to Africa. There is no solution other than that. If you can believe anything that I said, you see that the liberation of Africa is the only solution for us. The reason white people came to Africa is because Africa was bountiful and Europe was not. That's why they went every place else—they were looking for booty. They didn't have booty. That is true in both the ways that we understand it in our community!

Our problem is that Africa has been robbed and brutalized viciously. Evidence of the brutality done to Africa is our presence in this country, and we're worried about the prospect of having to go back to Africa? Isn't that something? That's a statement of the attack that was made on Africa. Africa was attacked, and Africa has all the answers, all the solutions. If it didn't have the answers and the solutions, white people wouldn't have gone there to solve *their* problems. They've kept Africa and her resources for themselves. It's really important to say that. Africa is where our history lies. Africa is where our future lies.

On my radio show this morning, I interviewed Brother Thami Ka Plaatje, who is the Secretary General of the Pan Africanist Congress of Azania (You call it South Africa.). He spoke at one of our meetings in London building for the African Socialist International a couple of weeks ago.

Thami talked about the significance of land to African people. He said that among the cultures when a child is born the umbilical cord is planted in the yard, and a tree is planted over the umbilical cord. It is a firm attachment to the land, and if a person goes away, and that tree under which that umbilical cord is planted seems to have a problem, then the community makes the assumption that something is wrong with this person, wherever he or she is in the world.

Today we are rootless. We have no connection to the land. The truth is, as much as we say that we are attached to America, what we really are attached to is Coca Colas and Big Macs and CDs and what have you. It's not America that we're attached to, because white people don't allow us to stay in one place in America long enough to get attached to it. Think about the place where you grew up, and the truth of the matter is that white people have moved you four or five times since the last time you were there. That community gets wiped out, displaced because they want the property, so they move you over to another community. We are rootless here. Africa is ours.

Our attachment to America is a false attachment. It's like sugar, which is addicting. Even though it's no good for you, you want it all the time, but it's killing you as you eat it. The more you use, the worse off you are. That's why all these Africans, in part, are suffering from things like diabetes. This false attachment to America has done nothing but brutalize and kill us. It kills us daily.

This is what Africans need to understand: the value of your labor does not disappear. The rate of exploitation of Africans has been greater since slavery. But even so, the value of our labor during slavery has not disappeared. Value doesn't disappear. The value of our stolen labor is now concentrated in all of the things that you see around you, even in the computers. Value creates more value.

That's a really important thing to understand, because people like to say, "Well, slavery happened a long time ago." They say, "Well, those slave masters don't exist anymore, and the Africans to whom it was done directly don't exist anymore. Therefore, it's over." But the reality is, the value is still there, concentrated in all of the value that you see around you. Value does not disappear.

Africans have to organize to liberate Africa.

Uhuru!

Barbarians in control

Technology is white power's weakness

This is the Chairman's response to questions from the audience during the discussion period following his presentation "Pay us the value of our stolen black labor!" that was given at the Uhuru House in St. Petersburg, Florida on September 1, 2002. It presents an insightful demystification of the power of imperialist technology.

The whole issue of technology is really interesting. What's clear to me is that barbarians have seized control of technology, and technology is driven in this really reckless, dangerous and anti-human way. Technology is a relatively recent thing to white people. I'm not slandering or race-bashing. The reality is that Africans were building pyramids before white people had even mastered fire. What happened is that white people conquered and stole the technology of Africans and others. Now the barbarians are in control of technology, and look at the direction technology is going with the barbarians in control.

Here you have a people who have not really achieved a certain level of civilization. It's as if you turned loose some apes in a roomful of dangerous, high-tech equipment. It's a very dangerous situation. I used the term "barbarians." That's a tribal name that comes straight out of Europe. The Barbarians were so violent and notorious that Europeans themselves used the term to describe the violent and destructive behavior of other Europeans.

The reality is that for the longest time in history, most of the

169

world has seen Europeans invading and attacking, being barbaric and uncivilized, a dangerous and treacherous kind of people. Since our conquest, they have the technology and now there is an enormous technological gap between the oppressed and the oppressor. This gap existed between the Vietnamese and America. The Vietnamese started fighting the imperialists with sticks and stones, and ultimately they were able to be victorious. It shows us America's vulnerability even with all of this technology.

September 11th was carried out with box cutters. Box cutters! Bush was talking about nuclear shields and things like Star Wars. But somebody with a box cutter got on one of these huge technological airplanes that they don't possess in the land that they came from, and used a box cutter to turn it against the imperialists.

We can't be afraid of their technology. When we were in London recently, someone raised the question of armed struggle. I wanted to get away from that. I can't even get y'all to come to a damn meeting, so how can we talk about armed struggle?

Somebody asked, "They have all these guns, so how are we going to fight them?" And the question is simple. You don't have a gun, you've got a rock. You take the rock and hit the enemy who has the gun. Then you take the gun, and now you've got a rock and a gun. Right? And then you take the gun you took from the enemy and shoot another enemy, and then you've got two guns. This is how it works, it's just like that. So, while it appears that they have control over the technology, much of the technology is accessible to us.

Imperialism is in a desperate situation. How do I know? Everything that George Bush is doing to the world is a sign of a most desperate crisis that the imperialists are confronted with. They are confronted with losing every damn thing they have. Our responsibility is to help them lose it, you understand.

Do you know what Jujitsu is? It's a martial art that uses the strength and power of the opponent against them. That's what September 11th was. It was a form of Jujitsu. They didn't have the airplanes and they didn't have the bombs and the missiles, but they had a damn box cutter, according to the U.S. It was a form of Jujitsu, and that's what we have to do, we have to use the enemy's power against the enemy. Technology is their weakness.

I used to work on *The Burning Spear* newspaper. I could lay out ten to fourteen pages a day, as long as I had some glue and some wax. Then they made these damn computers and I can't lay out anything! When the lights go out and the computers go down, though, I can still lay out a newspaper. The trap is when the monkey wrench goes into this technology, it doesn't work. So I'm not that concerned about it.

Let me tell you another example of technology used against them. I saw a documentary on television about Viet Nam. Some Vietnamese military officers were being interviewed. They said of the U.S. military, "You can't fight America from a distance. From a distance, America is powerful. They can shoot missiles and drop bombs from way up in the sky, and they are powerful there. But Americans are slow and clumsy. In order to fight them, you've got to grab them by the belt." And that's the problem—we haven't had the guts to grab this sucker by the belt. You grab him by the belt, and you can dance with him. This is what the Vietnamese did.

Huey Newton was right when he said that the will of the people is greater than The Man's technology. That's what we have to understand, that you cannot be intimidated by his technology. We can kick his ass, you understand. His technology cannot extract a boot from up his butt.

Yes, technology means destruction, too. Africa is currently being used as a pawn to impose genetically modified foods.[1] They starve Africa in a number of ways. There are about fourteen million people who are facing imminent starvation in Africa unless something is done. The U.S. is offering them genetically modified food. Zimbabwe and Zambia have refused to accept the food. The U.S. is waging a campaign of slander against them, because with all these starving people, they won't take genetically modified foods. Well, Europe won't allow genetically modified food either. The U.S. is really pushing this thing. Europe won't do it because white people are resisting it.

There are a number of reasons to resist genetically modified foods. They want to say that it's just rejected by people who are struggling against scientific advances. But the truth of the matter is that genetically modified foods can actually destroy natural food crops. It always gets out of the confines that they use it in. You can get a genetically modified plant that is supposed to, for example, be modified so that it is resistant to disease and pesticides. If that then escapes, as it will, into other kinds of crops, it's very dangerous. You can have weeds that kill natural crops but then can't die because they've been modified genetically. The genetically modified seeds can become the super-plants that will move out all of the other naturally grown crops.

White power has a patent on all of the genetically modified seeds, so you can't even get food without going through them. Nobody knows the consequences of consuming genetically modified foods over a period of time. So that's part of what we're talking about with technology running amok.

You can now eat a piece of wheat that looks like George Bush. They're actually making cross-species modifications of various foods, but that's a discussion for another time.

Uhuru!

---

1   Genetically modified (GMO) means that technology has been used to alter the genetic makeup of living organisms including animals, plants and bacteria, in order to produce desired effects.

Izwe Lethu i Afrika!

Build the Azanian Front of the African Revolution

This historic and powerful presentation was the keynote speech for the Eighth Congress of the Pan Africanist Congress of Azania held in Umtata in the Eastern Cape, in December 2002. The Chairman's words were met with exuberant singing, cheers and dancing from the large audience of hundreds of PAC members who had traveled from all over South Africa to attend the congress.

Brother President Mogoba, Secretary General Thami Ka Plaatje, Comrade Deputy President Pheko, the esteemed National Executive Council of the Pan Africanist Congress of Azania (PAC), Delegates, Guests, Brothers and Sisters, Izwe Lethu! [Audience: "i Afrika!"] i Afrika! [Audience: "Izwe Lethu!"]

I bring you greetings from the Central Committee of the African People's Socialist Party (APSP), from its mass organizations and membership, from our African brothers and sisters in the diaspora, especially those from the United States and London, UHURU! ["Uhuru!"]

"Uhuru" is the greeting of our Party and movement. Uhuru is the greeting that was made popular by Dedan Kimathi and the Kenyan Land and Freedom Army, popularly known as the Mau Mau. Uhuru, of course, is Swahili for "freedom" and so we in our Party greet each other with this word. Should you call our offices anywhere in the world, you will be greeted with the word "Uhuru." We say Uhuru because we believe that freedom should

173

be on the minds of African people twenty-four hours a day. [Applause] Uhuru! ["Uhuru!"]

A few days ago I talked to someone from the South African press. She asked me why was I here to be with the Pan Africanist Congress of Azania at this incredibly significant congress. I didn't think about it at the time, but I should have asked the white woman why *she* was here. [Laughter] It seems to me I have more right to be here than she does. [Applause]

I'll tell you why I'm here. I'm here in part because we are a Party of principle, and because we've worked with the Pan Africanist Congress of Azania for more than thirty-five years. [Applause] We've worked with this organization in an uncompromising fashion, even when it was popular in certain places in the United States for organizations to claim they couldn't decide whom they should support. [Laughter] We had to support the Pan Africanist Congress because we witnessed the African National Congress (ANC)[1] give away our Occupied Azania. [Applause and booing] We remember Joe Slovo's Freedom Charter that said that South Africa belongs to all who live here ["Boos" from crowd].[2] We had to support the organization of Mangaliso Robert Sobukwe[3] because it was the principled thing to do. [Enthusiastic applause]

On a practical level, I can tell you why I am here today. Someone mentioned to you that this is my first trip home to Africa. I have fought for Africa most of my life, but I have never been home until now. [Applause] It is fitting that my first trip home should be to Occupied Azania. It is fitting that my first trip home should be to a Congress of the Pan Africanist Congress of Azania. [Applause and cheers] It is fitting because I know the reason that I am here is because of APLA and Poqo[4] and the militants of the Pan Africanist Congress. [Applause] I could not be here except for the work that PAC has done. I recognize that.

It is a matter of principle and it is a consequence of the work that this glorious organization has done that makes it possible for me to be here. I thank you very much for allowing me to come home to be with my brothers and my sisters here in Occupied Azania. [Applause and cheers]

Another question was asked of me by the media. They asked, "Why do you think the Pan Africanist Congress has not done so well in the elections?" Well! I know why the PAC has not done so well in the elections. There is no mystery. I was in the United States and I saw the most powerful imperialist country in the world do everything possible to get the ANC elected. [Applause] I saw them do that! [Applause/booing] I saw U.S. president William Jefferson Clinton send his own campaign organizers to work for the African National Congress. I saw the money and experts who were sent here to work to organize in the name and interests of the African National Congress.

As a consequence of that, instead of having a direct settler colonial State, we now have a settler neocolonial State. [Applause and "Uhuru!"] It is a settler neocolonial State! As in any place on earth, the purpose of the State is to protect the status quo, the system that is in existence. Just as it was the responsibility of the apartheid State to protect the status quo, it is the responsibility of the settler neocolonial State to protect the status quo. [Applause and "Uhuru!"]

People who have spoken before me have talked about this status quo. It is a status quo where ten percent or more of the population still owns and controls eighty-seven percent of the land. [Audience: "Yes!"] This little handful of white people here in our country owns and controls land, with a territory that is four times larger than the United Kingdom and Northern Ireland combined! Something is wrong with that. [Applause] Something is wrong with that!

Sisters and Brothers, I want to be clear that I am speaking as the Chairman of the African People's Socialist Party. I want to say that in the event that there are representatives of the South African media here. I have to say that *I* am responsible for my statements. These are not, obviously, the statements of the Pan Africanist Congress. [Laughter, applause]

Seize power by any means necessary

In the African People's Socialist Party, we have had an analysis of the reality here in Occupied Azania for a long time, and we have understood that the fundamental question here is land. Now that you have a neocolonial settler State, its responsibility is to maintain the status quo, and it will do that by any means necessary. One of the means by which it maintains the status quo is the electoral process itself. [Applause]

From my perspective and the perspective of our Party, we say while it is important to take advantage of any possibility of capturing political power, a system that is established for protection of the system itself will not easily allow for a revolutionary organization to ascend to political power. [Cheers and applause] The revolution in Occupied Azania has not been completed. [Enthusiastic applause] It seems to me that it is the responsibility of revolutionaries to seize power that will lift the masses of people out of deprivation and misery. [Applause] Malcolm X said it before me, but I'll repeat it: we have to seize power by any means necessary, by any means necessary! [Cheers and applause]

I come now from a country where Africans were snatched up four hundred years or so ago and taken into a terrible condition of domestic colonialism. I'm talking about America, the strategic enemy of Africa, the enemy of all African people and the oppressed peoples of the world. America is the headquarters of world imperialism, which is the worst imperialism that has ever existed on the face of the earth. [Applause]

There has been an historic revolutionary movement inside

the United States and an historic connection with Africa. But this Black Revolution inside the United States has not succeeded up until now. In fact, the Black Revolution of the 1960s was defeated militarily in the United States. Many of you who are in this room know what I am talking about. You saw the assassination of Malcolm X. ["Yes!"]

You saw the assassination and murders of members of the Black Panther Party throughout the United States. ["Yes!"] You might have heard the then-U.S. attorney general John Mitchell declare that by the end of 1969 the Black Panther Party would be destroyed. If you did, you know that the United States government murdered at least twenty-seven members of the Black Panther Party that year and arrested more than seven hundred. On December 4, 1969, while he was asleep in his bed, the U.S. government murdered Fred Hampton who was the leader of the Black Panther Party in Illinois.

In the United States in the 1960s, struggles led by black liberals created a situation that called for the end of segregation. In other words, in the United States, apartheid was defeated a long time ago. We were hearing messages that our brothers and sisters in South Africa/Occupied Azania were fighting for the end of segregation here. I said I don't believe that! [Laughter] That's insane. Because when we talk about segregation or apartheid, we're only talking about the form that the oppressor State takes while it expropriates the value that is created by African workers, while it takes our land. With apartheid gone, they set up a system now where they give us the right to vote, and even when we vote, that vote doesn't mean anything! [Enthusiastic applause]

Look at the U.S. George Bush is the biggest terrorist in the world today [Applause]. He is in power because all the Negro liberals—all the black liberals—told us that the way to get free is to just vote. "If you just vote you can find freedom," they told us.

So all the Africans went out and voted for another white man— Albert Gore[5]—who represents another imperialist party in the United States. The other white man won the election numerically, but the Bush regime stole the election, disenfranchising all the Africans who live in the United States. ["Yes!"] And I'm told this is what my people are fighting for in Occupied Azania? I don't think so.

I have heard it said several times, that this congress of the Pan Africanist Congress of Azania is a crucial congress, and I believe that is true. Not only because of what is happening here, and not because I think the goal of the Pan Africanist Congress should be to represent itself as some credible opposition to the thugs who are in power in the form of the African National Congress. I think this is a critical congress because these are critical times in which we live, Sisters and Brothers. ["Yes! Yes!"]

When we look around us and we see the government of George Bush, the government of the United States, talking about making war against the peoples of the world, what we are looking at is an imperialism that is in serious crisis. It is in serious crisis. ["Yes!"] It is too blind to understand the nature of this crisis, or even the fact that it is in crisis.

It is boastful and arrogant in its ability to send troops to the Philippines, as there are now U.S. troops in the Philippines. It is boastful and arrogant in its ability to send U.S. troops into Colombia, in South America, as there are U.S. troops in Colombia right now. It is arrogant in its ability to send troops into Djibouti and Uganda and in its participation in orchestrating the Rwandan holocaust. In its involvement in Congo, the U.S. is arrogant.

Now the U.S. is talking about attacking the people of Iraq, after they have been bombing the Iraqis for eleven years already. Through sanctions the U.S. has been responsible for more than one and a half million Iraqi deaths since 1991. But the question that the U.S. cannot answer is why it is necessary for U.S. imperialism to make war against the world.

The reason it is necessary for U.S. imperialism to make war against the world, Brothers and Sisters, is because we live in a world that is configured economically and politically as a consequence of the thrust by Europe to conquer the rest of the world. It is an imperialism that was created by stealing the resources of all the peoples of the world. It is imperialism that is parasitic in its very nature. [Applause]

This imperialism is like a tapeworm. If you get a tapeworm in your stomach as a consequence of eating bad meat—that we shouldn't be eating too much of anyway—no matter how hard you work, no matter what you eat, you can't get any bigger. But the tapeworm is attached to your intestines and it doesn't have to do any work. No matter the fact that it doesn't do any work, it lives off *your* work, off your labor. You eat, but the tapeworm just grows bigger and bigger and bigger. [Laughter, applause]

Sisters and Brothers, you cannot talk this tapeworm out of leaving your intestines. You can't sing freedom songs to get it to leave. You can't go to the ballot and vote to make it leave, because if it leaves, it dies.

This is the nature of imperialism. This is the nature of international white power. It has constructed itself off the misery and the theft of the resources of the peoples of the world, and all over the world people are demanding Uhuru! People are demanding freedom, from one end of the globe to the other. This crisis of transformation, of people struggling for freedom, has made it necessary for George Bush to try to mobilize a military force that will bring back direct white power, direct colonial rule over the peoples of the world. This is the situation that confronts us.

This congress today is occurring in the context of an imperialism in crisis. This is one of the reasons that it is so important. This is one of the reasons why we have to advance the revolution that will raise up the African working class aligned with the poor peasantry from its position of misery and poverty to its historically required status as a new ruling class. ["Yes!"] That's why it is necessary.

One Africa, one African people

I want to point out that the African National Congress hasn't ever had to fight alone, as we have fought alone. I watched them in the sixties during the time when the Soviet Union declared that there were only six authentic revolutionary organizations in Africa. The ANC was one of them. The Pan Africanist Congress was not one of them. The Soviet Union gave money to the ANC. They gave them organizational training. They gave them military training and ideological training. They had a powerful international media that they used to win favor and friendship and resources for the African National Congress, all over the world. All over the world! ["Yes!"]

Oh yes they did!

Now the African National Congress is in government, after Poqo, APLA and the PAC did so much work to organize a revolutionary movement here that it made it necessary for imperialism to turn over the administration of the oppressor system to an African neocolonial party. That is what has happened. The ANC has been given the responsibility of administering an oppressive system, a system that speaks to the needs and aspirations of imperialist power all over the world. That is what it does. The ANC is the administrator for white power.

The question for us is: When will we, those of us who are African Internationalists, those of us who recognize that there is one Africa, one African people that must be united in order for Africa to be free, when will we start fighting? [Cheers, "Uhuru!"] Alone if we must!

Here are the choices that we are faced with. Here in

Occupied Azania, are we fighting to create another Kenya? Are we fighting to create another Uganda, where black people are apparently in power, but the masses of our people suffer the worst kind of misery?

I say "No!" I say that we have to unite Africans all around the world. We must unite! [Cheers, applause, "Uhuru!"] But it is not enough simply to unite. *We must unite under the leadership of the African working class and poor peasantry!* [Applause]

So, I have to come here to speak to the PAC. Don't tell me about the fact that the PAC only got a small percentage in an election. What the hell do I care about an election? I'm interested in *freedom!* ["Uhuru!" laughter, applause]

I've heard references made to the South African constitution, but law is simply the opinion of the ruling class. Anything that challenges the monopoly of power and violence in the hands of the ruling class is illegal. Slavery was legal in the United States. Apartheid was legal! So those of us who fought against it went to prison. We were killed. That happened here in Occupied Azania, throughout the Americas and in various other places around the world.

So, you will pardon me if I make the distinction between what is written on a piece of paper, whether in America or Occupied Azania, and the actual conditions of existence that confront our people. I have been to the squatters' camps. I have talked to the people in Soweto. I have talked to our impoverished masses who are living in one of the one and a half million so-called "houses" created by the ANC. [Laughter] I saw Mbeki[6] on television boasting about what he has done for our people with these houses. If the houses are so wonderful why doesn't Mbeki move into one of them? [Vigorous applause, cheers] I think this congress must resolve to put Mbeki into one of the ANC houses and see if he likes it. [Laughter, enthusiastic applause]

But we cannot struggle alone. The imperialists do not work

alone. When you in PAC put candidates up for the elections, you are going up against the entire imperialist world. It's not just the ANC. It's all the power, all the authority that's in America, that's in England, that's in Germany, that's in all the places where they are going to protect their interests. That is what you are up against. [Cheers]

Where is *our* power? Our power is in each other. Our power is in recognizing the necessity for African people worldwide to unite. We unite from the bottom up—from the workers and poor peasants—so that we overthrow neocolonialism wherever it exists. That's how we unite our people and our country. [Cheers]

Sisters and Brothers, things are bad for our people in Occupied Azania, but the truth of the matter is only seven percent of the formal trade of Africa is internal. That means that ninety-three percent of all that we call trade in Africa results in resources being stolen from Africa by America, Europe and increasingly by Japan.

We do not have access, ourselves, to Our Africa. We do not have access to Our Africa. We cannot have access to Our Africa as long as these imperialist-imposed borders separate us.

In the African People's Socialist Party, we are convinced that the African Revolution—wherever it exists on the planet Earth—has run into its limitations as long as it allows itself to be constricted or restricted, by the imperialist-imposed borders that separate us.

There is not going to be an American revolution by African people. I am a part of the U.S. Front of the African Revolution. Here in Occupied Azania, we have the Azanian Front of the African Revolution. [Applause] There must be a Kenyan Front of the African Revolution. We must raise up the concept of African Internationalism, so that in his consciousness every African on the planet recognizes who we are and what our responsibility to Mother Africa is. [Applause]

Africa gave the world civilization. It is irresponsible of us to allow Africa to continue to exist under its current conditions.

Build the African Socialist International

Sisters and Brothers, in closing, I want to say that I once heard a man, C. L. R. James, say that the future of the world is in the hands of the African working class. But unfortunately it is not in the heads of the African working class. [Laughter]

It is our responsibility to change that. I am hoping that we can enter into new relationships that demand a more principled stand by each of us. I have a responsibility to support the Pan Africanist Congress of Azania. We have never quibbled about that question. It doesn't matter that the ANC is in power. You don't switch alliances now that the ANC is in power. It doesn't matter. If we stand for principle, we are here because we see the future requires a unified Africa and the recapture of our land. We recognize that.

For more than twenty years now, the African People's Socialist Party and I have talked to Comrade Pokela and Uncle Zeph[7] about the fact that we are working to build what we call an African Socialist International (ASI). This is an organization of African socialists from all around the world who recognize that the future of African people is here, with a liberated, unified Africa. The ASI will work together to build a single revolutionary organization that can fight for the liberation of Africa everywhere on earth. [Cheers and applause]

When we talk about the African Socialist International, I want to be clear. We are not talking about that old, dead, tired Pan-Africanism, that allows folk who one day are Pan-Africanists when they are not in power, but once they win power they are only concerned about the little territory that they have now been allowed to administer.

I know I'm not supposed to say this because it breaks some

kinds of proper political norms, but the African People's Socialist Party built the first ZANU[8] solidarity committee in North America. We trained ZANU cadre how to go out among the Africans in the United States and win solidarity and support for our struggle in Zimbabwe.

We did this not as some kind of sympathy, but because the birthright of my children is Zimbabwe and Azania, just as it is the birthright of your children. [Applause and cheers] So, this was not charity work that we did. We toured ZANU throughout the United States. We helped them raise funds and did a lot of work. But once they went to power we can't find them anymore.

I say that I am happy that comrade Mugabe[9] has made the move around the land question. I am very excited about that. [Cheers] I am sorry he waited so long. [Laughter and applause] I am trying not to be cynical in believing that he may have only done it now to save his own political hide, because the masses of people in Zimbabwe were taking the land anyway. So, I won't be cynical about that.

But I do have a question because I read something in a newspaper article since I've been here. Brother President, I hope you will forgive me; I know it is a breech of etiquette. [Laughter] The article said that Comrade Mugabe was going to appear at the ANC's congress. I hope that is not true. [Laughter] I think Mugabe should be here! [Enthusiastic applause]

I think he should be here as a matter of principle because we worked with ZANU because ZANU told us that they were Africanists. They said they believed in a united Africa where all Africans would come together and be able to enjoy the benefits of Africa. ["Yes!"] How could Mugabe then go to the ANC, which says that Africa belongs to all who live here? [Applause, cheers]

There is no principle in that stance, I am sorry. [Cheers] I believe that we have to demand principled relationships among each other. We will not win unless we do that. We can not be a better ANC than the ANC is. We cannot run around trying to find a formula that will not upset anyone, like the ANC does. I'm telling you, that the ANC now has a copyright on sellout-ism in Occupied Azania.

What we have to do is stake out our base among the masses of the oppressed, as the Pan Africanist Congress has done. Then, regardless of whether anyone likes it or not, we have to strike out for the freedom of Occupied Azania, in solidarity with Africa and African people around the world. Izwe Lethu! [Audience: "i Afrika!"] Uhuru! [Audience: "Uhuru!"] Thank you very much. [Standing ovation, sustained applause, cheering and singing]

1   African National Congress was formed in 1912 as an organization working against apartheid in South Africa. ANC has been South Africa's ruling party since the elections of 1994.

2   ANC adopted the Freedom Charter in 1955.

3   Robert Mangaliso Sobukwe was instrumental in the break with the ANC in 1958 that led to the birth of the Pan Africanist Congress. He was PAC's first president. Sobukwe died in 1978.

4   The Azanian People's Liberation Army, known as APLA or Poqo, was the military wing of the PAC. Poqo means "for ourselves alone" in Xhosa.

5   Gore was vice president under U.S. president William Jefferson Clinton and the Democratic party candidate in 2000.

6   Thabo Mbeki is the current president of South Africa and the president of the ANC.

7   John Pokela was Chairman of the Central Committee of PAC, based in Dar es Salaam, Tanzania, from 1981 until his death in 1986. He is credited as the man who unified the party following a period of crisis for the organization. Zephaniah Mothopeng, popularly known as Uncle Zeph was imprisoned three times during the liberation struggle, the last time for ferrying arms and recruiting into APLA when he was seventy-five years old. He was elected PAC chairman in 1986 while in prison. He was released in 1988 and confirmed as PAC president in 1990 before dying the same year.

8   Zimbabwe African National Union which led the struggle for national liberation in Zimbabwe.

9   Robert Mugabe, President of Zimbabwe.

World summation

The crisis of imperialism
through the eyes of the oppressed

By the end of February 2003 it was becoming clear that U.S. verbal bellicosity toward Iraq was going to express itself in a new invasion of that already impoverished and brutalized country.[1] On February 27, Chairman Omali called together the local Uhuru Movement in St. Petersburg, Florida for a meeting to discuss the world situation. This discussion was designed to help our movement understand the underlying basis for the pending invasion and occupation.

The following is an edited version of the Chairman's presentation at that meeting. This presentation gives a thorough explanation of the real motive forces behind the current U.S. attack and occupation in Iraq. It first appeared in the April 2003 issue of The Burning Spear newspaper.

We're living in a world where more than half the people on earth live on less than two dollars a day. I'm convinced that it is not necessary to live in a such a world where the vast majority of the people don't have access to clean drinking water or enough food and shelter, where people are confronted with violence all the time.

I'm convinced it's not necessary to live in a world where ignorance is imposed upon masses of people on the one hand, while their wealth and resources are stolen and information is concentrated in the imperialist centers on the other hand.

I'm a revolutionary. I'm not involved in a movement to try to make a better imperialism. My objective—as arrogant as it may seem—is to transform the world. A lot of people have problems with that because an assumption of our own insignificance has been imposed on us by the social system under which we live.

In the African People's Socialist Party we understand that the fundamental contradiction in the world is one that exists between oppressed and oppressor nations. This is the most profound contradiction. It does not deny the existence of other contradictions, but this is the contradiction around which every other contradiction revolves.

We recognize that even as there are oppressed nations and oppressor nations, there are contradictions within the oppressed nations themselves. There are contradictions between men and women, between workers and bosses, between heterosexuals and homosexuals. There are similar contradictions within the oppressor nations.

I'm not saying that these other contradictions do not exist. My statement is that the most dynamic, fundamental contradiction—the one around which all the others revolve and the one which the others require for their existence—is this contradiction between oppressor and oppressed nations.

Capitalism is a parasitic system founded on slavery

This is the contradiction that began with the rise of capitalism itself. Capitalism was born as a world system. I'm not suggesting that there was never oppression or exploitation before capitalism. Of course there was. Slavery existed before capitalism. I'm not suggesting that contradictions did not precede the existence of capitalism.

Of course there were contradictions. But the ones that we are fighting, the ones that we have to contend with, the ones that set the terms for the relationships that we have in the world are those contradictions which were given birth by the rise of capitalism in the world.

This capitalist social system dominates the entire world. It's not feudal. It's not socialist. It's capitalist. Whether we are talking about capitalism as it manifests itself in the United States or Belgium or whether we're talking about capitalism as it manifests itself in Haiti, Burma or Congo, it is the same capitalist system that dominates the entire world.

Marxist[2] theory, as developed particularly by V.I. Lenin,[3] talked about imperialism as being capitalism developed to a certain stage. Lenin called imperialism capitalism that had become "rotten ripe," capitalism that had become "parasitic."

I pose to you that capitalism was born parasitic. There was never a time that capitalism was not parasitic. It was born off the slave trade. Marx referred to the "primitive accumulation" of capital, the accumulation that didn't come as a consequence of capitalist production, but was its *starting point*. Capitalism was born from the slave trade.

The slave trade created the world economy that was a precondition for the rise of capitalism as a world system. Things like the 1840–42 war against China, called the "Opium War" that turned China into a nation of junkies also gave rise to capitalism as a world system.[4] France got wealthy by turning Viet Nam into a drug colony.[5]

The tremendous amounts of loot and resources coming from places like this into Europe transformed the relationship for peoples who used to be free and independent. We previously had the ability to meet our own needs, but our resources were now going to what had been an impoverished and disease-ridden Europe.

Europe was not only poor and disease-ridden, it had no freedom. There was feudalism in Europe. There was no such thing as "home ownership" or the things that Europeans and North Americans like to brag about today. Those things all came as a consequence of the pillage that Europe initiated against the rest of the world.

The rise of capitalism as a social system was parasitic. It came at our expense and that of other peoples around the world.

Imperialism in crisis

We want to talk about the situation in the world today. We want to struggle to understand what is going on. Some things are very glaring to us.

We see a Bush administration[6] up against the entire world in its absolute urgency to deepen the war that was initiated some eleven or twelve years ago against Iraq.

We see millions of people in the streets protesting. We saw a few million here inside the United States. We've seen perhaps up to eighteen million people throughout the world marching, demonstrating against this genocide that the United States is intent on waging against the people of Iraq.

Folks are searching for answers. The African People's Socialist Party concluded some time ago that the whole empire, the imperialist system, is in a state of severe crisis. That's not to say that all the imperialists understand that there's a crisis, although some thinking imperialist leaders have expressed some recognition of this fact.

The crisis has its origin in a process that has been going on for a long time. It clearly began to manifest itself after the second imperialist war.[7] That's the war that the pundits like to refer to as the last honest war that America pursued. Of course that's garbage.

The second imperialist war, like the first one, like the Korean War[8] and like virtually every war that's been waged for the last four or five hundred years, was a war to redivide the world. There were no good guys in the second imperialist war. The "heroes" of that war—the ones fighting for "democracy"—were all countries and states that had colonies. As much as people like to talk about Hitler, the truth of the matter is that Churchill[9] presided over what the British like to refer to as "an empire upon which the sun never set." Hitler was a Boy Scout compared to Churchill. In that war, it was a group of cutthroats who were fighting to redivide the world.

Anti-colonial struggles emerge after second imperialist war

One of the significant things about that war is that it offered up a certain type of political space for oppressed peoples around the world. The empire was preoccupied being at war with itself. Oppressed peoples seized the opportunity to wage struggle for independence and freedom from colonialism. When you talk about imperialism, you're talking about white power that created itself off of the colonial domination of the rest of the world.

As a consequence of that war, in 1947 we saw independence in India. In 1949 it was China. In the '50s, revolutionary struggles emerged all over Africa. The Mau Mau[10] were fighting against the British in Kenya. Ghana achieved independence in 1957. Even Iraq, I think, became nominally independent from England in '55.[11] Of course, in '59 there was the magnificent Cuban Revolution that contributed to revolutionary fervor, particularly throughout the Americas.

In the '60s we saw the most magnificent struggle of the people in Viet Nam, who in the '50s had defeated the French before they saw colonialism propped up by the United States.[12] In the '50s, we also saw the people of Korea come close to total independence until the United States intervened to prevent the total liberation of Korea.

In many ways, the first humiliating defeat for the United States was the defeat by Korea. China came across the Korean border because it was clear that part of the objective of the United States was also to attack China. The Chinese pushed the

U. S. back across the thirty-eighth parallel. They ended the war by having an armistice that resulted in the Korean people being divided up even today.

We hear discussions about the North Koreans and the South Koreans as if they are two separate people. They're one people. They are people who have been divided just like the people of Viet Nam were divided and just like various peoples around the world have been divided—by imperialism.

These struggles for national liberation emerged after the second imperialist war. They just took off and created serious crises. The U.S. talked about the "domino theory." The backdrop to all of this of course was the communist "boogie man," represented mostly by the Soviet Union, and to a lesser extent China. Even though China sometimes gave more political support to struggles for national liberation, China was poor. When the U.S. talked about the communist boogie man they were really talking about the Soviet Union.

I would remind you that there was never an instance of real confrontation between the U.S. and the Soviet Union. The thing that made the Soviet Union such a terrible entity for imperialism was not the potential for direct contest between the U.S. and the Soviet Union. It was the fact that the Soviet Union supported struggles for national liberation in various places around the world.

The Soviet Union had to fight against encirclement by the United States and other imperial powers. So they would support anti-colonial struggles for national liberation around the world that challenged the U.S. power on many fronts. This was the contest. My point is that all along the real contest has been the contest for national liberation.

The Soviet Union was hated and dreaded because it would give a gun to people fighting in Nicaragua or Cuba. It would give a gun to somebody in some place in the world who would really change the fundamental relationships that existed between the oppressed nations and the oppressor nations of the world.

National liberation forces deprive imperialism of resources

Subsequent to the second imperialist war, we saw this escalation of struggles by people to win their freedom. In the process, they began to deprive capitalism of those resources that keep it strong. This has had profound consequences. Even now, as they try to explain the gouging that's being done at the gas stations, they talk about the impending war with Iraq as a solution. They talk about the troubles in Venezuela.[13]

How do you explain the fact that fundamental economic crisis can happen in America, England and other places as a consequence of what some poor, starving country is doing? The oil workers go on strike in Nigeria and the gasoline prices go up in St. Petersburg, Florida. It's because of this parasitic relationship.

This has been going on for a long time now. I can't say when the situation reached a critical level, but I do know that the struggles of oppressed peoples have contributed to the political crisis in this country and in other places.

Kennedy was assassinated as part of this crisis.[14] Subsequent to that, you had Lyndon Johnson who could not serve a second term as president because of the Viet Nam war. Following Johnson you had this crook Richard Nixon who was kicked out along with his vice president.

Then there was Ford,[15] who could only be there one term because of the deal that he had made to pardon Nixon. Following Ford, James Earl Carter, the Georgia plantation owner, was put forward in an attempt to resolve this crisis. There was also crisis inside of the U.S. itself that was brought about by the Black Liberation Movement of the Sixties. Our movement was making a fundamental ideological assault on the basic assumptions of Americanism and white supremacy, which in the final analysis is the ideological underpinning of America and imperialism in general.

James Earl Carter's presidency was a response to the crisis in the executive branch and the crisis that existed between the government and all the people in this country. Carter said, "Trust me, I will never tell a lie." That was his theme. His foreign policy was based on "human rights." Carter was trying to resolve the contradiction in this country among the people who had come to be so suspicious of the government. They did regular polls at the time that showed that sanitation workers were considered more trustworthy and popular than the president of the United States!

Peoples around the world, of course, hated the United States for how it was treating them. After what they'd done to Viet Nam, Cuba, Guatemala, Iran and all those other places, here's Carter with a human rights foreign policy. And who was his ambassador to the United Nations? Who did he put out to front this foreign policy? Andrew Young.[16] He put Young out to front this foreign policy for him so it wouldn't seem to be white power or white nationalism, but a Negro forwarding this policy.

Even as Carter was proclaiming "human rights" and saying, "trust me," he named Zbigniew Brzezinski as the national security advisor. Brzezinski has written books such as *Out of Control* and *The Grand Chessboard* that decried the fact that, from their point of view, the world was spinning into chaos and anarchy as a result of all these struggles of oppressed peoples around the world.

Carter's administration, through Brzezinski, created Osama bin Laden[17] and the modern jihad.[18] There was no such thing as jihad in modern history. They resurrected the idea from the Middle Ages to destroy the Soviet Union. They succeeded in doing that in Afghanistan. Through the CIA they created Islamic fundamentalism and organized Muslims from throughout the world to go into Afghanistan. They sucked the Soviet Union into a long, costly and deadly war, and then wiped it out.[19]

The situation with Osama bin Laden is what the CIA calls "blowback." That's when you put a program in motion and then it comes back and hits you in the face. Effectively that's what 9-11 was—"blowback."

Carter still goes to Venezuela and other places putting himself forward as the "nice imperialist." But, Carter had a problem in 1979 when he visited Iran. The Iranians had a huge banquet for Carter where he praised the Shah of Iran, who had been put in power by the CIA in 1953 after the U.S. overthrew the progressive government of Muhammad Mossadegh. The Shah was a dirty criminal tyrant and torturer who brutalized the Iranian people in ways that people in this country cannot imagine.

Carter said the Shah of Iran was the "island of stability in the Persian Gulf." Then he caught an airplane back to Washington D.C. and the Shah almost beat him here because the Iranian people ousted him. Carter's island of stability was overthrown and the mullahs[20] took power in Iran.

The Shah had been under U.S. tutelage, acting as the policeman of the United States in the Persian Gulf. He was so brutal, and the dictatorship was so severe, that the masses of people did not have the political space to organize. So, the churches became the centers of organization. That's how the mullahs were able to take power.

Carter and Brzezinski even played a role in creating Khomeini[21] with this modern day jihad as the Muslims took power in Iran.

Then, in 1979 the Iranians captured a nest of spies in the embassy in Tehran. A crisis emerged that was similar to what we saw happen after September 11th. This was a whole new experience for white people in this country.

The Iranians went into the embassy where the U.S. had shredded all the documents. The Iranians got all the shredded documents and pasted them together. They were selling them in the streets in Iran. These documents showed all the terrible stuff that the CIA and the United States government had been doing to the people there.

It was considered a real catastrophe. In that same year, 1979, the Sandinistas marched into Managua and overthrew Somoza,[22] who had been put in power by the U.S. and whose government was trained by U.S. forces. Crisis abounded.

Reagan administration calls national liberation movements "terrorist"

Then you had Ronald Reagan, this white guy on his white horse, attacking struggles of oppressed peoples inside this country and around the world. Reagan attacked the black movement and the African community in general, raising the most reactionary, racially-charged characterizations. The African community was taking all the shots. Reagan used terms like "welfare queens." He did this because there was a serious economic crisis that emerged in this country in part because of the success of the anti-colonial struggles.

Internationally there was the issue of the Panama Canal, which the U.S. saw as "our" canal.[23] The U.S. had created Panama. What they now call Panama had been a part of Colombia. The U.S. needed a canal for ships to pass between the Atlantic and the Pacific Oceans. That would save the Americans a lot of money. So the U.S. created a false revolutionary movement in what is now called Panama and then went in there to help their friends become independent. After their friends became independent, they gave the U.S. permission to build the canal.

Here was Reagan rescuing America from all of these things

inside and outside the U.S. White people in this country were not accustomed to being afraid. That's bad, because fear is a normal emotion. Most people experience fear as a regular condition of the oppression imposed on us. That isn't true for white people as a rule. In order to experience fear white people have to make up games like bungee jumping.

The world was closing down on America. The Iranians took "our" embassy. They were treating "our" guys so bad, holding them as hostages and not letting them come home.

Whoever heard of a situation where white guys can't go where they want to go when they want to go? Then, of course, there was America's so-called rescue attempt for the hostages in Iran. A grain of sand got into the helicopters, they crashed and the rescue was a failure.[24] It was just a mess out there.

There was revolution in Nicaragua. Revolution was threatening El Salvador. So, white people were afraid. They were also losing their money. We saw the emergence of the "angry white man." You saw the whole struggle against big government, which was, of course, government that was paying welfare and handing out food stamps.

Reagan took on these questions and he won the election. He won incredible support from the white population to try to return things to the way they used to be. Under the Reagan administration, you began to see a pattern emerge. His secretary of state was Alexander Haig. He was not a diplomat but a damn general, indicating how their foreign policy was going to be conducted.

I was in Nicaragua when Reagan took office. I'll never forget Alexander Haig declaring himself the vicar of foreign policy. He announced that those groups that had been called freedom fighters for national liberation organizations would henceforth be known as "terrorists." That came from the Reagan administration.

Reagan had a "moderate" imperialist as his vice president, George Herbert Walker Bush who was known as an ex-CIA agent. I don't know if you're ever an ex-CIA agent. I think it's like the Mafia. Once you're in, it's for life. You know too much.

They created this thing they called the "arc of crisis." They characterized Iran, much of the Persian Gulf, the Middle East and certain parts of Asia as the "arc of crisis." They recognized this crisis even back at that time.

We've been looking at this attempt all along to try to put the brakes on this process of people winning their freedom, winning their national liberation. All these struggles for national liberation always conflict with the national interest of the United States government. "Our" national interest is to have all the oil in the Middle East.

George W. Bush steals presidential election: denies Africans right to vote

Today the crisis is so profound that you saw most recently the theft of an election by Bush's son, George Walker Bush. I am talking about the public theft of the 2000 presidential election. That's not something that democracies like to do. Democratic capitalism likes to be a hidden dictatorship.

But now dictatorship rose up and bared its fangs for everyone to see. They actually stole the election in broad daylight. People saw them steal the election: "Stop the count. Stop the count!" It was televised. They stole the election by publicly disregarding the votes of the African population.

In my view, the political crisis is so severe that the Democratic party, certainly Al Gore[25] and those who he represents, could not even win the election. The Democrats had the *ability* to win the 2000 election but they wouldn't do what was necessary to win the election. To win the election, they would have had to call into question the Voting Rights Act of 1965. That Act was put into place exactly so the kind of thing that happened historically to the black community could not happen anymore.

Africans were denied the vote in Mississippi and Alabama. That's why the Voting Rights Act was passed in the first place. That's why people like Martin Luther King were out there dying. That's why people like Julian Bond[26] marched. That's why I nearly got lynched in Madison, Florida, when we tried to get the right to vote.

Not once did Al Gore invoke the Voting Rights Act, nor did he ever raise the question of the black community being disenfranchised. He would rather lose an election than raise up this contradiction that would mobilize African people against the system that had denied us the right to vote.

So, of course, he was not elected.

I think that was a reflection of the crystallization of the crisis that's emerging in this country. They stole an election. Then, having stolen an election, right away you began to see an attempt to take on the crises that exist in the world.

Bush creates war cabinet

Today we again see a general as a secretary of state. This is the third time that I'm aware that this has happened. The first time, of course, was Marshall[27] who was a general. This was after the second imperialist war when he became secretary of state, and the so-called Marshall Plan was initiated that white people in this country like to talk about. They say how we helped poor friends and poor Germany. In reality, the Marshall Plan nearly rendered Europe into a colony of the United States. It was no giveaway. The U.S. was raking in the loot and the resources.

Now we saw Bush make General Colin Powell secretary of state. Some people consider Powell a moderate imperialist. That's because they don't know Colin Powell. Colin Powell tried to cover up the My Lai massacre in Viet Nam.[28] In 1992, Colin

Powell was also working as part of the Reagan administration, along with Cheney, Wolfowitz and Rumsfeld.[29]

This crew created the plan that has been initiated now with the USA PATRIOT Act[30] and the preemptive strike. They had been floating these ideas around since 1992. Only now they're in power and have started implementing this stuff. Even Madeleine Albright,[31] of all persons, said that this group that's around the president has wanted to do this for more than ten years. We're not looking at a new phenomenon.

So, you've got this group that includes Colin Powell and Donald Rumsfeld[32] who previously was secretary of defense, if I'm not mistaken. You've got Richard Cheney, who's also been secretary of defense and who was CEO of Halliburton, the largest oil entity of its kind in the world.

There's Condoleezza Rice,[33] a frothing-at-the-mouth person tied to the oil corporations. There's an oil tanker named for her, the Condoleezza. Then there is this religious fundamentalist, Ashcroft.[34] You know, given the opportunity he would exchange the constitution for the bible. This is the crew that's in power.

Even as this is going on, there are other manifestations of crisis. I mentioned Brzezinski's books. There are others tied to these think tanks who are writing about the crisis, people like Samuel Huntington from Harvard University. He wrote *The Clash of Civilizations and the Remaking of World Order.*

Huntington opens his book up with a discussion about a demonstration in 1994 against Proposition 187 in Los Angeles. He was concerned because the Mexicans who were marching in that demonstration were carrying Mexican flags, not American flags. Huntington also began to anticipate the cultural clash between Muslims and others.

Then there's Pat Buchanan's book, *Death of the West.* It is another expression of the crisis. A lot of liberals like to discount Buchanan because he's supposed to be so far out. Buchanan,

Huntington and Brzezinski are running the same essential line. Buchanan was a speech writer for Nixon and Reagan. This guy is as legitimate as any other imperialist thug in the world.

Buchanan's concern is that by 2050 or sooner, white people will be a serious minority, making up only about ten percent of the world's population. White people are not reproducing, he said. Other people are reproducing. Even in places where there seems to be quite a few white people, they're old.

Buchanan decried the rise of the Muslims and the declining influence of Christianity, which he characterized as the ideological glue of the Western world.

All of these imperialist pundits are seeing the same kind of threat—the threat that is coming from hordes of oppressed peoples around the world. The world is descending into chaos because it is no longer being controlled by Europe and North America. That's the crisis that they're hell-bent on trying to resolve.

I don't know any more than anyone else in this room about who was responsible for the September 11th attacks. It can be argued effectively that the United States government did it. But that argument could represent the fact that liberals want to run away from another, for them more frightening, possibility. I think that some people might rather believe that the Bush regime orchestrated September 11th than believe that there might be Arabs and other people who are out there trying to find any way they can to bring America and imperialism down.

I was listening to a presentation I made some years ago when I said that if there were a nuclear accident that wiped out America, people all around the world would celebrate. That is an objective truth. I wasn't saying that to be alarmist. It is the truth because of the stranglehold that America has had on the oppressed peoples of the world.

I am biased on the side of the oppressed peoples. I've told you the foundation of my beliefs. I believe what I'm talking about. You can go to any library and pick out books that will show you the historical data that backs up what I'm talking about.

My concern now is that people in this country are the most politically backward people in the world. They base their politics on raw and naked emotion. How silly it is for a whole population, when talking about 9-11, to be saying, "I don't care why they did it." You ought to care why they did it. Hell, they might do it again!

To say, "I'd rather be stupid; I'd rather be dumb and ignorant," is just ridiculous. That's the kind of thing that permeates the political culture in this country. It makes it difficult to have the kind of discussion that we need to have if we're going to move things forward.

Either way the events of September 11th were a statement of crisis. The Bush regime could be so desperate that they would have done that. There's no morality in the politic of imperialism. I'm not suggesting that it's outlandish to assume that they would kill 3,000 people in the World Trade Center. Hell, they've killed more than that in Afghanistan in the last period, and regularly in other places.

Someone attacked symbols of U.S. financial and military power and they were willing to kill themselves in the process of doing that. That is a statement of crisis. In my opinion, this is something that needs to be recognized.

Bush regime attempts to recolonize world

Now the Bush regime is in a process of attempting to rescue the entire imperialist system. His objective is not simply to rescue imperialism, but to rescue imperialism in a way in which America would have absolute hegemony.

Last September, the Bush administration put forth the so-called Strategic Defense Plan which has three components to it:

One, it stated quite clearly that America is the most powerful country in the world, and that it would never allow any other country to become as powerful.

Two, it stated that if any power that is opposed to U.S. imperialism, in any region of the world begins to acquire weapons of mass destruction the U.S. would use preemptive attacks to wipe them out.

Three, the U.S. would attack unilaterally, by themselves, if necessary.

Their policy is world hegemony. Their objective is to recolonize the world. It is to stop the bleeding of the imperialist system that comes as a consequence of oppressed peoples around the world fighting and winning their freedom, whether it is in the Middle East or any place else.

Now, in my opinion and the opinion of the Party, the Bush regime can't do anything right. There's nothing right they can do.

The government says it is fighting against violence. It has characterized this massacre that it wants to commit against the people of Iraq as somehow rescuing the people from the violence of Saddam Hussein![35]

So, I'm truly, truly, truly concerned about that. I think that we are in a very serious and tenuous place in the world. We need to struggle for more political clarity and maturity in our movement. We need to be willing to look objectively at what America's about.

U.S. fighting in Asia, Africa and Latin America, as well as Middle East

There's another reason that I'm concerned. The situation with Iraq is obvious to everybody. What's not so obvious is what the U.S. is doing in all these other places.

They have now effectively declared war in the Philippines. Initially they were just going to send somebody over to help and advise in the Philippines. Now they say they are going in ostensibly to get Abu Sayaf.[36]

Who is America to go and get any damn body? I mean, they can't even get the white guy that sent out anthrax in this country.[37] There was a guy who was right over here in Seminole. They found him with weapons of mass destruction, but they haven't characterized him as a terrorist.[38] They didn't do to him what they've done to Sami Al-Arian.[39]

We're confronted with a serious situation, particularly in Africa. You read about the million Africans killed in Rwanda, because of so-called contradictions between the Hutu and the Tutsi. Many of those Africans died in 1998 and 1999. Every day you pick up the newspaper and read something about the situation in Congo. There's the situation in Ivory Coast. There's a near-situation in Central African Republic.[40]

Most people do not understand that what you're looking at in Rwanda, Congo, Ivory Coast and Central African Republic is a contest between France and the United States. France used to be the dominant force in these so-called francophone states.

The United States no longer recognizes the French sphere of interest in Africa. It has now moved to take all of it away from France. You're looking at proxy wars that sometimes have resulted in skirmishes between U.S. and French troops in Africa.

We're not just looking at what the U.S. is doing in Iraq. When we talk about peace, we have to be talking about a peace that comes as a consequence of national liberation. People have to be free.

Latin America has to be considered, also. The most dynamic force in the world is the struggle for national liberation. This is the most progressive force. Anybody who's standing in the way of that is standing in the way of progress, whether it's in the black community in America or in Bolivia which just had a major uprising. It's in a very unstable situation.

You don't even know half of what's happening in Colombia. I talked to a comrade who just got back from Venezuela. It's nothing like what you think because the media only lets you see what they want you to see. It's boiling in Venezuela. In Venezuela, comrades from the Fuerzas Armadas Revolucionarias de Colombia (FARC) liberation movement in Colombia are passing out leaflets on the streets.[41] It's that serious there. U.S. troops have made it clear why they went to Colombia. They went there to fight the revolutionaries.

Then in Brazil, which is huge, you've got a changed situation with the election of this social democrat, Lula da Silva.[42]

You know about the economy in Argentina.[43] It is an extremely volatile situation all over the world. There is no way that the U.S. can do what it wants to do and come out of it the way it wants to come out. It's attempting to recolonize the world, and it is serious. That is the context for everything that we're looking at right now, including this war that they're talking about making against Iraq.

This is the crisis that imperialism is looking at.

I'm not trying to find a way out of the crisis for imperialism, because everybody else lives in crisis. When more than half the people in the world live on two dollars a day, there is a damn crisis for the rest of the world. The fact that people are trying to resolve their crises is causing the crisis for the parasite that feeds off of them.

It seems to me that we're confronted with the question of how we move to unite with the vast majority of humanity that wants to be free! That's what we're contending with.

You have this interesting contradiction. It's not all what it looks like. Almost everything is up for grabs.

Europe fears U.S. hegemony over entire world

Europe is uneasy with the United States. It has been for a while, especially since the so-called Soviet threat has disappeared. Europe has been trying to move as rapidly as possible for unification.

It has been clear that there are two objectives of the European Union (EU). One of them is to contain Germany. Every time Germany flexes its muscles, it kicks everybody else's ass in Europe. So they want to contain Germany.

They also want to grow an economy and a military that are as strong as or stronger than those of the United States. They've even commented on this in their journals. This is one of their intentions. With the so-called Soviet threat gone, there was no reason why they could not do that.

Now, you have forces in Europe with their own interests that are separate and distinct from those of the United States. They have interests in Iraq. They want the loot from Iraq and Iran. France was trading seriously with Iran and Iraq. China was as well, although China's not part of Europe. These countries and entities want their own relationships. They want to look after their own interests. Sometimes that's in contention with the interests of the United States.

Now, everybody's concerned about the United States taking Iraq. They say that Iraq has more oil reserves than Saudi Arabia. In fact, they call it the second largest. They say that every time you dig a hole in Iraq you get oil.

The problem is that Europe is dependent on oil, too. So is Japan. If the United States sits astride all the oil in the Middle East, then they've got control of Europe, period!

That is the real concern on the part of Europe. Another concern is the arrogance of U.S. imperialism. It disallows other spheres of imperialist interest that I was talking about. It is quite blatant in its statement of world hegemony.

The U.S. today no longer even pretends that the Europeans are equal powers. They say this is how it's going to be and you fall in line or you get left out.

This is creating serious contradictions among the populations in Europe. There is a form of nationalism: European nationalism, French nationalism, British nationalism. They resent America telling Tony Blair[44] what to do. They are ashamed. They hate it. They write in newspapers that Blair is Bush's poodle.

Just yesterday, in the House of Commons, Blair received the largest defeat in the history of England. More than a third of his own party fought him against this war resolution. He won the resolution, but he won it because the Tories, many of whom were against him, carried the day for him. They said it was a humiliating defeat for Blair.

You've got all these people who hate that their fallen empire is a footstool for U.S. imperialism. There is a kind of nationalism in Europe that, even as it uses expressions about sympathy for the people in Iraq, is opposed to Europe being dominated by the United States the way it's being dominated. So, millions of people are in motion around that question.

You've got certain sectors of the ruling elite in England who are afraid of the European Union, because if Europe united like it's talking about, Germany and France are going to be the primary forces in Europe. To contend with them, England is hanging with the United States, come what may. That's going to be their seat at the table. They would be eaten up by a Europe dominated by Germany and France.

The U.S. is taking advantage of Europe in some interesting ways. The former Soviet states are being brought into the European Union and they are on the payroll of the United States. Rumsfeld is playing the "old Europe" against the "new Europe."[45]

He's telling Germany and France to go to hell, because he's got Hungary, Poland and the Czech Republic.

Because they're in the pocket of Uncle Sam, England is struggling with Germany and France about where they are trying to take Europe and the European Union.

The type of EU that France and Germany want is problematic. They want a closely knit, single economy and a single military. These new forces coming in are struggling for something loose. They're going to be the U.S. Trojan Horse inside this situation.

So, you've got a highly volatile, unstable situation where the U.S. is exposing itself to the whole world. That's no little thing. It's antagonizing many allies. One of the ways the U.S. gets to project its imperial power around the world is through military bases in these other countries that it's now making hostile.

You know there was a time when this contradiction we're looking at now might have caused a war among the imperialists themselves. The problem now is that the United States has a military budget that is larger than the next twenty countries combined.

No other imperialist power is willing to take on the U.S. The EU might have the muscle to try to push the U.S. around sometime in the future, but there is not a single one of the European nations that's capable of challenging the United States right now.

It seems France is going to jump on board once the war starts, because they want their own action in Iraq. France wants contracts for rebuilding and favorable business deals. It won't want to be left out of the business deals that are going to come with the conquest of that territory.

It's all cold blooded. All their moralistic nonsense has nothing to do with morality.

Driving force in history is national liberation

It's a volatile situation, but it's one that can bode well.

The problem is there are all the millions of people out there opposed to imperialism, but they lack organization. The people need organization! In any case, oppressed peoples everywhere, including the black communities and barrios in the cities and towns are moving forward. They are no longer going to live like this. That stand is defining the historical trajectory that we're moving along today. Bush is trying to stop history but it will not work.

Revolutionaries struggle to understand the historical trajectories and join them to facilitate the birth of a whole new kind of social system. That, in the final analysis, is what we're fighting for.

People have to choose sides. The driving force in history is national liberation. There's a real attempt to recolonize the world directly under white power. I believe everything they do will deepen this crisis as opposed to lessening it for them.

Uhuru!

1 On March 20, 2003 the U.S. invaded Iraq for the second time in twelve years, following more than a decade of deadly economic sanctions and regular bombings.

2 The theory of Karl Marx, 1818–1893, the German philosopher, political economist and revolutionary, author of the *Communist Manifesto, Capital* and many other theoretical works.

3 V.I. Lenin, 1870–1924, revolutionary, political leader and theoretician, was the driving force behind the Russian revolution of 1917 and the formation of the Union of Soviet Socialist Republics (USSR).

4 In the early nineteenth century, Britain, the biggest drug cartel in history, began forcing tons of opium on the Chinese people, creating massive addiction among the population and extracting enormous wealth for the British. The Chinese resisted this imposition of drugs in what is called the Opium Wars of 1840–42 and 1856–60 when the British navy, built off the trade in African people, overpowered China.

5 One third of France's colonial revenues came from the opium trade imposed on the French colony of Viet Nam, where the French in 1918 had 1,512 dens and 3,098 retail shops for the sale of opium.

6 U.S. president George W. Bush.

7 Second World War.

8 Korea was divided into North and South Korea at end of second imperialist war. When the Korean people attempted to reunite their country the U.S. invaded. The U.S. War against Korea was 1950-53.

9 Winston Churchill was the prime minister of Great Britain from 1940 to 1945, during the second imperialist war.

10 The Mau Mau was a guerrilla force that rose up out of the struggle of the Kikuyu people in Kenya in the 1950s against the genocidal colonial rule of the British. The Mau Mau was led by Dedan Kimathi.

11 Iraq won its official independence from British colonialism in 1932, but Britain retained control of Iraq, only turning over its last air bases in Iraq in 1955.

12 Viet Nam won its victory over the U.S. on April 30, 1975 when the last ten remaining U.S. marines were forced to leave the country.

13 Venezuela is the oil-rich South American country now governed by populist leader Hugo Chavez, whom the U.S. unsuccessfully attempted to overthrow in 2002. Hundreds of thousands of people came out to defend Chavez, forcing the U.S.-backed military forces to reinstate Chavez as president.

14 U.S. president John F. Kennedy was elected in 1961 and was assassinated November 22, 1963.

15 Gerald R. Ford was U.S. president 1974-77.

16 Andrew Young was a top aide for Dr. Martin Luther King during the Civil Rights Movement and was vice president of the Southern Christian Leadership Conference. He served two terms as mayor of Atlanta, Georgia. Currently he is on the board of director of numerous corporations including Delta Air Lines, Argus, Host Marriott Corp., Archer Daniels Midland and others.

17 Osama bin Laden is a Muslim resistance fighter accused by the U.S. of masterminding the September 11th attacks.

18 Jihad is often translated as "holy war." However, the Council on American-Islamic Relations (CAIR) states that jihad "does not mean 'holy war.'" Rather, it refers to "a central and broad Islamic concept that includes the struggle to improve the quality of life in society, struggle in the battlefield for self-defense . . . or fighting against tyranny or oppression."

19 In 1998 Brzezinski admitted in an interview with France's *Le Nouvel Observateur* that he and CIA director William Casey had cooked up the idea of trying to provoke a Soviet invasion of Afghanistan by providing covert aid via the Pakistani intelligence services to the Mujahideen (Muslim resistance fighters in Afghanistan). "What is most important to the history of the world?" Brzezinski reportedly told the paper, in its January 15-21, 1998

issue. "Some stirred-up Muslims or the liberation of Central Europe and the end of the cold war?"

20 Muslim clerics.

21 Ayatollah Ruhollah Khomeini was the Iranian head of State after the people's overthrow of the Shah's regime. Khomeini was in power from 1979 to 1989.

22 The Sandinistas are the Frente Sandinista de Liberación Nacional (FSLN, the Sandinista National Liberation Front), the revolutionary force which overthrew the U.S.-backed regime of Anastasio Somoza in Nicaragua on July 27, 1979.

23 In 1977 U.S. president James Earl Carter had signed a treaty ostensibly to turn over the Panama Canal to Panama on December 31, 1999. One of Reagan's campaign promises was his commitment not to "lose" the canal.

24 After the ousting of the U.S.-backed Shah by the people of Iran in 1979, he was granted medical treatment in the U.S. In response, a crowd of Iranian people took over the U.S. embassy on November 4 of that year, taking ninety people hostage. On April 4, 1980 U.S. president Carter sent in helicopters in an attempt to rescue the hostages. After three of the eight helicopters were damaged in a sand storm and eight people were killed, the operation was aborted. On January 20, 1981, the hostages were released after 444 days.

25 Al Gore was the vice-president under U.S. president William Jefferson Clinton and the Democratic party presidential candidate in 2000.

26 Julian Bond was a Civil Rights leader and one of the founding members of the Student Nonviolent Coordinating Committee (SNCC). He was a Georgia state senator and is currently the Chairman of the NAACP (National Association for the Advancement of Colored People).

27 George C. Marshall, 1880-1959, was a general who was named secretary of state in 1947 under the Truman administration.

28 On March 16, 1968, U.S. soldiers slaughtered, raped, tortured and murdered 347 Vietnamese civilians in the village of My Lai. Colin Powell was the officer who covered over this atrocity.

29 Richard Cheney is the vice-president under George W. Bush. Paul Wolfowitz was the deputy secretary of defense under George W. Bush and is now the president of the World Bank. Donald Rumsfeld is the Bush's secretary of defense.

30 A reactionary law passed just after September 11th, 2001 that seriously abrogates human and constitutional rights.

31 Albright was secretary of state under U.S. president William Jefferson Clinton in 1996.

32 Previously Rumsfeld was an economic adviser for president Richard Nixon (1969-73). He then worked in the Gerald Ford administration as White House chief of staff (1974-75) and as the secretary of defense (1975-77). During the 1980s Rumsfeld served in various capacities as an advisor to the Ronald

Reagan administration.

33 Rice was the national security advisor under George W. Bush's first term. She is currently secretary of state.

34 John Ashcroft was the attorney general during George W. Bush's first term as president.

35 Saddam Hussein was the leader of Iraq from 1979 until he was ousted in the U.S. invasion of 2003.

36 Abu Sayaf is an armed self-defined Muslim liberation organization in the Southern Philippines.

37 In 2002 it came out that a Jewish Zionist in the U.S., Dr. Philip M. Zack, may be behind the mailing of anthrax to the offices of senator Tom Daschle, news commentator Tom Brokaw and others. Zack, who worked at the U.S. Army's center for research of infectious diseases at Ft. Detrick, Maryland, initially tried to blame the anthrax mailings on an Arab colleague. Despite mounting evidence against him, Zack has apparently never been arrested.

38 In August 2002, police in Seminole, Florida arrested Dr. Robert J. Goldstein after a search of his residence found more than fifteen bombs and the components to make up to forty more, along with thirty to forty weapons including semi-automatic weapons. Also found was a list of fifty Islamic worship centers in the Tampa-St. Petersburg area and other parts of Florida. Goldstein was charged with "one count of possessing destructive devices and one count of attempting to damage and destroy buildings by means of explosive devices."

39 Dr. Sami Al Arian, a Palestinian professor of computer science at University of South Florida, in Tampa, was arrested on February 20, 2003 in a pre-dawn raid of his home by the FBI and Joint Terrorist Task Force. Al Arian and others were charged with fifty counts of racketeering and conspiracy to commit murder. Al Arian, who has long been a supporter of the Palestinian cause, has been labeled a "terrorist." Unlike the case of Dr. Goldstein, no weapons of any sort were found in his apartment.

40 The situation in these and other African countries is grave. The mass murder of over 800,000 people in Rwanda in 1995 was instigated and backed by U.S. and Western imperialist interests. In Congo, more than five million people have been slaughtered since 1998 in proxy-wars backed by the U.S. to maintain control, in particular, of the mineral coltan which is an essential ingredient for the manufacture of cell phone and computer technology. Ivory Coast and Central African Republic, former French colonies, are, as the Chairman explains, victims of the intra-imperialist battles between France and the U.S. for control of resources there. Ivory Coast has had eight or more coups since 1999 as one neocolonial government succeeds another. Central Africa Republic is one of the poorest countries in the world.

41 The revolutionary movement led by FARC-EP ("The people's army") in Colombia is said to have 18,000 members and has liberated or has strong control of thirty to forty percent of Colombia's territory. FARC-EP stands for Fuerzas Armadas Revolucionarias de Colombia-Ejército del Pueblo.

42 Leftist former union chief Luiz Inacio Lula da Silva, known as Lula, was elected by a landslide as president of Brazil in October 2002. Despite his promise of a progressive administration, Lula is now widely unpopular in Brazil because of his anti-worker policies, in addition to the fact that he has postponed promised reforms and has continued following the dictates of the U.S. controlled World Bank and International Monetary Fund put in place by the previous president. At the World Social Forum in Porto Allegre, Brazil in January 2005, Lula was booed by the thirty thousand participants, while Venezuela's Hugo Chavez was cheered.

43 The U.S. government and IMF and World Bank policies fueled the collapse of the Argentine economy in January 2002.

44 British prime minister.

45 Rumsfeld made the comments playing "old Europe" against "new Europe" on a 2003 tour to the continent.

Victory to the people of Iraq!
Peace through national liberation for all oppressed peoples!

The Chairman gave this electrifying three minute speech at an anti-war rally in Oakland, California, on April 5, 2003.

The march and rally were sponsored by a white left coalition called the People's Nonviolent Response Coalition that decided they would build a peace rally in Oakland, which is populated predominantly by African, Mexican, Asian and other peoples, as opposed to holding it in San Francisco which is predominantly white.

Although the coalition put out a call for Oakland organizations to participate, members of the Uhuru Movement had to fight fiercely against a hostile and unprincipled white left for the Chairman to be able to speak on the program. Despite the fact that he was put at the end of the program with only a few minutes to speak, the response from the crowd was profoundly enthusiastic.

The war that we are protesting today started a long time ago. Here we are, in Oakland, California, looking out on part of a territory stolen from Mexico. I'm talking about California, Texas, Arizona, New Mexico, Utah and other states stolen by the U.S. government.[1]

Here we are in Oakland, California, in a country where there are still concentration camps, also called reservations, where the Indigenous people are forced to live on their own land. We are talking about looking out and seeing Africans in this country where one out of every ten of us, if we are men, is locked up in prison. We are looking out at Filipinos who are oppressed by the U.S. We are seeing all of these peoples right here who have been under U.S. invasion for more than four or five hundred years. [Cheers and "That's right!"]

When we look at America and imperialism, we are not just looking at bad policies by George W. Bush. We are looking at an America that is a predator State. It is a predator State now; it has always been a predator State! America is an imperialist country. It is the worst empire in the world. The fact is that right now, even as we are talking, people are being murdered by U.S. imperialism throughout the Middle East. But they are not only being killed in the Middle East; they are being killed in Colombia, they are being killed in the Philippines. U.S. imperialism is intervening in Venezuela. It is intervening in Congo, the Central African Republic and other places throughout Africa.

We recognize that if there is to be any peace on earth, it is going to come as a consequence of our people uniting to defeat U.S. imperialism once and for all. When we stand here today, it is not enough to simply be for peace. We have to be for social justice. We have to be for self-determination. We have to be for self-determination for the people of Iraq, self-determination for the people of Occupied Palestine, self-determination for the people of Colombia. We have to be for self-determination for the people of the Philippines, self-determination for Africans, and Mexicans and Indigenous people, who live right here in the U.S.

In the final analysis, it is not going to be enough for us to say, "Stop the war." We are going to have to unite with the oppressed peoples of the world. That is the only way that we will ever know peace. It is the only way we will know peace. We have a responsibility not to simply stand for peace, but to pick sides.

The truth of the matter is that the progressive force in the world today is that force that is driving for self-determination, for national liberation. U.S. imperialism is on the other side of the question. It is not enough—in the final analysis—for us to say, "Stop the war against the people of Iraq." Ultimately we are going to have to understand that it will be necessary for us to say, "Victory to the people of Iraq in their struggle!" We are going to have to pick sides. U.S. imperialism is empire. [Applause and cheers]

It is a dirty, nasty war that black people understand, that Indigenous people understand, that the people of the Philippines and the Americas understand, that the Mexicans understand. More and more of the peoples of the world are coming to the same conclusion that we are coming to. This is just the latest chapter, the latest imperial war.

Sisters and Brothers, in the final analysis, if we want to stop imperialism in the Middle East, if we want to stop it in the Philippines, if we want to stop it in Africa and other places, we are going to have to make it fight for its life right here in North America. [Cheering and applause]

All power to the people, and Black Power to the African community! Uhuru!

1   The U.S. war against Mexico (1846–1848) stole Texas, California, Utah, Arizona, New Mexico, Nevada, Colorado and Montana from Mexico.

Touch one, touch all!

African workers and poor peasants, unite

During the annual weekend conference to build the African Socialist International in London on July 27, 2003, Chairman Omali gave this presentation that mobilized the audience made up of Africans from around the world. The slogan "Touch one, touch all!" elicits an exuberant response from African people everywhere. Through the African Socialist International we will no longer have to endure in isolation imperialist attacks on African people any place on the planet.

Uhuru!

I want to express my appreciation to Comrade Luwezi[1] because he is one of the most committed revolutionary forces that I know. He does incredible work leading the Party's international work—work that happens here in London, as well as in Africa and other places. And I want to thank all of you for coming out.

These are incredibly significant times in which we live. As African people, we do not have the luxury of simply being bystanders as history continues to be made at our expense. Everywhere we look in the world, wherever African people are, we are suffering. We are suffering from various forms of violence, including police violence here in London or in New York, in Liberia or in Nigeria. Everywhere we are located we are facing some form of violence imposed on our lives. We are experiencing extraordinary poverty, which is the most irrational, insane reality possible.

Here we are the people who gave rise to civilization. We came from the place that gave birth to humanity. There was no such thing as the human species until life emerged in Africa. This says more clearly than anything that Africa is nurturing to life; Africa is not hostile to life. Today, you look at the devastation, the violence, the starvation, the famines being imposed on Africa. These conditions did not arise naturally. Human life arose from Africa. Our suffering today is the result of the imposition of this oppressive social system and the hostile reality that has brought us poverty and suffering everywhere we are.

All of us have had to ask the question, why are we poor? We look around and see that white people are rich and we are poor. You see that white people live well, but we live poorly. We are the ones who face violence. The explanation we are given—no matter where we live on the planet Earth—is that white people do well because they are civilized, they are thriftier and they work harder. We are told Africans do poorly because we are less civilized, we do not know how to save our money, and we don't work. The reality is we're in the shape that we're in precisely *because* we work. If working hard provided wealth, then Africans would be the wealthiest people on earth. The reality is we came into contact with white people precisely because they wanted us to work. So it's not a matter of us not working.

All around the world African people are trying to understand what's happening to us. We make the mistake of blaming our children, our neighbors, ourselves. We are blaming ourselves for our own oppression. We don't act like white folk. They have defined for us how our society should be. The fact is white people are rich precisely because *we* work hard. What has happened is that we have been stripped from our own resources. Whether we live in Africa or in the Caribbean, in Brazil, America, or England, we have been stripped from our own resources. If we had possession of our own resources, then we would be the wealthiest people on earth.

We created the wealth. This capitalist system that we suffer from was born as a consequence of our enslavement. Sometimes, so-called white communists tell us that we cannot emerge from our poverty and our oppression until we go through the capitalist process. But the fact is, we've gone through the capitalist process because capitalism was born from the slave trade. It was slavery and the rape of Africa, among other things, that gave rise to capitalism.

You cannot escape from capitalist-imposed oppression by trying to be a capitalist. Our escape is going to come from destroying this system that imposed this reality on us. If you live as a slave, you're not going to be able to cajole the slave master to give you your freedom. The slave master will never free you, because it is your slavery that keeps him fat, that sends his little ugly children to school. It is our slavery, our resources that make this possible. You think you can take him to church maybe, change his heart, save his soul. Then he might say, "Ok, I understand now, here are your resources." No, it won't happen that way.

We are one African people

What it's going to take to free us, Brothers and Sisters, is simple. All you have to do is look at what it took to put us in this situation, and it explains clearly what it's going to take to get us out of this situation. If we find that any place in history anywhere, that we got into this situation through voting, through singing civil rights songs, through prayer, then that's it, let us start a choir. [Laughing in audience]

We all know that is not how we got here. That's important for us to understand. It is also important for us to know that we have been robbed of the knowledge of ourselves, which is fundamentally important. We have been robbed of our consciousness, the understanding of who we are. Malcolm X characterized this phenomenon as similar to having collective amnesia. All over the world, here we are, the people who gave rise to civilization. We created libraries, universities, great monuments. Yet we don't have any understanding of our significance because we have been separated into Jamaicans, Haitians, African-Americans, Black-Brits and Negroes. We call ourselves black and all kinds of weird things, because we don't know that we are all Africans.

We talk about each other as if we're so different, "You know how those Jamaicans are. You know how those Haitians are." Right? This is obscene. The reality is that we must come to understand that wherever we are, whether it's in Jamaica, whether it's in Trinidad, whether it's in Haiti, whether it's in North America, Canada, Brazil, Britain, Nigeria, France, whether it's Somalia, wherever we are, we are one people. We are Africans. And I don't mean some kind of hyphenated Africans. We are one African people! [Applause]

I'm here to tell Nelson Mandela and Thabo Mbeki over in Occupied Azania, that I was mad as far back as 1955 when they created the so-called Freedom Charter. You know what the Freedom Charter said? It said that South Africa, as white power calls it, "belongs to all that live there, black and white."[2] What the hell is he talking about?

If you go to what they call "South Africa" today under black rule, you know what you'll find? The white people, who are ten percent of the population, still own eighty-seven percent of the land. You will find that forty-three percent of the black people in South Africa are unemployed.

Fifteen million African people live in shanty towns built from rubbish just to put a roof over their heads. In many instances, there is no water, or only one water faucet for a whole community. There is no electricity in many instances. This is the thing they call "Black Economic Empowerment."[3] This is the deal the black government made with the white corporations who still control our resources there. They give these big shot Negroes a piece of the action at the expense of our people in Azania.

Even back in 1955, I understood that what the Freedom Charter was doing was giving away not just the birthright of the black people who live in South Africa, it was giving away the birthright of your children and my children as well. Do you understand? I was in Florida when I heard about what the Freedom Charter was doing, and I was mad as hell. Because I know one day we're going home to Africa. I don't know about the rest of you, but I'm going home.

Fight back wherever we are

I can't go yet though. I can't go yet because I have a responsibility in America. No matter where we are in the world, if we have a problem, America's got something to do with it. If there's dirty water, if people are dying of terrible diseases, if you've got a headache, if you're living in the world, America's got something to do with it. So I've got a job in America. Every time I go to Africa, it's so hard to leave. Africa is so magnificent, so beautiful! I've waited so long to go home, and when I got home, oh my goodness! But I can't stay, because that demon America has to be dealt a deathblow. American imperialism must be destroyed! [Applause]

Although I'm living in America, I'm not trying to integrate America. Malcolm X said that's like trying to integrate into a burning house. My job is not to integrate with America. My job is in the U.S. Front of the African Revolution.

We have a slogan, "touch one, touch all." This slogan gives us the capacity, wherever we are in the world, to fight back. If the British government attacks you here in London, then African people around the world have the responsibility to respond to that attack. In South Africa, or Sudan, Africans may not be able to respond to an attack by the U.S. or by imperialism, but we must respond. We say, "You touch one, touch all." That has to be our slogan as a people.

You know Mother Africa, our mother, is raped every day. Only seven percent of the formal trade that happens in Africa is between African people. Ninety-three percent of what they call trade is white power looting Africa. They steal every damn thing we got, and then they slander us. It's like Malcolm X said, they break your legs and then they accuse you of not being able to run. They slander us.

Some eighty-three percent of the gross domestic product of Africa goes to pay what white people say is a debt to them. That means that only seventeen percent of what Africa produces is left in Africa. These boot-lickin', vomit eatin' Uncle Toms, these neo-colonialists, these petty bourgeois forces who have been created in the image of their masters take their part off the top. The rest of Africa is lucky if we get five percent of what we produce. And we are supposed to live on that.

Our resources are leaving Africa, coming to England, to America. In Africa, you look at television, you see these magazines and you see your resources, all this wealth. You say "I must go to England. I must go to France." You don't even know it, but you're chasing your own damn resources. That's why we're here, chasing our own African resources into England. Then they blame us for being here. They say, "You're causing us economic problems," when it's the rape of Mother Africa that brought us here. That's what brought us here, and it made them rich. Well, dammit, we're coming to get everything you took from us! [Applause]

Since the time of the second imperialist war, we have seen the development of struggles for national liberation. These struggles have had a cumulative effect on the ability of imperialism to easily extract other people's resources, which they stole to build capitalism in the first place and which are needed for its continued existence. There is no longer a dynamic imperialism. It used to be something that was constantly growing. Now, you've got an imperialism that's attacking people in an attempt to hold onto what they've already got, because people around the world are struggling to take back their resources.

Guess what's missing in this process. Africa. Africa and Africans. You know why? Because no people on earth have ever won their freedom without first building an organization of professional revolutionaries. You may have a job as a bus driver, a ditch digger, or a brick layer, but your *profession* is revolution.

Uhuru on our minds

Every morning I wake up with nothing on my mind but the intent to destroy imperialism, and I work to make that happen. I go to sleep with that on my mind. That's why anytime you greet one of us, we say "Uhuru." We say "Uhuru" because it means freedom. We say it because it was a slogan that was given to us by the Kenyan Land and Freedom Army, under the leadership of Dedan Kimathi. They were called the Mau Mau.

"Uhuru" should be on our minds twenty-four hours a day. In order to win our freedom we have to build an organization, a cadre of people with the discipline and commitment to fight and bring down imperialism. Our organization has to be able to unite African people all over the world. We cannot win our freedom without that.

What imperialism did was disorganize us by dispersing us throughout the world. It gave us new names and identities. Now, what we have to do as part of the process to win our freedom is to understand that we are one people. We have to engage ourselves in a process of reorganization. Most importantly, we have to understand what social force is capable of leading this revolutionary process to its conclusion.

The African Liberation Movement has run into its limitations as it attempts to fight within the context of the borders that imperialism has created for us. There's not going to be a South African revolution. There's not going to be a Black-Brit revolution or Negro-American revolution. It's going to be an African Revolution. For us to be free, we have to be able to unite all of Africa with a revolutionary organization led by African workers and poor peasants. Our job is going to include bringing down those neo-colonial entities that hold up the false, imperialist-created borders, with weapons that they got from the imperialists to keep our peoples oppressed.

Some people say that we've already had revolutionary struggle. But these were struggles of an anti-colonial movement under the leadership of the African petty bourgeoisie, the middle class, created in the image of their masters. When they come to power, they get their cars. They get a lot of money, and they get white women. The masses don't get anything but hell. Nothing but hell! South Africa is the most recent example. Remember when Nelson Mandela was our hero? [Audience: "Not mine!"]

There are Negroes out there right now whom you are cele-brating, and it's going to take you a little while before you find out who they really are. They represent a social class, a social force. But the black petty bourgeoisie is a tiny social force. In all of Congo, there were only four Africans that had graduated from university.[4] It's a tiny social force, the African petty bourgeoisie. You know all of them by name. You can count them. [Laughter]

It's a tiny social force, but any time they get ready to go into power, they say "I'm speaking for black people." and you get behind them. You rush and help them win their objective. They get what they want but you're still where you were before, except now you're worse off! When the imperialists give them their cut, there's even less for you! Now they can do anything they want to do to you, and you can no longer say that it's white people oppressing us. The imperialists can now say, "Oh no, it's not us. It's Mobutu!" Isn't that right?

So we have to identify the only social force capable of taking the revolutionary process to its conclusion, and that is the African workers and poor peasants. Now, somebody said "Damn, I'm not a worker because I haven't had a job for seven years!" But the reality is, if you had an income, you would only be able to get it through selling your own labor power. Imperialism has determined that many of us are unemployed workers.

African workers ourselves must take the lead

The reality is that some of us are intellectuals, and others of us come from the middle class. The middle class as a social force is traitorous. Generally speaking, it is a class that is self-alienated. It is alienated from Africa. They are Africans who don't want to be Africans. Occasionally, there are individuals from the middle class, the petty bourgeoisie, who will abandon the interests of the middle class. Even though it seems to have a lot going for it right now, it is a dying social force. As a class it is a dying class. So some forces abandon the interests of the African petty bourgeoisie and unite with the interests of the African working class. Amilcar Cabral called this "committing class suicide."

The terms have to be set by African workers and poor peasants. In much of Africa, of course you know, they have not even allowed the working class to emerge yet. There is mostly peasantry. But the truth is that if Africa is ever going to be developed it is going to be as a consequence of having a strong working class. Who creates value? Banks don't create value. Professors don't create value or wealth. Wealth comes as a consequence of human beings, working people, using their labor to transform resources to meet our requirements as human beings.

A tree is just a tree. It has all kinds of abilities but it can't shelter you until a worker transforms it into a house. We say that the people who produce the wealth ought to be the ones who control the wealth. It makes no sense that we come together collectively and produce all the wealth and then eighteen people in Chicago own and control it. Only the workers, in the final analysis, have an objective interest in destroying this kind of system and create a system that will liberate us all.

The thing that's before us now is whether we are willing to step forward, to take control of our own future. There's a kind of welfare mentality that's been created in our community, a colonial mentality, if you will. Not just here. There are places in Africa where we don't even know how to farm anymore. White power stopped the farming. They drive up in trucks now, throwing bleached flour and United Nations provided stuff off the trucks, so that now we're starving. They throw this stuff off the trucks, and we scramble and fight each other to get our hands on it. It's incredible what imperialism has done to us. We are always waiting for someone to do something for us.

The reality is that it's the working people ourselves who are going to have to step forward and assume the responsibility for leading.

In the final analysis, the African working class must become the ruling class. The only way we can do that is through a seizure of power. I hope you will step forward. Let's go to work and build the African Socialist International and change these circumstances in which we live.

I'd like to leave you with a slogan from the Pan Africanist Congress of Azania, which at one juncture was a pretty important social organization in history. This is a call and response slogan: "Izwe Lethu i Afrika." It means "Africa is our land." Because, if you don't have the land, you don't have anything! I say Izwe Lethu, which means "the land is ours." You say "i Afrika" which identifies the land. Then I say "i Afrika" and you say "Izwe Lethu."

Yeshitela: "Izwe Lethu!" Audience: "i Afrika!"

Yeshitela: "i Afrika!" Audience: "Izwe Lethu!"

Yeshitela: "Uhuru." Audience: "Uhuru." [Applause]

1 Luwezi Kinshasa is the Director of International Affairs for the African People's Socialist Party

2 The African National Congress (ANC), the party of Nelson Mandela and Thabo Mbeki, adopted in 1955 the Freedom Charter, written by Joe Slovo. The ANC is today the ruling party of South Africa.

3 Black Economic Empowerment (BEE) is a program of the South African government that claims to "redress the imbalances in South African society created by apartheid."

4 Because the Belgians kept Africans from education, there were only four African university graduates in the Congo at the time of independence, June 30, 1960.

You can't *fix* imperialism
The occupation began in 1492

The following presentation was made by Chairman Omali Yeshitela on October 2, 2003 in Oakland, California at a forum called "The occupation began in 1492," sponsored by the African People's Solidarity Committee (APSC).[1]

The forum was an attempt to win white people, or North Americans, to unity with the fact that while the U.S. was in the midst of a brutal attack on the people of Iraq, the solution is not simply "peace" but the right of the Iraqis and all oppressed peoples to national liberation. The forum also raised the issue that struggles for national liberation exist inside the borders of the U.S. as well for African, Indigenous, Mexican and other oppressed peoples.

Other speakers on the panel included Quetzaoceloacuia, leader of the Barrio Defense Committee; Matthew Shenoda of the American Arab Anti-Discrimination Committee; Kawal Ulanday of the Committee for Human Rights in the Philippines; and Penny Hess, Chairwoman of the African Peoples's Solidarity Committee.

Uhuru! I'd like to express my deepest appreciation to all of you tonight for coming out, as well as to the African People's Solidarity Committee that made this important event happen, and a really special thank you and appreciation to the presenters who have preceded me.

I thank you, Compañera Quetza, for the most important work that you do, this lonesome work over in San Jose[2] and other places in defense of the rights of Indigenous peoples here and particularly forwarding the Mexican National Liberation Movement.

I thank Kawal, whom I've known for a very long time, who is struggling to forward the movement for the liberation of the people of the Philippines, and I thank Comrade Shenoda. I think it's important that Comrade Penny Hess, who provides tremendous leadership for the African People's Solidarity Committee, is here today. These comrades in the African People's Solidarity Committee have struggled mightily to try to win white people, North Americans, to come and intervene in a progressive and positive way in the future of the world.

Something I would like to say to the white people, the North Americans[3] who are here, is that the folks who spoke about the struggles of Arab and Palestinian people, who spoke about the struggles of the Filipino people and explained what is happening to the Mexican people, are making special presentations geared just for you. They are trying to educate you about the conditions they face and the struggles their people must wage. These comrades are part of struggles for national liberation. When they have discussions with people from their own community, from our own community, our objective is to lead our people into motion, to mobilize them to destroy the relationship that we have to imperialism.

My primary responsibility is to organize African people all around the world to reclaim our history, to reclaim our resources, to reclaim our freedom. That's my responsibility. That's my obligation. That's the obligation of these other comrades towards their own people. So, I think it's really important that folks from the white community who have the opportunity to hear this, begin to take a stand on the right side of history.

We are living in a very critical time in history. Although a lot of people don't recognize it, there is a profound crisis happening right now. Imperialism is in its death throes. It is in a crisis that resembles the death throes of a dying beast. It is this crisis that makes it necessary for us to say that the occupation started in 1492. This crisis today is a reflection of something that started a long time ago.

It's important for us to have this discussion beginning with the premise that the occupation began in 1492. This is an attempt to begin to seize the leadership from those who would treat the crisis of imperialism as something that is only important to white people in America.

White peace movement covers over crisis of imperialism

This crisis of imperialism is reflected in the war in Iraq, the U.S. attack on the people of Iraq, the attack on the people of Afghanistan and the theft of their resources—the naked white colonial domination of those folk. These attacks represent a crisis of imperialism that George Bush and the rest of them are attempting to solve.

But the peace movement, the anti-war movement, doesn't recognize this. In fact, it moves in such a fashion as to cover up the crisis. It attempts to *solve* the problems of imperialism, instead of deepening the crisis of imperialism. You have a peace movement that tells me that a march for peace is somehow patriotic!

It's a peace movement that keeps asking the question, "Where are all the black people?" The reality is that most of us have been at war with imperialism for hundreds of years and the question has always been, "Where are all the white people who are going to stand in solidarity with us and join the right side of history?" Where have you been?

People get born into a situation that gives them the impression that it's always been like this. So, when you see the Filipino or the proud African, Mexican or Indigenous people, when you see the Arab and other folk living in circumstances of oppression imposed on us by colonial domination, you just take it for granted. You think this is the way it's supposed to be. Africans are supposed to be killed in the streets of Oakland and throughout this country by the police.

When you read that since 1998, some five million African people have died in Congo, it doesn't cause a stir at all. That's the way it's supposed to be! I have seen Mexican people in Northern San Diego County with their plastic Safeway bags climbing up into the mountains where they live in the caves. Then they come down at dawn to pick the fruit and the vegetables for white people, and that's just the way it's supposed to be! Nobody gets upset about it. The only time you see white people upset is when there is an assumption that somebody is coming to take the resources back that belong to them. Then we see them upset. Then we talk about peace movements and the rest of that.

So, the attacks on September 11th, 2001 made somebody upset. It's that way because for the longest period of time it has not been necessary for white people, for North Americans, to worry about what America was doing to oppressed peoples around the world. Don't give it a second thought. Just go to the mall and do all those things that make you feel good. White people never had to pay a price.

But now, it's very clear that it's possible for the oppressed to bring the war right here—to put the war down in Manhattan or Oakland or anywhere. Then it becomes necessary for white people to start to question what's going on, to start to ask about what the U.S. is doing to oppressed peoples all over the world. That's the juncture at which white people begin to want to have a "peace movement."

The reality is that we don't need peace. We need exactly what Che Guevara called for in the 1960s: "Two, three, many Viet Nams!" Instead of just a simple demand for peace, white people have the responsibility to stand on the side of the oppressed peoples of the world who are fighting to change their relationship to imperialism. That's the question that's before us.

When we look at what's happening in Iraq, we have the responsibility to stand on the side of the Iraqi people, and to do it even without the caveat that usually accompanies some feeble expression of solidarity. You know what I am talking about: "I'm against Saddam Hussein." Hell, no! What you need to do is apologize to the world for being for George Bush, for being for William Clinton, for being for American imperialism. If Saddam Hussein lived to be a thousand years old, he could not commit the offenses against humanity and against Iraq that U.S. imperialism has committed! That is the reality that confronts us.

The U.S. is enacting the USA PATRIOT Act and now all the North Americans are concerned about how, "We ain't got no rights." Oh, please. Please! Suddenly everybody wants to get a lawyer. You want to know about rights? Ask the compañeros in the barrios about rights. Ask the Africans who live in our communities about rights. Ask them about when the police come to the street corners and say, "Give up the corner." Ask them what they'd better do if they want to survive it.

There has never been freedom of speech, freedom of assembly or freedom of expression for Africans in America, nor for the other oppressed peoples who are here. People live in concentration camps—even in these days right here in this country—that are called reservations. It's not like we don't know whose land this is. It's not like it's a mystery that there was somebody here when Columbus and the rest of them arrived.

It's important for us, I believe, in talking about these contradictions to look around the world. We're talking about American imperialism in the Philippines, in Colombia, in Iraq. Look around the world. You see a terrible kind of situation, and we're seeing things inside this country like the PATRIOT Act.

Capitalism born from the theft of resources of oppressed peoples

It's important for us, I believe, to recognize that in the face of all of these contradictions that we see in the world, there is one profound contradiction around which all of the others revolve. It's important to recognize that the fundamental contradiction is that capitalism itself has its origin in the conquest of the lands, the liberties and the right to self-determination of the masses of oppressed peoples of the world.

This is the foundation of the whole capitalist system. This is the foundation. You talk about white women being oppressed? Well, hell, white women are oppressed on the *pedestal* of the oppression of the Africans, the Indigenous, the Arabs, Filipinos and others.

This conquest and oppression of the majority of the peoples on the planet is the context that gave rise to the capitalist system that white communists say that they hate so much. Karl Marx said that wage slavery in Europe—even the *concept* of wage slavery—has its origin in the real enslavement of African people. He said that wage slavery—meaning white peoples' jobs— requires as a pedestal, slavery pure and simple in the New World.

He should have been able to say after that, if you want to get rid of wage slavery or capitalism, then what do you do? You get rid of the pedestal, which is slavery pure and simple. But he didn't say that. He came up with a non sequitur. Wage slavery, he said, in Europe, requires as a pedestal slavery pure and simple in the New World. Therefore the way to end wage slavery, or capitalism, he wrongly concluded, is for the workers to seize power. The "wage slaves" then seize power, right? And that happens upon the damn pedestal pure and simple that sits on the backs of Africans, Indigenous and other oppressed peoples.

This means very simply that a white workers' movement, a white women's movement, a white homosexual movement or any white movement is a movement for white rights sitting on the pedestal of the rest of us. That is why you get entirely different responses from oppressed peoples around the world than you get from white people anywhere in the world when you are discussing the crisis of imperialism.

The question before us is not whether we are for peace, but whether we are for freedom, whether we are for national liberation, whether we are for the right of the peoples of this earth to live a decent life. There shall never be peace as long as there are oppressed peoples on this earth. There shall never be peace! Nor should there be peace. Nor will I allow there to be peace as long as I am alive! Nor will I stand by without challenging other people to struggle against peace.

Our responsibility is to build a revolutionary response to this tyranny that has been imposed on us. Where does it come from? We talk about Marx's term "slavery pure and simple." He also coined another term, which he characterized as the "primitive accumulation of capital." He said we must envision an accumulation of capital that was not a consequence of capitalist production but was the *starting point* of capitalist production. He called this "primitive accumulation of capital."

What was this primitive accumulation of capital? It was the raping of Africa. The attack on this land right here, now called the Americas, became a part of the primitive accumulation of capital. It was the attack against China in 1841 and 1842 by the British—the so-called "Opium War" that forced China to be a nation of junkies. It was the war against the people of Viet Nam, which France held for a hundred years as an opium den. France brought more wealth out of Viet Nam as a result of imposing drugs on the Vietnamese people than they got out of any other French colony. It was rape and pillage around the world. It was the attack on the Philippines that left millions dead and stole their land. It was the theft of our rights, the theft of our resources, the impoverishing of the rest of us.

This is where the wealth and power of the U.S. and the whole white world came from. This gave rise to capitalism. The slave trade was a prerequisite for the rise of capitalism. It was the trade in African people that created, for the first time in history, a world economy that was a precondition for the rise of capitalism. Capitalism arose in the world as a world system. It arose in the world as white power. White power was born on this earth as capitalism.

Human life originated in Africa

I want to say a few words about Africa. Africa is the most slandered continent, and its people are the most slandered people in the world. First of all, I am not an immigrant to America. I am a captive. I did not come here looking for a better way of life. I *lost* a better way of life as a consequence of having been brought here. By now, most people recognize that Africa is the origin of human life. Beyond that, it is the origin of human civilization itself.

Some people have speculated that the Sphinx in Egypt may be 15,000 years old. You go to any museum in any city of any consequence in Europe or North America and you find the stolen resources from Africa and stolen treasures from other peoples around the world. You find locked up bones and other kinds of marvels. Every other week on the History Channel there's another different explanation for how the pyramids might have gotten built, something they still can't replicate.

In Africa, you have a whole continent that was transformed into a place where human beings were bred to be put into colonial slavery and scattered around the world. The vicious attack on Africa is something that will never be fully exposed until we win our freedom. But the entire ecosystem of the Atlantic Ocean was changed by the attack on Africa.

Insurance companies would insure the ships' loot—enslaved human beings. As Africans got sick, ship captains would just throw them overboard. African lives were meaningless to them except as property that was heavily insured. The sharks learned that if they wanted to eat well, they just followed the ships from Africa across the Atlantic. Whole schools of sharks literally followed ships that brought Africans to this country. The brutality is indescribable.

I have read that there was a time when Portuguese ships alone nearly encircled Africa just for the purpose of bringing out human beings. By 1500, some seven hundred tons of gold had been brought out of Africa by Portugal alone. Some people have suggested two hundred million African people in all were captured from Africa and brought into slavery.

I don't want to hear another word by Bush or anyone else about Gadaffi[4] or Saddam Hussein or anybody else being "evil," because the enemy of the peoples of the world is imperialism. U.S. imperialism is the worst imperialism that has ever existed on the face of the earth, and in the history of humankind.

Imperialism not just bad policy!

Our Africa is under assault. So, Africa, where is the peace movement? How can it be that in five years, since 1998, five million Africans died from U.S.-backed wars in Congo, and there's not a single murmur that's coming from anybody? Or if it comes, it comes in the form of condemnation of Africa?

How is it that in just a matter of months, a million Africans can die in Rwanda directly as a consequence of U.S. policies? In Rwanda and Congo people are dying because the U.S. is fighting France for domination of this territory so they can steal resources that were previously considered a part of the French sphere of interest.

Imperialism is not just a matter of bad policy. You can

condemn George Bush for the rest of your life, but the next president is going to be just the same. Bush wasn't responsible for Viet Nam. He wasn't responsible for the Philippines. It was Thomas Jefferson who raped a thirteen-year-old enslaved African child named Sally Hemmings and made babies by her. It was George Washington who owned slaves. It was Kit Carson who murdered the so-called "Indians." It was all the heroes of America who committed all the crimes against the people.

We're not talking about George Bush. We're talking about imperialism. Every policy that comes from imperialism will be a bad policy. Imperialism doesn't have the capacity to have good policy. Our responsibility is not to fix imperialism, but to destroy imperialism!

There's a whole bunch of money that's being made teaching people to "unlearn their racism." I am not interested in racism, and frankly I don't care if you like Ray Charles or not. In the final analysis, we're not struggling against the ideas in your head. The struggle is for power over our lives. You can still dislike Omali Yeshitela and African people. I don't give a damn. But what's important is whether or not you believe in freedom and national liberation. That's the question that confronts us. That's the question that confronts all oppressed people.

Racism is the ideological foundation of imperialism. This concept of the supremacy of white people was born out of slavery. Racism was the philosophy that was created to justify the bestiality of the enslavement of Africans. The fact of the matter is that Europe and white people themselves were born out of the slave trade and out of the attack on the rest of the world.

There was no such thing as "Europe" or "Europeans" or even "white" people. There was no concept of a collective body of folk who were recognized as Europeans throughout the world until the seventeenth century. Europe was just a group of territories of warring tribes. It was Europe's attack on Africa, on the

Indigenous population of the Americas, on the Asian and Arab peoples, that created a common collective consciousness. It was a consciousness of genocide and a culture of violence that united all of these folk in stealing the resources of the rest of the world. This is what gave rise to the idea of the "white" person as an entity, as a social concept.

We're not fighting against an idea. We do believe that it's important for Europeans to look at yourselves and make a decision about whether or not you're going to join the rest of humanity. But our responsibility is to organize and mobilize to win our freedom whether you're with us or not.

Don't resolve the crisis—deepen the crisis!

Our objective here is to move beyond simply talking about this thing and to get busy. Go ahead and organize. Do not give them space to try to resolve the crisis that they are confronted with. *Deepen* the crisis for them by really identifying what the contradictions are. The profound thing that has been impacting on and pushing imperialism into crisis since the second imperialist war[5] is that the masses of colonized people around the world have been struggling for independence. From India to China, from Viet Nam to Nicaragua, from Africans inside the U.S. to the Iraqis and Palestinians today, oppressed peoples everywhere are demanding their national liberation, self-determination and sovereignty.

This is the profound crisis that Bush is trying to resolve. Neocolonialism—white power in black and brown face—has failed. Now they're trying to reimpose direct white colonial rule on the rest of the world. It ain't going to work. It didn't work then; it ain't going to work now.

To us it doesn't really matter whether or not North American or white people here or in Europe get on board and stand in solidarity with us. We are making the struggle with or without you.

It may only matter for your benefit, because, in my view, it is white people who need to end your voluntary isolation from the rest of the peoples on earth. Unless you do that you will never be secure.

How in the hell do you think you're supposed to be able to sleep comfortably at night, when all the resources that belong to all the peoples on the planet are in your community, and sometimes in your house? This is the reason that so many white people are nervous and anxious. There isn't enough Valium to solve that problem.

The thing is that you can end this isolation and join the rest of us. Turn loose your whiteness and join the rest of us. Recognize your relationship to the rest of humanity and turn against white power and imperialism. That's what you are being called on to do here tonight.

Either way, Africa's going to be free. Either way, Africans are going to be free! There used to be a saying, "The more sweat in peace, the less bloodshed in war." That's why we do this sweating right now.

In our Party we believe that we are now in a time that we refer to as the "Final Offensive on Imperialism." Imperialism has nothing dynamic about it anymore. It's no longer a powerful imperialism that can easily control the world with one phone call. It's an imperialism fighting for its very life, fighting to hold on to what it's got. Our responsibility is to make that impossible.

White people have a choice: to stand on the side of this dying imperialism or to stand with the oppressed peoples of the earth in our struggle to liberate ourselves and bring true peace and justice to the world. We must get organized. Thank you so much.

Uhuru!

---

1   The African People's Socialist Party formed the African People's Solidarity Committee in 1976. Made up predominantly of white people who organize

in the white communities, APSC works under the direct leadership of the Party's strategy to build white solidarity for the struggle for the liberation of Africa and African people.

2 The Barrio Defense Committee, led by Quetzaoceloacuia, is based in San Jose, California.

3 The African People's Socialist Party uses the term "North American" for white people as a way of taking the question of identity away from the racial connotations inherent in the term "white." The Party makes it clear that the struggle is not against "white racism," ideas in white people's heads, but one for African people to win national liberation and state power. Therefore, the stand that white people must take is in solidarity with the struggle of African and all colonized peoples for national liberation from imperialist state power.

4 Muammar Gadaffi is the leader of Libya.

5 Also known as the Second World War.

U.S. guilty of crimes against Africans

Now we need state power to enforce the verdict

On November 15, 2003, the twelfth session of the International Tribunal on Reparations for African people was convened in Philadelphia, Pennsylvania. The two-day hearing reaffirmed the guilty verdict of the first session of the Reparations Tribunal, which was held in Brooklyn, New York in 1982, initiated by the African People's Socialist Party.

That tribunal convicted the United States government of genocide and numerous human rights violations against African people, and produced insurmountable evidence that the U.S. owes $4.1 trillion in reparations to African people in the U.S. for labor alone. Ensuing sessions of the tribunal continue to substantiate the guilty verdict with hearings that gather testimony from African people on the many faces of African colonial oppression and exploitation in the U.S.

During the twelfth session in 2003, more than three hundred people gathered in Philadelphia to witness the weekend proceedings, which featured testimony from scores of African people before an international panel of judges. Chairman Omali served as the People's Advocate for the hearings, and the tribunal was convened by Chimurenga Waller, president of the International People's Democratic Uhuru Movement.

Among those who testified were Charles Barron, New York City Councilman; Pam Africa of Friends and Family of Mumia Abu Jamal; Lawrence Hamm, People's Organization for Progress and many other victims of police, prison and educational abuse.

The panel of judges included Dorothy Lewis, National Coalition for Blacks for Reparations; Mohammad Chehab, Arab activist; Judy de los Santos, Unión del Barrio; Patricia Lumumba, African Socialist International,

240

London; Penny Hess, African People's Solidarity Committee.

The following electrifying presentation by Chairman Omali was given at a special session called "Reparations now! A just demand," held on the evening of the first day of the 2003 tribunal. Other testimony during the special session was given by African scholar Dr. Leonard Jeffries of City College of New York.

I would like to express my profound appreciation for all of you, and for the incredible presenters who preceded me. I'm truly humbled just to be in the company of these people whose testimonies and presentations clearly reveal their commitment to the struggle to build a better world. I am also humbled by your presence. I think there is something significant about the fact that you have come from many different places, including this city, to participate in the emancipation of our folk.

All of the testimony we've heard today clearly indicates that there is no justice for African people to be found in the court system in this country, and that this court system was born from our enslavement. It is, in fact, a system that was created for the purpose of maintaining and protecting the status quo.

The reality is that if you have a society that is born out of slavery and the destruction of the Indigenous population, you can expect that the laws, the courts, and every other social, legal and political institution born of that, will justify slavery and genocide. They cannot represent anything other than that.

I think that this court that we are holding today is a part of the process to win back our freedom. The testimonies we've heard up to now clearly indicate that more than anything else, we need our freedom. In fact I think that if we sum up everything we've heard today, we would understand that the biggest problem we've got is that somebody stole, somebody expropriated, not just our wealth, not just our gold and that kind of thing. Somebody expropriated our right to be a self-determining, self-governing, self-respecting people. That is the fundamental issue that we're confronted with!

In any society on earth that is split between Haves and Have-nots, you will see what we call the State. This is particularly true if the Haves represent the folk who have everything as a consequence of expropriating the land and resources of those who have nothing.

The State is an instrument of oppression. That's what it's there for. It's there to maintain the status quo. The State is that thing in every city in this country that stands between hungry people and the grocery stores that have food overflowing from the shelf. The State is that which stands between people that are sick—sometimes with curable diseases—and hospitals with empty beds. It doesn't matter how sick you are, if you don't have money, you can't get in one of those empty beds. The thing that stands between us being able to do that, in instances where it's possible, is the State.

The State is the police department. The State is the court system. The State is the jails, the prisons. The State is the army, the navy—all of those things are instruments of state power.

The State legalizes itself. It doesn't ask permission. It legalizes itself. The State can write down that slavery is legal. If you are a slave and you try to escape slavery, you have broken the law. In fact, Nat Turner[1] was brought before a court and tried. They murdered him as a consequence of that trial. It was a legal trial.

Our court is real but we must have state power

In 1982, we convened the first tribunal on reparations where Dr. Leonard Jeffries gave his magnificent presentation that still thrills everybody today. He chronicled all of the horrors, all of the terror and hardships imposed upon African people. That testimony was followed by witnesses from all across this country, Africans who came to testify about the things that had happened to them. That tribunal was our trial. That trial was based on international law.

It wasn't like what they do in this country today, where they create a constitution, which says that such things as trying a person twice for the same crime is prohibited. They say that out of one side of their mouth, and out of the other side they say, "We are going to put you in jail forever, not for what you did this time, but what you did two times ago—three strikes and you're out." That is nothing but double jeopardy. We don't do that kind of thing in this tribunal, which is based on international law. We brought a panel of judges to hear this evidence based on international law.

In 1982 the panel of judges made the determination that this government was guilty of, among other things, genocide against African people, based on the United Nations Genocide Convention[2] that was put together in 1948, at a time when Africans all over the world were still living under colonial domination. At the time, the majority of people on earth were living under colonial domination. It was a Genocide Convention that had no intention of representing African people.

The white man who wrote the Genocide Convention was a Polish Jew who went all over the world and throughout this country campaigning for the adoption of the convention. This man coined the term for genocide, but he said that genocide didn't have anything to do with black people in America!

So we held a court, *our* court. African people could come to this court without fear, unlike the courtrooms in this country where you're terrified every day. People walked in freely.

We gave the United States government and its representatives the right to freely stand up and defend themselves before the people. But none of them have the courage to stand before you.

Our court came up with a verdict. It said among other things, that all of these courageous African men and women, who in the face of the terrible things that this government has done to African people in this country, risked their lives, their happiness and their freedom and stood up for black people, and are now locked up in prison are prisoners of war. They are political prisoners.

Our court said they should be freed. This tribunal said, among other things, that the United States government owed African people a minimum of $4.1 trillion just for labor alone. That was up to 1982.

The question that was before us then, as it is before us now, is what is the difference between our court and their court? Certainly justice is one aspect of what is different about it. But the other thing that makes it more significant is that if they want you in their court, they'll send an army out to get you. They won't just come here to North Philadelphia to get you, they'll come at you in Baghdad; they'll come at you in Panama. They'll get you if they can, wherever you are.

We subpoenaed George W. Bush, and we subpoenaed his daddy. We subpoenaed Cheney and Reagan, along with a lot of former and sometimes current representatives of the United States government, both on the national and the local level. None of them showed up here. What then is the difference between our court and their court? The difference is that they have *all the instruments of state power.* They have the power to enforce a verdict.

We have just begun, Brothers and Sisters. We've created this court, but we don't have the other instruments of state power. What did I say they are? I said they are the police department, the jails, the army, the navy, the air force. That's what's missing. When we have this discussion, we are not playing. Our law and our justice are real law and real justice. The only thing missing at this juncture is the *power to carry out the verdict!* That tells us what we have to do.

It's not a matter of being able to write good appeals to the U.S. Supreme Court or some other court. It's about being able to carry out the verdict that you make in your court. Malcolm X said it better than anybody else: "You don't take your case to the criminal; you take your criminal to court." And that's what we have to do here, that's what we're about.

We have to discuss this also in the context of history even as it unfolds before us today. Historians find themselves—Dr. Jeffries would tell you—with the problem of always having to work backwards. You weren't there then, so you take the evidence that you have now and work your way backwards. That's how we unfold the history, and begin to see some things that are happening right now.

We see that George W. Bush and the United States military invaded Afghanistan, and right now they are occupying Iraq. They have gone back into the Philippines and Colombia. They have attempted to overthrow the government of Venezuela. Everywhere you look you see this vicious force in motion. There's a connection to what they are doing now in places like Iraq, Afghanistan, Colombia, the Philippines and Venezuela, to their attempt to strangle Cuba. I'm telling you, all of that is tied to the history of African people and has brought us to this court today.

Africa's wealth and power were stolen

Dr. Jeffries told us we need a systems analysis. The fact of the matter is we need to understand something about this system and where it came from. Did God, in all her wisdom, just bestow all this wealth and all these resources on white people, and all this misery and poverty on the rest of us? Is that how we explain it? As a child this is one of the things that I tussled with day in and day out, because everywhere I looked, black people were poor and white people had everything. How did it happen that way?

When I was a youngster they were more frank in their discussion. They'd say, "You're not as civilized as white people." They'd say, "White people are civilized and have been civilized for a long time. That's why white people have everything and you've got nothing." They would also say things like, "You've got nothing because white people are thrifty, and you are not. You just don't save your money. You act crazy on Friday nights and waste all your money." This was the explanation that all of us labored under, with our heads down, humiliated, having no other understanding, no other evidence of what really happened.

But today we understand more clearly what the hell did happen. The reality of the matter is that in the beginning of this process, it was Africa that had the wealth. It's important to say that even as white people in Europe were learning to master fire, Africa had created magnificent civilizations. I'm not just telling you this because I'm some kind of black nationalist who wants to make you feel good, even though you have the right to feel good knowing who you are and where you came from. It's important to discuss this because when somebody robs you of your history, they rob you of your memory of yourself, and part of the way that you know what you can do is from knowing what you have done. It's important for them to take that memory away from you.

Brothers and Sisters, in a four year period between 1347 and 1351, half the white people on earth died. Some people say it was only one third, but even so, a third was a lot of people for a particular society to lose in four years. The white people died of bubonic plague, pneumonic plague, and other diseases. For the next fifty years there was an ongoing decline in the population of Europe. It is totally impossible for any society to have a meaningful economy if half the people die in four years. The plague wasn't prejudiced. It killed artisans, cooks, bakers, every damn body. In fact, the disease had such an impact on Europe that people wrote that literally you could smell Europe from a continent away. People were simply just dying.

There is a nursery rhyme that children sometimes sing today, "Ring around the roses, pocket full of posies." This rhyme originated during the plague in Europe. The children go 'round and 'round, and then they all fall "dead." They talk about "roses," because on white skin, the disease looked like a rose with a ring around it. Pocket full of posies referred to the fact that white people literally carried pockets full of flowers to cover the stench of their own bodies rotting from the plague, as well as the dead around them. Many people wouldn't even bury the dead, they'd just run away. Wives would leave husbands and their children because they didn't understand what was causing the death. Isn't that something?

Now this is the same Europe that we are told one day just woke up and had some kind of intellectual itch sending them exploring around the world, just to find out what was on the other side. Sometimes they say they were looking for spices. That's a hell of a statement. I mean, I understand it when your neighbor knocks on the door and asks if they can borrow a cup of nutmeg. But to send out ships all across the ocean to get some nutmeg, you must be in bad, bad shape!

Europe was starving and impoverished. It sent those ships around the world to rescue itself. This was no civilizing mission. If the mission was to civilize, it was to civilize Europe, which rescued itself with the rape and pillage of the rest of the world.

When Columbus left Europe, there was an estimated seventy million white people on earth. The estimate of the number of Indigenous, so-called "Indians" living throughout the Americas ranged between fifty million and three hundred million. When Columbus landed in what is now called Haiti, there were something like nine million Indigenous people there.

Four years later there were only two million left. Now you won't find an Indigenous person in Haiti. By 1888, ninety-eight percent of the Native people of this hemisphere had been killed. This was a part of the process of the accumulation of capital that gave rise to European capitalism.

I haven't even talked about what they did to Africa. I mean the attack on Africa is so profound. They changed the entire ecosystem of the ocean with the so-called "slave trade." I've read that sometimes there were so many ships, in particular Portuguese ships, surrounding Africa to capture Africans to bring us into what they call slavery. It was like when you are coming into the Philadelphia airport and the airplanes can't land right away, and they have to put them in a holding pattern.

There were so many ships encircling Africa coming to get black people, to work black people, that they had traffic problems coming in. They were bringing so many Africans out of Africa, that the sharks learned to follow the ships with Africans all across the Atlantic from Africa to the New World because they knew that they were going to eat well.

It wasn't simply because Africans resisted and jumped off the ship, or killed their babies rather than have them go into slavery, or sometimes died on the trip! Africans did that, but there was more. There was the insurance industry that grew up out of the slave trade. Lloyds of London,[3] for example, was born directly from slavery. The ship owners would insure their cargo, which was stolen black bodies—us, right? They would put more Africans on the ship than the ship could hold. If an African got a headache or looked like he was sick, they'd just throw him overboard, knowing that they would be reimbursed by the insurance company for the life of an African person.

It was a vicious system. Even if everything they said about Saddam Hussein was true, he'd have to live to be older than the mythological Methuselah to do anything comparable to what America and U.S. imperialism and capitalism have done to us.

This is the way the wealth was accumulated. In this country, they put the so-called "Indians" in mines, and worked them from "can't see" in the morning to "can't see" at night, sometimes in the water up to their chest, bringing out gold and silver that was taken to Europe.

And you talk about the resources stolen from Africa! As an example of what was done to Africa, Portugal alone by 1500, took seven hundred tons of gold out of Africa. This is part of the rape of Mother Africa, and of her children, of Africans ourselves, who were taken and scattered throughout the world. This is the origin of European and white power.

Democracy and wealth in Europe at expense of African people

Somebody was talking about the royal trading companies and slavers. A lot of people like to talk to us about the democratic revolutions in Europe. They like to attribute these democratic revolutions to European philosophers like Descartes and Rousseau. They say these guys just came up with these ideas about democracy and inflamed the imaginations of Europeans who were then inspired to overthrow the nobility. No such thing.

The reality is that Europe was poor. When Columbus left Europe he had finally gotten money from Isabella of Spain. She was broke and, according to the story that I read, she had to go out and pawn her jewelry to get enough cash for Chris for his trip.

Europe was broke. But when Europe's nobility started sending thugs and pirates, like Francis Drake, and the rest of them out as looters around the world, then guess what? The thugs and pirates started piling up all the money. In fact, they amassed more money than the nobility.

Have you heard of the struggle for free trade? Well the demand for free trade came out of Europe when these up-and-coming thuggish pirate entrepreneurs said "Hell, the King and the Monarchy have a monopoly on selling Africans. We want a piece of the action. We demand free trade!" That's exactly where free trade came from. White people demanded their rights, their freedom to sell black people. They would sell your mama too, you understand? The reality is that all this wealth came from slavery.

Then there was wealth that came from China too. The British fought a war against China in 1841–42, where the British demanded that the whole nation of China become a nation of junkies. It is called the Opium War. The French held Viet Nam for more than a hundred years as a drug colony. Most of the colonial resources that the French brought out of Viet Nam were in the form of drug money. This is the origin of the wealth that white people got.

In the 1930s there was a bank robber whose name was Willie Sutton. Somebody once asked him, "Willie, why did you rob banks?" He answered, "Because that's where the money is." It's a simple question.

If you want to know why the hell the Europeans left Europe and came to the Americas, why they went to Africa, why they went to Asia, it's because that's where the loot was. They didn't have it in Europe, so they went to all of these other places, raping and pillaging. As a consequence of this wealth that they were stealing, you saw Europe transformed with wealth on the one hand, and you saw Africa, Asia and the Americas become impoverished and oppressed on the other.

Once we had wealth. We had democracy. Europeans had never, never, never known democracy. I say that despite the myth of Greek democracy that they throw in your face. The reality is that in ancient Greece, only twenty percent of the population was free. Eighty percent of the people were enslaved. So they didn't know anything about freedom!

They talk about how "a man's home is his castle." Not if you came from Europe! When the Europeans left Europe, they lived in feudalism. And the only ones who had castles were the nobility. The ordinary white person didn't own anything, except maybe the plow that he used to sharecrop. In the system that they called feudalism only a small part of what he grew went to his family, and the rest went to the nobility. This is the real world. This is the history that you need to know in order to be armed to do what you have to do in order to be free.

All of this wealth was flowing into Europe, and it was transforming Europe. This provided the material basis for the democratic revolutions and the industrial revolution. The democratic revolutions were brought about by white people who, as I said, became the new capitalist class, a new social force. The capitalist class rose up as a consequence of slavery, as a consequence of stealing the resources, the silver and the gold from the rest of the world. They then became more powerful than the nobility and built movements to overthrow them. The capitalists created what they called a democratic system. Ain't that something? Bourgeois democracy. And so now, every white man had the right to sell his labor any way he wanted. A whole new system was born.

How many people here are familiar with *A Christmas Carol* by Charles Dickens? This story was born out of the capitalist hardships imposed on white people in Europe. A movement emerged among white intellectuals to try to humanize capitalism. In *A Christmas Carol* you've got Scrooge, who's symbolic of the capitalists. "Bah humbug." Right? He didn't believe in Christmas. He was so bad he was even mean to Tiny Tim. Scrooge didn't have pity on anybody, so he became symbolic of the capitalists. During this period, children were working in the factories, and sometimes they were being maimed. So Europeans wanted to humanize capitalism.

They thought they were catching hell. The problem that the Marxists and white people in general have always had is that they can see the problems and difficulties of the white worker at what they call the point of production. They can see the worker who is working in the auto plants and other places and that they are not getting paid what they think is the value of their labor power.

But what the Marxists and others did not see is the African in Guyana and Guinea who dug the bauxite out of the mines that went into making the aluminum before it even got to Detroit, you understand? What they cannot see are the Africans who are dying in Congo for this precious metal called coltan that goes into making every computer and every cell phone that's being used by people around this country. They like to simplify, and they want you to believe that all of us are in the same boat. Well hell, we were in the same boat during slavery, except they rode up there and had the whip, and I rode down there in the holds of the ship. And that's effectively the same kind of relationship that we've still got today.

Trade in African people precondition for rise of capitalism

So this is what brought about the emergence of this whole vicious social system. Capitalism was born as a world system. It didn't just start in the nineteenth century. The first capitalism occurred in the fourteenth century in Venice. It came out of the crusades, when the white folks were making this holy war, as they call it. They said they were looking for the Holy Grail as they attacked the Middle East. They never found the Holy Grail, but they found a lot of loot, right? As a consequence of these looting expeditions they were able to establish capitalism right there in Venice. It couldn't be sustained because the crusades couldn't sustain the capitalist system.

Later on, the most fundamental thing that gave rise to capitalism was the trade in African people. It was the trade in African people that was responsible for the creation of colonies throughout the Americas. It was the establishment of colonies throughout the Americas that created for the first time in history, a world economy. People had traded with each other before, long before the white people were involved, but there was never an economy hooked up, a single economy, before the trade in African people. This was a precondition for the rise of capitalism in the world. Capitalism arose as white power in the world. This led to the emiseration of the rest of us, and wealth and power and democracy at our expense for the white world.

Are reparations due? Are reparations a just demand? Sure enough!

I want to say that this is not our land. I say, this ain't our land. I know your name might be on the mailbox, but the reality is that this land is the land of the Indigenous people that they call Indians. Many of the Indigenous people, those who remain, are still stuck on concentration camps that they call "reservations." They have a life span in their forties in this country.

Our land, now, as it has always been, is Africa. Some people have struggles with that. They say, "I ain't no African. I've been here a long time." Again, Malcolm said it better than anybody. He said, "Chickens are sometimes born in ovens, but that don't make them biscuits," right? There is a saying at home in Africa, that you can go to the forest and you can cut down a tree. You can strip the branches from the tree and drag it to the river. You can throw the tree into the river, and leave it there for a thousand years, and it will never turn into a crocodile. If we got on the ship in Africa as Africans, then when we got off the ship in Jamestown, Virginia, we were still Africans. We were Africans then; we are Africans now.

I think it's fundamentally important for us to come to terms with that. If you don't understand that, we shall always be victimized. Marcus Garvey[4] understood it. He said we had to organize ourselves everywhere. There are at least a billion of us worldwide. But if we allow them to divide us into Haitians and Jamaicans and African-Americans—that hyphen is a chain—into Kenyans and Nigerians, into Kikuyu and Ashanti, into Baptists, into all of those other kinds of things, we shall always be victimized. We are African people!

Our oppression, our struggle is the same no matter where we are on earth. We're fighting the same struggle no matter where we are. This is the U.S. Front of the African Liberation Movement. Key to our liberation, our program here is the question of reparations. When we say reparations, we mean we want the whole damn deal. You understand what I'm saying? I'm not on some symbolic quest. I'm talking about the stuff that's necessary for human beings to live. That's what it's about.

African people have been separated from our resources whether we are in Africa or whether we are here in America. The law functions as an instrument to maintain our separation from that which belongs to us—either as a consequence of what we have created or what our ancestors have created. This separation took them to early graves.

So we say, "Yes, reparations are ours." Young Brothers, young Sisters, you have to understand that this system won't work unless we cooperate on some level. Look at what's happening with Massaoui,[5] the brother they say is connected with Al Qaeda or something like that. He won't cooperate at all. He has no respect for the institution. You cannot respect the oppressor; you cannot respect your oppressor at all.

At that juncture where African people understand that we are due reparations, we can throw off the illusion that's been imposed on us that the American system has suffered because somehow black people have lived off the welfare of white people. Then our people can understand that it is not we who have imposed a welfare burden on America. It is America that has lived off of the welfare of Africans for at least four hundred years.

When Africans begin to understand this, you can see that young brother or young sister standing before that judge, being told that he or she is charged with stealing. You can see this young African looking this thug in the eye and saying, "I know who the real thief is. I reject this concept of me being a thief, because everything you've got—the suburb that you live in, the tree-lined community that you go to in safety every day—has come as a consequence of what you have stolen from my people, from me. You have inherited the wealth that was created by my mama, my grandma, and I'm going to take it back no matter what you do." That's where the power is.

The only way we get out of this is through struggle. You can't write a good enough brief for white folks to turn us loose. The way that works is, you write a brief and then you go to court and say, "Judge, look out the window." When the judge looks out the window he sees a well-armed body of forces standing there. The judge will say, "Well damn, I think this person is innocent, innocent, innocent."

We are in a struggle to build ourselves an instrument of state power. That's what this tribunal is about.

I want to close with this. We are indeed in the struggle. There are so many injustices that have been done to our people and to so many peoples around the world. But I would ask you to remember this: a particular system was born out of our oppression that has established the context of our struggle today.

Our oppression is older than capitalism, but capitalism is the dominant system today that controls our world, that's responsible for our condition everywhere on earth.

Uhuru!

1 Nat Turner was an African preacher who led a powerful uprising of enslaved Africans in Virginia against the white slave owners in 1831. Turner and his forces killed fifty-five white people on several plantations before the rebellion was defeated by armed white citizens and state militia forces. Turner escaped and hid out for six weeks before he was jailed, tried and hanged along with sixteen other African people. The Nat Turner rebellions struck terror in the hearts of Southern plantation owners.

2 The United Nations Convention on the Prevention and Punishment of the Crime of Genocide, adopted by the United Nations General Assembly on December 9,1948.

3 The British company Lloyds of London, one of the biggest specialty insurance companies in the world, accumulated its wealth by insuring slave ships in the seventeenth century.

4 Marcus Garvey, 1887–1940, organized the Universal Negro Improvement Association (UNIA) and its coordinating body, the African Communities League. He published the newspaper the *Negro World* in several languages and toured the Americas speaking to large audiences of African people about his vision of African independence. The UNIA had millions of members in eleven hundred branches in more than forty countries. Garvey launched ambitious business ventures, notably the Black Star Line shipping company.

5 Zacarias Massaoui is being held by the U.S. for supposed connections to Al Qaeda and the September 11th hijackers.

Jesus was a revolutionary
So why is your preacher such an Uncle Tom?

This presentation was given at the regular Sunday afternoon mass meeting at the Uhuru House in St. Petersburg on Feb. 8, 2004. Here Chairman Omali cleverly shows the parallel between the struggle led by Jesus to free the Jews from Roman colonial domination and the struggle of African people today to liberate ourselves from U.S. colonialism. In the process he exposes the corruption of the parasitic, sellout preachers who are always working to keep African people oppressed and pacified.

Uhuru! I'm not a preacher, but I brought a Bible to this meeting because our community is filled with institutions called churches, which are filled with people who are followers of Jesus. The churches in many ways have become instruments to keep African people away from struggle, yet if the historical Jesus was real—and there is evidence that he was real—he was a revolutionary.

I'm going to tell you what your preacher won't tell you, and I'm going to use the scripture to prove it to you. You don't have to be defenseless when you listen to your old silver-tongued, slick, bootlicker preacher. The real question is: If Jesus was a revolutionary, then how come your preacher is such an Uncle Tom?

At the time of the birth of Jesus, the Jews, like most people in the Middle East, were dominated by the Romans. The Jews were living under colonial domination just like African people are today inside the U.S. and around the world. The Romans had what they called an "empire;" they were imperialists.

An empire is where a government not only dominates and rules its own people, but it conquers and dominates many other peoples around the world. The Roman empire was comparable to what America is today. America is an empire. It tells people what to do, and if you don't do it the empire will attack you. That's how Rome was, except it was more honest. It openly called itself an empire. The U.S. has always tried to hide this, although more and more, thinking representatives of white power today are referring to America as an empire. Except they don't call Bush an emperor, they call him the president!

Rome was not large enough to have an army that could be over all of the people in the empire. They were stretched too thin just like the United States now is stretched too thin in Iraq. They're trying to get Iraqis to be lackeys and to run Iraq for the United States. The fact is, you can't have enough armies and soldiers to hold down the entire world. So, you have to have the ability to inflict pain and brutality against the people and then you get some of their own to run it for you by rewarding a sector of the oppressed population.

The same thing was true when Rome was the key force in the whole world and the Jews were dominated by the Romans. The Jews didn't want to be dominated by the Romans, because no thinking human beings want to be dominated; they want to be self-determining. You can't have national dignity if every time you look up there's someone telling you how you have to do things. So, living under Roman domination at the time of Jesus, the Jews had the same problems you have today.

The Jews had what many people refer to as a religion. But it's not exactly religion. The reality is that every culture, every society, has for itself an explanation of its place and destiny in the world. You won't find a society that does not have for itself an explanation that has come out of its own experiences as a people. The Jews had a way of life built around their own philosophy, and this philosophy is tied up into what you now call the Bible.

The Jews had certain leaders who best interpreted, best understood and best expressed the notions that were in this philosophy that is found in the Bible. These were the teachers and the priests. I'm not talking about what white folks have taught you about religion: going to church every Sunday, or to Bible study. I'm talking about a way of life. This is how all peoples emerged. They had a way of life. Their philosophy grew out of this way of life and informed the people how they should act.

The Romans were violent and oppressive everywhere. The people who were oppressed by Rome wanted to find a way out. The Jews had this belief that some day a "deliverer" was going to come, a messiah, someone who would deliver us. The Jews wanted to have their own government and their own kingdom. They believed that somebody would come and lead them to their own kingdom right here on earth. They wanted to get out of the domination of the white people from Rome.

There were all kinds of organizations among the Jews, just like there are organizations among you. There was an organization called the Sadducees. This was an old Uncle Tom organization comprised mostly of rich Jews. They were real rich religious Jews. Just like today, back in Jesus' day you could be under foreign domination and still get rich if you carried out the Roman's oppression for them against your own people. The Sadducees had a nonviolent approach to everything.

There were the Pharisees. They were another Uncle Tom sellout group. The Pharisees believed in a legalistic approach to everything.

The Romans used the Sadducees and the Pharisees and created a neocolonial institution called the "Sanhedrin," through which the Uncle Tom Jews exercised the law.

There were also groups like the Zealots. The Zealots were violent revolutionaries. You can check your Bible history. John the Baptist was a Zealot. He was a guerrilla, a revolutionary. How do I know he was a guerrilla? I know because John was acting sort of like Nat Turner.[1] Read up on Nat Turner and then read about John the Baptist and see if they don't sound alike.

According to the scriptures, John the Baptist was also Jesus' cousin. He was born about six months earlier than Jesus. John the Baptist had a great following. Many people thought that John the Baptist was the Messiah and that he was going to lead them to this kingdom right here on earth. John was running around baptizing people and telling them to "change your ways, Brothers and Sisters. Change your ways." He was trying to get them to come out from under the Romans. They said that he wore clothes that were made out of camel's hair, and ate grass-hoppers and honey. This is somebody living off the land. This is a guerrilla. Check it out!

John was getting in trouble because he was talking about Herod, a super Uncle Tom Jew. Herod was called the King of the Jews, because his whole family, for generations, had been appointed by the Romans to be over the rest of the Jews. John was running around trying to bust Herod, because you can't get to the white man 'til you get through these Uncle Toms. John was trying to organize the masses of people. He knew he had to bring down these Uncle Toms before he could get to the Romans.

Herod wanted to do something about John, but he was scared because the masses followed John. Except on one day, Herod's wife's daughter did this dance. This must have been one hell of a dance, because Herod said "I'll do anything you want, because this dance was so great." Herod's wife told her daughter, "Tell him to give you John's head on a platter, because John's talking about us." Herod didn't want to do that because he knew it would be a political problem. But he had made this promise in front of people, and so he busted John and cut off his head.

But before John had his head cut off, Jesus came to him to

be baptized. Y'all know the scripture, right? What did John say? "You're the man!" Isn't that what John said? He told Jesus that he was the one. So that means that Jesus must have been a Zealot too.

A lot of people claimed to be the Messiah during that period. Many people thought John was the Messiah. But John said, "No, this is the one, right here. Jesus is the Messiah." The Jews are still waiting for a messiah, a deliverer, today. Those people who thought Jesus Christ was the deliverer became known as Christians. This is where the term comes from. Christians were the group of Jews that thought they could follow Jesus to get rid of the Romans. There was no such thing as what you now call "Christianity," because Jesus wasn't a Christian. Jesus was a Jew.

Revolutionary organizers

Jesus had a program. He had an organization. He pulled together into his organization twelve key people, each of whom had unique skills and talents. He sent them out as organizers. If you want to know how to organize, you should read the Bible. It tells you how to organize, who to see, and when you get there what to do. He sent these organizers out there to organize Jews—only Jews.

In Matthew 10:5 it says, "These twelve Jesus sent out with the following instructions: 'Do not go among the gentiles.'" A gentile is somebody who's not a Jew. "Do not go among the gentiles or enter any town of the Samaritans." Samaritans are people who are of mixed marriages, Jews and Gentiles. He told them not to mess with anybody who's not a Jew, and don't mess with anyone who's hooked up with white people. That's what he said. It's in Matthew 10:5.

He also said, "Go rather to the lost sheep of the house of Israel, and as you go, preach this message: 'The Kingdom of

Heaven is near.' Heal the sick. Raise the dead. Cleanse those who have leprosy. Drive out demons. Freely you shall receive. Freely you shall give. Do not take any gold or silver or copper for your belt. Take no bag for your journey or extra tunic or sandals or staves, for the worker is worth his keep." In other words, don't take anything with you. You're an organizer. Go among the people. The people will take care of you. That's what it says right here in this Bible.

Jesus was an organizer in dangerous circumstances. If you were caught, the Romans would bust you and do something terrible to you. This is Matthew 10:11: "Search for some worthy person there and stay at his house until you leave. As you enter the home, give it your greeting. If the home is deserving, let your peace rest on it. If not, let your peace rest on you. If anyone will not welcome you or listen to your words, shake the dust off your feet when you leave that home or town." He's saying that if they don't listen to you, just check out.

Now, Jesus was concerned. He knows about the dangers there. If you go to Matthew 10:15, you know he's talking about danger and this ain't no religious instruction. He says, "I tell you the truth. It will be more bearable for Sodom and Gomorrah on the Day of Judgment than for that town. I am sending you out like sheep among wolves. Therefore, be as shrewd as snakes and as innocent as doves."

You understand? In Matthew 10:17, he says, "Be on your guard against men. They will hand you over to local councils and flog you in their synagogues. On my account you will be brought before governors and kings as witnesses to them, and to the Gentiles. But when they arrest you, do not worry about what to say or how to say it." He's sending them out as organizers in a dangerous situation. The Romans will bust you up. They'll put you in jail. They'll do terrible things to you.

He says, again, in 10:21, "Brother will betray brother to death and a father his child. Children will rebel against their parents and have them put to death. All men will hate you because of me, but he who stands firm to the end will be saved. When you are persecuted," he says, "in one place, flee to another." Get out of there. Split. Do the work.

A lot of people like to tell you that Jesus was a pacifist who believed in nonviolence, but Jesus was not a pacifist! If you look at Matthew 10:34, you find very clearly that Jesus was not a pacifist: "Do not suppose that I come to bring peace to the earth. I come not to bring peace, but the sword." Ok, so Jesus said, "I come strapped." You understand? You have to be clear on that in order to understand who's most like Jesus.

So Jesus came to deliver his people from Roman domination, and they pulled together an organization to try to do it. He belonged to an organization that believed in struggle. The Romans were always trying to trap Jesus. This wasn't a religious question. They weren't trying to send Jesus to Hell. They were trying to send him to jail!

You go from Matthew 22:16 to 22:22, and it says, "Then Pharisees went out and laid plans to trap him in his words." They didn't have tape recorders, which is what they use now to back up the snitches. They sent their disciples to him with the Herodians. "Teach us," they said.

"We know you are a man of integrity and that you teach the way of God in accordance with the truth. You aren't swayed by men because you pay no attention to who they are. Tell us then, what is your opinion? Is it right to pay taxes to Caesar or not?" Caesar was the emperor, the one dominating everybody. Why would they raise that question? Because the Romans were a foreign government that occupied them, so why should they have to pay taxes to the Romans?

It's like here in St. Petersburg. Why should we have to spend $12 million of our taxpayers' money to go downtown to the Bay Walk[2] entertainment complex when Bay Walk ain't even for the black people? The Jews raised that question because they wanted him to say the wrong thing. This is no religious question. This is a political question. This is a question that can get you put in jail.

"But Jesus, knowing their evil intent, said, 'You hypocrites, why are you trying to trap me? Show me the coin used for paying the tax.' And they brought him the dinars, and he asked them 'Whose portrait is this, and whose inscriptions?' 'Caesar's,' they replied. Then he said to them, 'Give to Caesar what is Caesar's and to God what is God's.'"

In other words, "I'm not answering that question. You're not sending me to jail because of that!" Jesus was trying to deliver the Jews from Roman domination. The Romans and all of the Jewish sellouts were trying to keep that from happening.

Here in St. Petersburg recently, Rev. Murphy had the police chief and the whole police department at his church, talking about how good it is to lock up the black people. But Jesus was not a snitch. He did not work for the police. The snitches were the ones who turned Jesus in to the police.

There was an agent in his organization, named Judas. Judas said, "Look here. I'll turn him over to you. Give me a little bit of money, and I'll turn him over to you." He said, "You'll know who it is, because I'm going to kiss him." Jesus met him in the garden and Judas kissed him on the cheek. Isn't that in the scriptures?

That ain't nothing new. There are snitches in this organization. There are snitches all around, people who have lost themselves, who don't even belong to their communities and their people anymore. They work for the white man. They sit up in your meetings pretending, and then turn you over to the white man. That's how Malcolm X died. That's how Martin Luther King died. You understand?

When Judas kissed him in the garden, a whole crowd of people came to arrest Jesus. They had swords and clubs. So Jesus said to them, "Am I leading a rebellion that you have come out with swords and clubs to capture me?" Then he says, "Every day, I sat in the temple courts teaching and you did not arrest me." You know why they didn't arrest him when he was in the courts, right? Because of the power of the people! They were scared of the people. So they caught him when he was by himself in the garden. He says now you're coming to bust me for a rebellion, this is what you came for... *inciting to riot.*

Jesus was quite clear on what he was about. When he was before Pontius Pilate, the Roman governor over the Jews, the governor asked him, "Are you the King of the Jews?" And Jesus' response was, "Yes. It is as you say." In other words, "You said it, I'm the one. I'm the King." I'm looking at Matthew 27:11.

I'm saying this because you've got all of these Uncle Toms who are trying to be like Jesus. But Jesus kicked over the money tables. He said, "You guys are a den of thieves." He kicked over the money tables, and said, "you guys are just making money here. Most of you are just working with the Romans, working with the empire." It's like the Uncle Toms in our communities.

Jesus had a revolutionary program

Jesus wasn't a pacifist. At the last supper Jesus said, "When I sent you without purse, bag, or sandals, did you lack for anything?" "Nothing," they answered. "But now, if you have a purse, take it, and also a bag."

This is when Jesus knows he's going to die, you understand? "And if you don't have a sword, sell your cloak, and buy one." If you don't have a piece, sell your suit, you understand, be naked if you have to, but get yourself a piece! "If you don't have a sword, sell your cloak and buy one."

And his disciple said, "See lord, here are two swords." "That is enough," he replied. This is the Jesus that these Uncle Toms say they believe in. The Uncle Toms are the ones who condemn the masses of the people, support the emperor and the empire, and work against the interests of their own oppressed brothers and sisters. Jesus was clear on that. He was against the rich Jews. He said it would be easier for a camel to go through the eye of a needle than for a rich man to get into heaven. Why? If you are rich under colonial domination, you cannot work for the independence of the people. You get your wealth by being tied to white power.

You've got to be free from white power to overturn white power. It's what Malcolm X was talking about when he talked about the "House Negro" and the "Field Negro." You see, it's the House Negro who lived with the white man, in the white man's house. If the people in the field come and try to burn down the white man's house, well you're burning down the House Negro's house too. The House Negro's going to snitch on you because he's got a stake in the existence of slavery. This is what Jesus was talking about.

Jesus had a program. Jesus had a health care program. He sent out his disciples and said, "Go heal the sick," didn't he? Jesus walked around healing the poor and oppressed. He had an economic program too. Listen to me. He was a socialist. How the hell do you think it's possible for somebody to feed 5,000 people with five loaves of bread and two fish except through planning and cooperation? You can't do anything by yourself. You get everybody together—that's when you find out that collectively you've got more than you think.

Jesus was serious about struggle. He was bringing the message of revolution to the Jews, to free the Jews from Roman domination.

For many, many years, the thing that made Christianity spread like wildfire was the fact that Rome dominated so much of the world. In every place, people around the world heard about this group of people who were rising up against the Roman empire. In the beginning, Christianity was this movement against the Roman empire, against domination. All the people who were dominated by Rome took it up. Even some Romans who hated what their empire was doing to other people took it up as well.

Things got so serious that Rome was still fighting these followers of Jesus who were organizing insurrection all over the empire for a couple of hundred years. It got so serious that Rome was feeding the Christians to the lions. Then they got hip.

In 313 A.D—313 years after Jesus was born—the emperor was no longer Caesar. It was a man named Constantine. Constantine said, "Hell, we don't have to keep killing them. We'll join them." So Constantine joined the Christians. He became the top Christian. Much of the Bible is just various writings that Constantine pulled together. This is the emperor who the Jews had been fighting against. Now the emperor becomes the chief Christian. He's over all of the other Christians.

The Roman Catholic Church has the same structure that the Roman empire had. As I read this, you can see that some of Jesus' stuff got through into the Bible, but the emperor made sure that whatever he didn't want in there didn't get in there.

When Jesus and the other Christians were going out, they were fomenting insurrection against Roman domination. Now the emperor is in charge of Christianity, and he uses Christianity to co-opt the insurrection and try and save the empire. So everywhere people are oppressed, all over Latin America, all over the world, you see that Christians are led by Rome. You see Catholicism and other Christian religions all over the oppressed countries of the world, because Christianity is no longer the religion of the oppressed, it is the religion of the oppressor.

Africans in this country were attracted to Christianity because it was the religion of the oppressed. That's why we used to sing that song, "Go down Moses, way down in Egypt's land. Tell old Pharaoh, 'let my people go'..." Now you have sellouts who go to Pharaoh to lock his people up. That's what was happening at Rev. Murphy's church, isn't it? "Say, 'lock my people up.'" [Laughter]

When I was a child, when a baby boy was born, the old women would go over to the child and say "Is this the one?" Through the Christian tradition of looking for a deliverer, Africans were looking for somebody to deliver us from this hell.

Just like the emperor Constantine integrated into Christianity, the Negroes here integrated into white power, and when they integrated into white power, the Christianity in our community turned into something else. It had now joined the emperor. The moment it joined the emperor, then Christianity was no longer something to fight the emperor, it became something to keep us oppressed.

I'm talking about this today because, if you look around us, we are dealing with a contest of ideas. We are contending with the philosophy that they call Christianity that these preachers are using against our community. You need to understand it so that you can go ask Rev. Chickenbone to tell you the truth. "If Jesus was a revolutionary, Rev. Chickenbone, how the hell are you such an Uncle Tom?"

In the African People's Socialist Party, we've got the same programs Jesus had. We've got a Wellness Center to heal the sick. We've got a gym where you can go and get fit, don't we? We fight against the oppressors—every time you look at us, we're fighting against the oppressor. Just like Jesus, we want our own government.

Ours is also a message of deliverance. It was brought to us by Marcus Garvey[3] and others who told us that if you want your freedom, then you strike out, because Africa is our homeland. Africa is freedom.

This is how you value freedom. You've got to have your own philosophy. You can't use somebody else's philosophy to win your freedom. If Christianity were what it was when Jesus was around, the Christians would be trying to put Rev. Murphy on the cross. Instead, the empire is trying to put Mtundu[4] on the cross. In fact it's the Murphys and the rest of them who are acting like the Pharisees and Sadducees, always trying to trap you and deliver you up to the white man, and to the emperor.

We are the ones who carry the legacy of Jesus, not the hand-kerchief-head, chicken-eating preachers, who've delivered the people up into servitude. And so we ought to act like it. I've quoted scriptures here and you can look it up for yourself. You don't have to believe me.

We're in a war, and key to this war is the battle of ideas. You have to believe in your freedom in order to win it. If you don't want freedom, you won't get it. If you don't strike out for freedom, you won't get freedom. Jesus believed in freedom. John the Baptist believed in freedom. John was an organizer and Jesus was an organizer too. Jesus was able to win a whole bunch of people to him because he was able to heal people. He brought a program to the people. He brought people an understanding of how they had to love each other and get along with each other.

Somebody said, "Well Jesus, I want to go with you, but there's been a death in the family." Jesus said, "Let the dead bury the dead," because the most important thing you can do right now is to make this revolution. Isn't that what he said? He said "Let the dead bury the dead." We've got work to do, because the Romans are trying to deal with us. Jesus would never accept any excuse, and he turned around a whole bunch of folks.

I think it's a decent question for you to be able to ask your preachers about the revolutionary Jesus. If you look around, you will see that your preachers act more like Pharisees and Sadducees than Jesus.

Our liberation is going to come with our own philosophy, and our own philosophy is that which is going to liberate Africa and give it back to African people scattered around the world.

Uhuru!

1   In 1831 Nat Turner, an African preacher, led a powerful uprising of enslaved Africans in Virginia against the white slave owners. Turner and his forces killed fifty-five white people on several plantations before the rebellion was defeated by armed white citizens and state militia forces. Turner escaped and hid out for six weeks before he was jailed, tried and hanged along with sixteen other African people. The Nat Turner rebellions struck terror in the hearts of Southern plantation owners.

2   The city of St. Petersburg, Florida, gave $12 million to the developers of the downtown Bay Walk entertainment complex which caters to the white tourist trade and is hostile to African people, especially young Africans.

3   Marcus Garvey, 1887–1940, organized the Universal Negro Improvement Association (UNIA) and its coordinating body, the African Communities League. He published the newspaper the *Negro World* in several languages and toured the Americas speaking to large audiences of African people about his vision of African independence. The UNIA had millions of members in 1,100 branches in more than forty countries. Garvey launched ambitious business ventures, notably the Black Star Line shipping company.

4   Mtundu Dialobe is an Uhuru Movement organizer who was facing five years in prison for speaking out against an incident of police brutality against another African at the Bay Walk entertainment complex in St. Petersburg, Florida, in 2002. Through the efforts of the International People's Democratic Uhuru Movement, which held weekly demonstrations at Bay Walk for eight months, all charges were later dropped against Mtundu and Bay Walk agreed to change some of its anti-black dress codes.

Get off your lily white asses!

The peace movement must stand with the struggle for African liberation

On November 7, 2004, five days after the U.S. presidential election, the African People's Solidarity Committee (APSC) held a march and rally called "Stop America's Other War; March for Social Justice," in St. Petersburg, Florida.

Similar APSC-sponsored events had taken place in Oakland, California and Philadelphia, Pennsylvania during the previous month. A primarily North American or white organization, working under the leadership of the African People's Socialist Party, APSC organizes in the white communities building political and material support for the African liberation movement.

At the rally the Chairman gave this impassioned presentation, which ruffled the feathers of many white leftists, Democrats, pacifists and other opportunists. The Chairman challenged all those so-called progressive white people who so enthusiastically campaigned for candidates John Kerry of the Democratic party or Ralph Nader of the Green party, both with white programs that do not address the struggles of oppressed and colonized peoples. He criticized a movement that so easily protests a U.S. attack thousands of miles away while stepping over African and other oppressed peoples struggling for national liberation inside the U.S.

Uhuru!

I'd like to express my appreciation to all of you for coming out today. It's really important that the African People's Solidarity Committee (APSC) has made this event happen. In the last couple of weeks, I have participated in a March for Social Justice sponsored by APSC in Philadelphia, Pennsylvania, and in Oakland, California. It's a variation of a mobilization that this organization has done now for more than twenty years in various places around the country.

This mobilization is being held in solidarity with African people in this country and around the world and with oppressed peoples around the world. It is not something that's being done for African people. It's a mobilization for white people. It's a mobilization that attempts to bring white people in line with the rest of humanity. It's a mobilization that gives white people, or North Americans, an opportunity to end this terrible isolation that you have from the rest of humanity.

On September 11, 2001, a lot of illusions were shattered. For white people in America, there was a contemptuous ignorance of the world, based on gluttony, full stomachs, sated personalities and souls dulled by the fact that all of the resources of the world were coming here. For so long, it seemed to be that it was possible to have all of the resources coming here at no cost at all. This was notwithstanding the fact that half the people on earth are living on two dollars or less a day. Notwithstanding the fact that in Africa, people live on approximately one dollar a day, while in Europe, a cow lives on government subsidies of two dollars a day. That means that a cow in Europe is better off than a person in Africa.

Then, of course, there is the United States. Other speakers have talked about Amadou Diallo and Abner Louima.[1] We've seen the street crimes unit of St. Petersburg, Florida recently created—a street crimes unit that is based on the same New York unit that killed Amadou Diallo and brutalized Louima.

The street crimes unit here holds grown black men down in public in front of places like Church's Fried Chicken, and gives them rectal searches. The street crimes unit stops grown African men on the street and demands that the men cow down to them, and speak to them as if the African men were children. This is the America that the rest of the people of the world know.

You would think that after the events of September 11th, people would say, "Let's find out what the hell is going on." Clearly the illusion of American invulnerability was destroyed. This is despite the fact that America is taking billions and billions of dollars of public monies and giving it to arms industries, creating the illusion of invulnerability by building nuclear shields and things like this.

But in one fell swoop on September 11th, all of those illusions were destroyed. Americans—white people—found that just as Africans and other peoples around the world can die from a single incident, so can white people die like this too.

It was extraordinary to hear the whining, the blubbering, the fear that white people experienced. The reason it happened like that is because white people have been isolated from the rest of the world. You have assumed a separate identity from the rest of humanity. You can watch on television an African woman whose breasts have shriveled to the extent that she cannot feed her own baby, and not feel a kinship with that woman because you are white, because you are a so-called "American."

This is the world in which we live. It is a world where the original inhabitants of this land live in concentration camps, places called "reservations," where African people are stuck in other kinds of concentration camps, sometimes called "ghettos" or "housing projects" or prisons. African people were brought here as captives, whose labor was forcibly employed to develop a rotten, filthy, exploitative economy on the stolen land of the Indigenous population.

This is the America that everybody in the world understands, and we thought just briefly that on September 11th white people would peek behind the curtain of illusions, these comfortable illusions that have been made possible by a certain kind of satisfaction while living off of other people's resources. The truth of the matter is that the bread that goes into the mouth of a white child in America has been snatched from the mouth of oppressed peoples around the world—and sometimes even right here in this country. That is an objective reality and we call on people to recognize it.

Opportunist patriotism from the right and the left

Now, we just had the presidential election. We came to it with the U.S. having more than seven hundred military installations scattered around the globe to keep the rest of the world suppressed. We come into this election at a time when in Congo alone, over the last few years, nearly five million African people have been murdered as a part of a contest between France and the U.S. to maintain control of that turf. That's just recent history.

We come to this election at a time when the U.S. has reintroduced its military presence in places like Colombia, when it's obviously attempting to overthrow the government of Venezuela. This is a time when they are attempting to starve Cuba, because the courageous Cuban people stood up and defeated U.S. imperialism by overthrowing an Uncle Tom neocolonialist puppet that they had placed there. We come here with the experience of Viet Nam, where we saw the victory of the heroic mass of Vietnamese people, upon whose shoulders all of humanity rode in this terrible war of brutality that the U.S. imposed on them, attempting to hold them in colonial domination.

You would think that with the events of September 11th, white people would open their eyes to the Africans who live right in the same cities where you live, and who've died terrible deaths, and who are treated like animals and beasts.

You would think that September 11th would allow you to peek behind the curtain. For a moment that almost happened. But you have in this country a deep and profoundly opportunist kind of patriotism, a social patriotism based on rotten, racist ideological perceptions. It's on the left, and it's on the right.

You have on the right an obvious assumption by the United States government and white people in general to dominate the rest of the world.

From the left, what we hear is, "What about the white people? What about the workers. What about the women?" The left is not supporting what this march is calling for, to unite with the struggle of African people, unite with the Indigenous people who are being oppressed right here.

I'm told that we should support John Kerry. Well, I'm not going to support John Kerry, or Ralph Nader, who is Kerry-lite. Of course Kerry is Bush-lite, right? But what is the politic of these great white hopes that are held out for the rest of us? We're told that the fundamental issue is that of same-sex marriage or social security for the elderly or freedom from fear of colonial subjects from around the world who are coming to get their resources back and might blow up the mall. The issues, we are told, are protection for your sons and neighbors and relatives who are soldiers occupying somebody else's country right now. Those were the essential issues being articulated in this election.

There was no discussion about Venezuela. There was no discussion about Cuba. There was no discussion about seven hundred U.S. military bases that are holding the world in oppression today. There was no discussion about street crimes units that are destroying African communities, that are destroying the manhood and peoplehood of a whole nation that's being occupied right here in this country. There was no discussion of the Indigenous population of this country living in concentration camps with a life span of forty-six years. There was no discussion about any of that, neither by Kerry, nor Bush, nor Nader or any of them.

I really appreciate this mobilization, because we are in a contest. There's a convenient illusion under which many people are pursuing political life in this country. Somehow, I'm told, there's a great divide in this country. There's a radio station here that every liberal in this area holds up as the greatest thing that's happened since slavery. That is WMNF, a station that they call "Radio-Active." This notoriously white left, white nationalist station likes to argue the difference between the Republican party and the Democratic party.

Here is something you need to deal with. In a country such as this, the bourgeois elections are nothing but nonviolent contests between contending sectors of the white ruling class for control of the State. Sectors of the ruling class vie for power so that they can be more effective in pursuing their own economic interests. It's a nonviolent struggle between opposing and contending sectors of the white ruling class State. That's all it is.

The Democratic party is not a revolutionary organization— never has been, never will be. In fact, they used to be openly the party of the slave owners in this country. I'm saying that in this country, they use the election as an example of democracy.

Even in Israel, a brutal white nationalist, white settler-State that sits on the backs of the Palestinian people, they have elections! They are democratic, even though at the same time they are using Apache helicopters to murder, assassinate and brutalized the Palestinian people and hold them down. They do this so the white people can vote in elections, so it's democratic.

They love elections until they are in Venezuela and the U.S. can't get the right person elected. Or let's say it's in Haiti, where somebody who is trying to advance the interests of the African people gets elected. Then the U.S. sends a military force to kidnap the president in broad daylight, put him on an airplane and take him to a French-held colony.[2] So this is the electoral democracy that they believe in.

All of the white people in America, who have more access to the internet, great libraries, newspapers and news media outlets than anybody on earth, pretend ignorance of this reality. The rest of us know it, but white people pretend ignorance. It's an ignorance based on gain, based on a gluttonous appetite that makes it inconvenient to recognize what's happening to the rest of the world.

Democracy for white people at the expense of the oppressed

Democracy is just a form of the capitalist State, and the State is an instrument of repression, regardless of the society. The State comes into being when you have a situation where there is a split between the haves and the have-nots, between the exploited and the exploiters. The State is an organization to maintain the status quo.

What are the arms of the State? The police, the military, the prisons, the court system, these are organs of the State. They are in place as long as there is injustice in society. What is it that stands between abandoned houses in any urban center and homeless people?

Why the hell should people be homeless? There are empty houses everywhere. But if the homeless put themselves into those houses, then they will face the power of the State, which sends the police to kick them out. The State uses repression to maintain the status quo and to protect the private property of the owning class in this country and around the world.

Right around the corner here you have supermarkets with food overflowing from the shelves. But in the same city, there are hungry people who have nothing to eat. Sometimes you see them with styrofoam cups, standing outside of 7-Eleven's and under freeway bridges. What is it that stands between those hungry people and all of that food in those supermarkets? It's the police, it's the State. The State is the organization of violence, of coercion, to maintain the status quo, to maintain the imposition of this kind of unjust social system on the people.

Whichever sector of the ruling class it is that controls the State apparatus will be able to pursue their economic interests in the best possible way. So, if you've got an interest in securing all of the oil in the world, the oil barons and everyone tied to the industry will create some animal, some creature like this dumb guy who's currently the president. I'm not picking on him because he's dumb, because Kerry is a smart guy, and he has the same role as the dumb guy. Whether it's the smart guy or the dumb guy, they both do what the corporate bosses want them to do.

The oil companies want to take all of the oil on earth. They want to control the planet forever. Not only do they want to control the Middle East, they want to control Europe too. Why do you think Europe is creating a European Union? Europe is in a contest with the United States. It wants to build an economy; it wants to build a military; it wants to build a force that can contend with what the U.S. is doing.

It's not that Europe loves the oppressed peoples of the world; Europe doesn't want to be treated as if they are colonized, so they are trying to build up their capacity. Whoever controls the oil in the Middle East controls more than the Middle East. They control Europe; they control Japan, because Europe and Japan rely on the oil in the Middle East as well.

So all of these oil guys get together, and back somebody who wants to be president. All the people who make munitions, make airplanes, make tanks and the rest of it, back the candidate as well. The candidate runs for office and gets elected. As soon as he is elected, he struggles for absolute control of the State. If he wants the oil then he's got to attack somebody, and if he's going to attack them, then he's going to have to be able to win your support to do it. So there is the election, and you call yourself a Democrat, most of you.

I know there are a lot of card carrying Democrats out here. The truth of the matter is though, they will let you join the party, but the party is a party of the white ruling class, dummy! It's not your party. The Democratic and the Republican parties are both parties of the ruling class! They will let you sign your name, and they will give you a piece of cardboard with your name on it. They will give you a precinct number, but you are not part of the core group.

The next time they come to the Hilton and have a big time Democratic leadership meeting, you show up there with your little membership card and tell them you want to come in. Then you'll find out what the State is. At that juncture they will introduce you to the State. That's not your party, it's their party, but they need you to join it. They need you to come out and vote for their interests, in the name of democracy. That's why they created all of this drama about how this is the most important election ever.

Why do they need you to vote? Because they intend to dominate the world. They need you to join the army. They need you to say, "I don't support bank robbery, but I support the robbers. I don't support arson, but I support arsonists. I don't support the war, but I support the troops." You dummies! So you send your children to war. They need you. They need to know that this is the base of support they've got for killing the Iraqis.

Now, some people say that Bush can't do it this time, because the country is split fifty-fifty. They say Bush doesn't have a mandate. Garbage! The truth of the matter is, the vast majority of white people voted for George W. Bush. The only reason there is the appearance of a close vote is because twenty-five percent of the Democratic party is African. The only reason all those Africans are behind the Democratic party is because my party—the African People's Socialist Party—is weak, because the Black Movement is weak.

The Black Movement is weak because it was destroyed by the United States government militarily, in public view. Every time a leader, even today, raises his head, this government, this media will attack him. All of the white left and all of the white liberals will stand aside and let it happen. They will apologize for the government when it does it.

The Black Movement is weak right now because, in this country, you've got police terror in the African communities. There is terror from the street crimes units, doing the kinds of things they did to Amadou Diallo and Abner Louima—doing what they did to Marquell McCullough[3] and TyRon Lewis[4] here in St. Petersburg. Our movement is weak because they terrorize the African community to keep it from rising up.

White people who love democracy in Iraq can't even get off your lily white asses and take a stand right here in America. I'm especially offended by you rotten, filthy pacifists. You love peace so much on the one hand, but on the other hand I've never seen one of you stand in front of a police car heading in the direction of the black community. I've never seen you do a single thing about police terror right here. Instead, you tell me, "My solution is to vote for Kerry."

Kerry is a tool of the white ruling class. The last five hundred years of world history has been a history of imperial white power. This history is coming to an end right now, before your eyes. That is what September 11th was about.

Peoples around the world today are organizing to end this, and we are in a contest right here. The question for all of us is how long are you going to continue participating in the Democratic party, or some other instrument of imperialism? When will you be able to break with America and join with the rest of us in this struggle?

When will you be able to recognize your own humanity? When will you be connected to the rest of the world instead of some white conception that was created for the exact purpose of separating you, and using you as tools to be used against the rest of us? This is the question that you are confronted with, because we are in a contest, and our movement is weak. But my objective is to make African people free, to win a revolution, to destroy imperialism so that it cannot impose its will on oppressed peoples around the world.

My objective is not to rely on Nader or Kerry or Bush, or anybody else to guarantee the future of African people, either here or around the world. My objective is to direct Africans to their own selfish interests, and to help organize them under the leadership of the African working class. When we are able to do it, my objective is to win our freedom by any means necessary.

So here is a contest in which we are involved. Can you support the demand for Marquell McCullough's family to be compensated by the city of St. Petersburg for his murder by the police? Can you support the demand for TyRon Lewis's family to be compensated for his murder? Not because we believe in a pay off, but because we know that the U.S. government will continue to do these kinds of things until there is a price to pay.

It is also important for you to take this stand, because it's necessary for white people to end your isolation from the rest of us, and join in this process. Here is the contest. At some juncture, I will call on the African community to not keep on demanding that the white system does something to correct its own problems. My call will be for the African people to employ the right of self defense. I will say that if he comes at you with a gun, and you know the only thing that separates you from him is a gun, then you need to get your own gun. If you've got a gun and he's got a gun, at least you can stand up to each other as equals.

We say:

All power to the people!
And Black Power to the African community! Uhuru!

---

1 Amadou Diallo, an African born in Guinea, was killed on February 4, 1999, by New York police who shot forty-one rounds at him as he stood unarmed in the vestibule of his apartment building in the Bronx. Abner Louima, an African born in Haiti, was brutalized and tortured on August 9, 1997 in Brooklyn by New York police who forced a wooden stick into his rectum.

2 Jean Bertrand Aristide, President of Haiti, was ousted by a U.S.-backed coup on February 29, 2004. He was kidnapped by U.S. forces and taken to Central African Republic.

3 Marquell McCullough was killed on May 2, 2004 by St. Petersburg police who shot nineteen rounds through the windshield of his pick up truck where he sat unarmed. McCullough was seventeen years old.

4 TyRon Lewis, eighteen years old, was killed on October 24, 1996 by St. Petersburg police. Lewis was shot with his hands up in front of a crowd in the busiest intersection in the African community. The murder sparked a major African community rebellion that night and three weeks later when the police attacked the Uhuru House after the grand jury exonerated the killer cops. Lewis' killing was the central focus of years of mass organizing by the Uhuru Movement for economic and social justice for the African community.

Advanced detachment
The revolutionary Party of the African working class

This brilliant article presents a complete, all-sided understanding of why the African working class must have a political party of its own that represents its interests. Chairman Omali lays out the aims and work of such a party in the context of the political history and current situation in which the struggle for African liberation is being waged.

This is the only article included in this book that predates 1990. It was chosen because its relevance is perhaps even greater today than when it was first written. This is an edited version of "The History and Role of the Proletarian Party of the Black Working Class," that first ran in the June, 1985 issue of The Burning Spear *newspaper and which was printed as a pamphlet in 1986. Because of its significance it was published again in the May 2003 issue of* The Burning Spear.

In this version Chairman Omali has elaborated on certain points by adding footnoted comments. To differentiate from other endnotes that simply provide information, the Chairman's notations are designated as "OY 2005."

Political parties have not always existed in human society. Indeed, they represent a rather new feature of human society. Political parties emerged with the development of capitalism in Europe. They developed with the growing bourgeois-defined assumption of democracy that accompanied the bourgeoisie's rise to power.

The existence of political parties is a recognition of class contradictions in society. It denotes the role of the political organization of the people as a means of acquiring and keeping political power.

For African people, both on the Continent of Africa and elsewhere, political parties are even more recent. This is because the European bourgeoisie came to power as a consequence of the slave trade in Africa. Even as it was promoting democracy for itself in Europe, the European bourgeoisie used every available resource to immobilize, disorganize and suppress the African. This is why class contradictions inside Africa never reached the sharpness of Europe, except as an extension of the power of the European bourgeoisie in the form of African slave catchers or others who carried out the will of the oppressors against the masses of African people.[1]

For Africans then, the external white enemy became such a dominant force that it served to unite the broadest sectors of our community as one oppressed community. This muted or made secondary the contradictions *inside* our community. Africans generally expressed the situation as "the white people against the black people." When, by some chance, there was a white individual who stood in apparent support of the demands of African people, or when there was an African who betrayed the demands of black people or our movement, African people would generally sum this up as due to the personal qualities of the individual involved. This was a "good" white man or a "bad" or "Uncle Tom" black man.

The features of class began to achieve definition as early as the first quarter of the twentieth century. The struggles of Marcus Garvey[2] with W.E.B. Dubois[3] and the communist articulations of the African Blood Brotherhood[4] in the 1920s were early examples of class struggle inside the African community. It was only in the 1960s, though, that the actual, objective conditions emerged sharply enough for the class contradictions inside our oppressed, colonized community to become consolidated.

The movement of the 1960s was immediately influenced by the concrete, material developments of the fifties. During the 1950s the alliance between our movement and the liberal bourgeoisie consolidated itself in mass struggle. In the process our movement began to achieve a revolutionary character. This movement activated the African victims of U.S. colonialism as conscious participants, and impacted on the consciousness and practical life of all the peoples inside the U.S. This powerful movement overthrew the immediate form of capitalist rule of the Southern white ruling class,[5] and achieved legal democratic rights for African people.

This struggle became sharp and definitive in the South in the fifties because of the convergence of two important factors— one subjective and the other objective.

The subjective factor was the longing by colonially oppressed Africans for freedom from foreign rule, for dignity and for a better life without brutality and material want.

The objective factor was the tremendous growth in the industrial production capacity that followed the second imperialist war waged in the 1940s to redivide the world among capitalist powers. The war resulted in the U.S. becoming the world's greatest imperialist power, which now possessed—either directly or indirectly—the colonial raw materials that were previously held exclusively by European powers.

This growth in productive capacity multiplied the need for industrial workers almost overnight. These workers could only be found in the South among the African sharecroppers and other toilers who were trapped in a labor-intensive form of the capitalist system. This system required the most oppressive, backwards and terroristic political methods for its maintenance.

For the Northern capitalists it was absolutely necessary to acquire these workers in order bring about capitalist expansion and imperialist economic development. This led the liberal industrial sector of the white ruling class to support and encourage the black movement of the South against the kind of Southern capitalist rule that had prevailed since the Civil War.

This was a struggle against a particular form of capitalist rule, and not capitalism itself. Like the liberal white ruling class, the black petty bourgeoisie was only interested in limited revolution. In this way, the alliance between the black petty bourgeoisie and the liberal white ruling class consolidated the leadership of the black petty bourgeoisie over our movement.

Birth of the African proletariat

The outcome of this alliance, however, was something that neither the liberal bourgeoisie nor the black petty bourgeoisie could predict, namely the emergence of an African proletariat rising up from the bowels of America itself. This proletariat rapidly became conscious of its own aims and interests, which were not only in contradiction with the aims of colonial white power. They were increasingly in contradiction with the aims of the colonized black petty bourgeoisie as well. As these contradictions in aims and interests began to crystallize, differences in ideology and tactics begin to crystallize as well.

An inconsistent though generally materialist philosophy of "black nationalism" began to emerge out of the aims of the African working class. Black nationalism began to reject the idealist and obscurantist philosophy of the liberal black petty bourgeoisie. Martin Luther King's "dream" of a better day in America as a consequence of the moral regeneration of whites of the oppressor nation was challenged by the "nightmare" as defined by Malcolm X. The African proletariat, facing objective reality in America, raised the demand for Black Power to determine our own black destiny.

The white liberal bourgeoisie required that the black petty bourgeoisie uphold the philosophy of nonviolence as a condition for its support. By the mid-1960s however, philosophical nonviolence met its fate in the flames of black rebellion that consumed city after city. We were seeing the first full-fledged generation of urban African workers powerfully come to political life as a colonized proletariat becoming conscious of its own class interest.

During and subsequent to this period, revolutionary black parties began to emerge. We came to understand the nature of political parties, not as simple associations of people who have the same general beliefs, but as repositories of particular class interests. We saw that parties are the political instruments of particular classes, the projectors and protectors of the will and interests of particular classes, the political concretization of the economic interests of particular classes.

Political parties are organizations of the most advanced representatives of a particular class. The tasks of political parties are directly tied to the material interests of the classes they represent.

Sometimes elements of a particular class are not aware of their own class interests. There are people from the white ruling class, for example, who are drunks or drug addicts, or even insane. Sometimes elements of the ruling class are wife beaters, bed wetters, or lazy ignoramuses who are unconcerned and disdainful of the overall interests of the capitalist-colonialist ruling class.

Nevertheless, some members and representatives of the white ruling class take it upon themselves to organize into political parties, which represent and look out for the interests of the entire class, including the drunks, wife beaters, etc. We call these people the advanced or activist elements of their class.

What are the interests of the U.S. capitalist-colonialist class? The most fundamental interest of the capitalist-colonialist ruling class is the perpetuation of the capitalist system and itself as the ruling class. This fundamental interest gives rise to other interests:

Economically, there is the interest to eliminate all economic competition, both domestically and internationally. The interest of the capitalist-colonialist ruling class is in dominating the natural resources and markets of the entire world.

Politically, there is the interest in restricting the political liberties of the peoples of the entire world. This is an interest in crushing any political liberties that do not facilitate the economic domination of the U.S. capitalists. It is an interest in restricting the development of any independent political expression that would challenge the hegemony of U.S. capitalism.

Ideologically, the interests of the white ruling class are served by idealism and obscurantism, which covers over reality. This keeps the oppressed and exploited peoples, especially the African working class, separated from an understanding of their own material interests. It keeps oppressed and exploited peoples ignorant of science and a scientific approach to an examination of the nature of class exploitation and national oppression. Ideologically, the interests of the white ruling class give rise to ideological imperialism, the imperialist imposition of its worldview, aims and ideology onto oppressed peoples. Imperialist domination of ideology is consistent with the economic domination of the capitalist system.

During the sixties, black political parties began to emerge from within the colonized African population in the U.S. as a result of the internal pressures of class contradictions. As these contradictions began to crystallize, they revealed a colonial society that was much more complex than before.

Before the movement won our legal democratic rights, it was all of "us" (blacks) against "them" (whites). The U.S. government was not generally recognized as an agent of a particular class and social system. Our movement, under the leadership of the black

petty bourgeoisie, courted the various U.S. presidents assidu-
ously, hoping to find a "good" president who was sympathetic to
the general democratic aims and demands of the movement.

By 1965, after a decade of most intense struggle, our
movement won the vote and our legal democratic rights. In the
process, the black petty bourgeoisie was growing as a result of
the effectiveness of the movement and the intervention of the
liberal white bourgeoisie. With the vote and legal rights, the basic
aspirations of the black middle class were, in effect, realized. For
them the movement had reached its goal.

For the new generation of fully mobilized African workers
that was thrust onto the scene as the main social factor in the
U.S. political life, its aspirations were far from being met by
gaining legal democratic rights. The attempts by the petty bourgeoisie to moderate the Black Liberation Movement, to decelerate
it and direct it toward liberal bourgeois democratic sops, were
met with the cries of "Burn, baby burn," in Los Angeles and
"Black Power" in Mississippi.

At this point the independent aspirations of the African
working class became clear. This new clarity fueled efforts to
build independent political parties by and for the colonially
oppressed African population. Nevertheless, our inexperience
frustrated our efforts at party-building. More often than not, we
were unable to build parties that clearly identified the class
interests they served. Generally we were not able to show that
the African working class had an interest in overthrowing the
colonial oppression of our whole people.

The party-building movement was successful, however, in
creating party formations that raised principles of unity going
beyond the limitations of the liberal black petty bourgeoisie.
Those who could unite with militant anti-colonial principles that
clearly distinguished African workers from the black petty bourgeoisie joined the party and were able to characterize themselves

ambiguously as revolutionaries and black nationalists. Such parties began to characterize sectors of the movement that were trapped inside the limitations of reform as Uncle Toms and sometimes as the black bourgeoisie.

None of these parties was capable of raising up the interests of the black working class as the hegemonic interests of the party. Although it was the pressure of the black working class resistance and struggle that pushed this party-building process forward, it was essentially petty bourgeois nationalists—often revolutionary—who were leading this effort. The black working class was yet to seize leadership of its own revolutionary movement, even as history was pushing events in that direction with growing urgency.

Black Panthers, first black worker's party

The Black Panther Party, which emerged in 1966–67, came closest to being the party of the African working class.[6] For the first time in the history of our movement, an independent black political party had identified itself as a socialist or communist organization, with socialist or communist revolutionary objectives.[7]

Inherent in this identification was the assumption of a worldview with the interests of the African working class at its center. Certainly the vast bulk of the membership of the Black Panther Party was working class, and its Ten Point Program and Platform raised fundamentally working class demands.

The Black Panther Party (BPP) gave the colonially oppressed African working class more experience in leading its own struggle than any organization before it. Nevertheless, it muddled its own effectiveness with an ideology that mystified the character of the black working class under colonialism. Instead of elevating its membership to the highest stance of the African working class, the Black Panther Party idealized the traits of the lumpen proletariat, a non-working class element of unstable and unemployable people, as the leadership of the Revolution. In this process, the BPP mistakenly identified colonized unemployed black workers, who sometimes have lumpen tendencies, as the lumpen proletariat.[8]

Nevertheless, the Black Panther Party provided the closest thing to a revolutionary center that our movement had ever experienced. Although incorrect on some essentials, the BPP introduced the question of class struggle to our movement, a question that was briefly taken up within a large sector of the African working class itself.

Bourgeois democracy and the parties of the white ruling class

The parties of the white ruling class inside the U.S. are the Democratic and Republican parties. The objective of the Democratic and Republican parties is the perpetuation of the capitalist social system, which rests on the foundation of African oppression. Although both of these parties are capable of prattle about democracy, the democracy they talk about is only a description of the form of the U.S. State, which exercises capitalist rule with its organs of coercion such as the police, army, the courts, etc. Besides being "democratic," the capitalist State can take the form of dictatorship or monarchy, among others.

Neither the Democratic or Republican party is capable of talking about overthrowing the capitalist social system. Neither party will ever be able to bring about democratic self-determination for the broad mass of African people. This is because the capitalist social system within the boundaries of the U.S., perhaps more than any place else, rests on the foundation of African oppression going back to the days of what is called slavery.

The Democratic and Republican parties have been excellent tools of the white ruling class precisely because they appear to give African workers, oppressed peoples and even the general white population a choice in the U.S. They give the illusion of providing alternatives and freedom of democratic participation in American political life.

The Republican and Democratic parties make it possible for the white ruling class to monopolize political, economic and ideological power while obscuring the class interests that they represent. Since oppressed peoples, like sectors of the bourgeoisie, are often ignorant of their class interests, African workers generally attempt to pursue their class interests within the parties of the white ruling class, especially the Democratic party in this period.

Within the U.S. and most capitalist countries there is generally, but not always, more than one capitalist party. This allows the bourgeoisie to wear two hats, a kind of "good cop, bad cop" routine. In this way, the bourgeois social system protects itself by passing political power to one bourgeois party when the other has come into disrepute with the people.

The fact that the people can vote for one or the other bourgeois party gives the impression of political free will by the masses and acts as a social pressure release valve, blunting the development of class struggle. This is what is called bourgeois democracy.

Actually the people have not exercised free will, which presupposes information and science. Freedom is the recognition of necessity, which is prerequisite to exercising free will. Within the U.S. and other places where more than one capitalist party dominates political life, elections are means of nonviolent struggle by different sectors of the ruling class for control of the State.

The various social forces are not organized into their own independent class parties and engaged in conscious class struggle, one against the other. Instead, the American two-party system mobilizes African and other oppressed workers into the service of a sector of the white ruling class as it engages in intra-class struggle with another sector. The two-party system obscures the class interests of the exploited workers and oppressed peoples, reducing them to reserve forces for one sector of the bourgeoisie or another.

The question of class struggle within the U.S. has always been difficult enough even without the two-party duplicity of the bourgeoisie. This has to do with the parasitic nature of the capitalist system. Within the U.S., this parasitism stems from a social system built on stolen land, the massacre of hundreds of thousands of Native people and the enslavement of African people.

The entire white population—workers and bourgeoisie alike—and all social forces and classes that benefit from the development of the "New World," find their happiness and freedom from political oppression and material want at the expense of the life, liberty and development of Indigenous and African peoples.

Hence, there is a material, economic basis for the political unity that exists between the North American bourgeoisie and the general white population. This political unity is directed against the African, Indigenous and other colonized peoples here and around the world, in defense of the capitalist social system.

The parasitic nature of the capitalist system is the basis for the political and ideological leadership of the modern U.S.-based African proletariat. The African working class is the only social force that has the exact combination of qualities which makes it an absolute, volatile opponent of the capitalist social system.

Along with the Indigenous people, the oppression of the African people represents the foundation upon which the capitalist social system rests. The nineteenth century philosopher Karl Marx termed this economic relationship "primitive accumulation...an accumulation not the result of the capitalist mode of production but its starting point." The African population exists as a domestic colony upon which the U.S. capitalist system was founded.

The African population is a colonial population within the belly of the U.S., a factor with explosive social connotations in and of itself. In addition, the African population is essentially made up of workers, with estimates ranging from eighty-eight to ninety-four percent of U.S.-based African people falling into the working class.

Racism or white nationalism, the ideological foundation of U.S. and world capitalism, has as its basis "primitive accumulation," the material foundation of the U.S. and world capitalist social system that was born and maintained at the expense of African, Indigenous and other oppressed peoples.

Inside the U.S., the class struggle against the capitalist-colonialist social system is centered in the colonized African population, which constitutes the true proletariat. Through the Black Revolution of the Sixties, the African working class came to understand that the bourgeois parties are opposed to our genuine interests.

When the black working class was organized into its own party in the sixties with the Black Panther Party as its legitimate representative, the African working class became a formidable opponent to the U.S. capitalist system. The threat of organized African workers was so great that the chief of the U.S. secret political police declared the Black Panther Party the greatest threat to the internal security of the U.S. since the Civil War.

The war against the Black Revolution

When the black working class was organized into its own party, with its class and national interests summed up in the form of a political program opposed to colonial rule, the Democratic and Republican parties had to call into force the repressive arms of the State. These parties of the bourgeoisie were incapable of engaging in successful ideological and nonviolent political struggle with the black working class. It took an all out urban war against the black working class in the sixties for a return to imperialist class peace and the reinstatement of the facade of a two-party system supposedly representing the class interests of all the people.

This war saw African workers stand up alone not only against armed police organizations, but even armed military forces usually reserved for foreign U.S. intervention. In Detroit this included the Eighty-second Airborne Division. In urban areas throughout the U.S., military tanks and an assortment of other sophisticated armaments were deployed against the unarmed black working class communities.

The military offensive, directed by the Democratic and Republican parties, was faced with the immediate task of putting down a massive movement with insurrectionary characteristics similar to that presently occurring in Occupied Azania (South Africa). This military offensive, or counterinsurgency, was designed to destroy the will of the entire African working class to struggle by crushing their independent organizations, particularly the Black Panther Party.

The U.S. ruling class used its military power, its state power, to defeat the independent, revolutionary capacity of the African working class, the only internal social force that made it necessary to defend the capitalist social system. The African working class was the only social force inside the U.S. that was capable of challenging the bourgeoisie for power, the fundamental question for any revolution.

For all these years subsequent to the military defeat of the Black Revolution of the Sixties the bourgeoisie has expended a tremendous amount of energy and resources in keeping the African working class politically disoriented, disorganized and unable to come together organizationally in its own class interests.

The methods for this have ranged from open white ruling class bribery of nonproletarian social forces, to naked terror against the African working class itself. Evidence of the African working class in the popular culture has nearly disappeared. Michael Jackson, Jesse Jackson, Prince, and Lionel Ritchie have become the stereotypes of the acceptable African within the U.S. On the occasions when black working class elements are allowed to emerge as acceptable, it is as followers of Jesse Jackson into the Democratic party. Or it is as fictionalized pathetic, poor black working class children who manage to escape colonial poverty through being adopted by well-to-do white petty bourgeois families, as seen on television sit-coms.

A significant sector of the liberal black petty bourgeoisie accepted neocolonial roles in the bourgeois Democratic party. This is payoff in material resources and prestige for administrating the African working class in areas where white direct colonial rule would be unacceptable. The Jesse Jackson presidential campaign was a manifestation of this, along with the bombing of an African working class community in Philadelphia by a black mayor and a black city manager.[9]

In the years since the sixties, the white women's and homosexual movements have become virtual scabs on the Black Revolution. These movements are incapable of raising up and supporting the Black Liberation Movement which is the quintessence of the class struggle within the U.S.

The black petty bourgeois neocolonialist puppets and the women's and homosexual movements are conscious opportunist movements. They offer up the battered carcass of the collective African working class to the altar of capitalism as offerings of class peace in exchange for privileges for themselves. They all attempt to mute and obscure class struggle and call on the people to join the Democratic party to achieve their aims.

With the defeat of the Black Revolution of the Sixties, our independent working class organizations were destroyed and the mass of black workers were disorganized and dispersed. A variety of petty bourgeois social forces, mostly tied to the Democratic party, united with the white ruling class in assuring class peace. Such unity means the muting of any class struggle that has the interests of the African working class at its center.

This is the context of the significance of the existence and struggle of the African People's Socialist Party.

Strategy for revolutionary African working class party

Organized in 1972 from surviving black working class organizations of the sixties, the African People's Socialist Party pulled together the best elements of the class subsequent to the defeat of our movement. While we are a revolutionary party, we understand that our task for this period is not to make the Revolution, but to build the capacity of the only consistently revolutionary social force within U.S. borders, the African working class. This means that our primary task is to build the African People's Socialist Party.

We must address our strategy for building a truly revolutionary African working class party. This is necessary because at least one petty bourgeois, U.S.-based African organization claims party-building as its main task. This party does not distinguish its main task from its general aim, hence the "task" of party-building has for all practical purposes, become its general aim. This party uses the slogan of party-building to obscure class struggle, to maintain the class peace which is necessary for successful bourgeois colonialist rule.

For the African People's Socialist Party, fundamental to the task of party-building is the need to smash the class peace. Otherwise, sectors of the black working class might remain ensconced within the Democratic party. Additionally, the millions of African workers who have rejected the false choice of the two white ruling class parties will be unable to see that we must do more than just turn our backs on this pitfall. We must join and support our own independent parties in order to achieve our own separate class interests.

For the African People's Socialist Party, the task of party-building is always a process deeply rooted in solving the concrete, practical problems of the Revolution for the period. A key, fundamental problem today is the reorganization of the black working class into its own independent revolutionary party. We are not, however, talking about party-building for its own sake. For us the task of party-building is for the purpose of solving the most fundamental problems of the Revolution. We are informed of the practical problems of the Revolution by our ability to sum up the period in which we live and assume the task of party-building.

Our summation of this period informs us that objective conditions for revolution are ripe. The U.S. capitalist-colonialist class is engaged in several undeclared wars, a fact which currently divides the ruling class.

The conditions of existence for the black working class are reaching new and greater levels of desperation, and the use of overt police terror against the colonially oppressed African workers is becoming more blatant every day.

These conditions are evidence of the general crisis of imperialism. Although the election of Ronald Wilson Reagan as U.S. president was designed to confront this crisis, it continues unabated, nationally and internationally. Clearly, the objective conditions for the African Revolution are very strong.

However, currently there are key weaknesses that we face in the subjective factors for revolution. These include the general state of disorganization of the African working class. This disorganization is facilitated by opportunism on every level. For example, there are the so-called revolutionary black parties that are fearful of class struggle and black working class hegemony over our own movement.

There are the silver-tongued, bourgeois-sponsored, neocolonialist black petty bourgeois stooges, whose prestige, appearance of power and material resources are dependent upon their ability to speak for the masses of unorganized black workers. There are the "communists," "socialists" and "leftists" of all stripes, who can wear such appellations only so long as the African working class is voiceless and unable to impress our own version of class truth on the political life of the U.S. There are the women's and homosexual movements and every other social force that faithfully serves the U.S. bourgeoisie, and who remember with fear and trepidation the undiluted power of the Black Revolution of the Sixties.

In practical terms party-building today means, first and foremost, concrete work designed to activate the best of the class into political motion around concrete programs. Our immediate aim is to achieve absolute political hegemony over our movement and class in the process. Party-building means providing leadership for the class even when the party is small and has not yet fully achieved its desired capacity.

For example, although small, the African People's Socialist Party has been able to ignite a social movement in Oakland, California. The Party has successfully mobilized elements of the African working class. With the Party at its center, this movement has been able to mobilize social forces of various nationalities into the service of the African working class and away from absolute unity with the bourgeois colonialists.

Although most of the African workers in Oakland are not Party members, the leadership of the Party in the city has made it possible for African workers as a whole to experience an organized fighting capacity around real, concrete, social needs. The Party-led Uhuru Movement in Oakland has led a campaign to successfully challenge the basic assumptions of bourgeois property relations. For the first time since the sixties, the Party has put the bourgeoisie on the political defensive in a struggle with African workers.

In 1984, the African People's Socialist Party put an initiative on the electoral ballot in Oakland calling for community control of housing. Known as Measure O, the initiative called for residential rents to be set no higher than twenty-five percent of the average income of a neighborhood. Measure O also called for abandoned houses to be turned over to homeless people. Essentially a land reform measure, the initiative won twenty-five thousand votes, a quarter of the votes cast, despite a half million dollars spent to defeat it by Oakland landlords and realtors.[10]

Thus, our small Party, in the process of party-building, was able to provide leadership for African and other working class elements in a fashion greatly disproportionate to our physical size. More than this, the voters who were won to a working class stand in that election stood against the leadership of the bourgeois parties with whom they are registered.

The party-building process must awaken the black working class to practical participation in its own political life. This is why party-building is not an abstract process. Real political struggle must be coupled with real, practical leadership of the class when building the party. The party must be capable of mobilizing and leading the African working class and various social forces of various nationalities if it is to be worthy of the name "party."

Today we are confronted with a period when the last significant political lesson to be summed up by the black working class is military defeat. Still reeling from the U.S. military assault against our movement of the sixties, the masses of African workers today are restless. They have not yet, however, again concluded that their own interests are summed up in the African working class party, or that joining the party is worth the risk to life and liberty that may be suggested by party membership. Nevertheless, African workers must still have the leadership of the party available to them and be able to claim the party as their own.

For the African People's Socialist Party, the party-building process is an open one. We believe the African working class and our allies should have some idea of what parties are and what their functions are. We think our supporters should have a better grip on what it is they support and whether their support is what it needs to be.

The African People's Socialist Party is a revolutionary African working class party, the only such party in the U.S. We are organized around a common General Program and policies that were ratified during our First Party Congress, the highest body of the Party, comprised of representatives of the entire membership.

Our General Program and our policies are the practical, concrete manifestations of our revolutionary theory of African Internationalism. African Internationalism is Pan-Africanism developed to its highest stage, Pan-Africanism during the age of imperialism.[11] African Internationalism unites the African people of the world in a revolutionary process to liberate Africa under the leadership of African workers and poor peasants.

The theory of African Internationalism is ever-developing with the new experiences of the international working class, African and otherwise. It is based on a scientific method of investigating and analyzing social life. It recognizes that the current oppressive circumstances of African people have their base in the slave trade, the fundamental feature in the development of world capitalism.

The scientific method of investigating social life employed by the African People's Socialist Party is called dialectical and historical materialism.

By dialectical we mean that our approach to the investigation of all phenomena is all-sided, taking into consideration the past and present. Dialectical means that we take into account the relationship of a phenomenon in motion to all other phenomena, even as phenomena come into being and die away.

By materialism we mean that our analysis of phenomena is based on an investigation of a phenomenon itself, not requiring an explanation of phenomena outside of it.

By historical materialism we mean the application of the principles of dialectical materialism to the investigation and interpretation of society and social life.

The opposition of the African People's Socialist Party to the U.S. government and the capitalist social system, which rests on our colonial oppression, is total and absolute. There are no circumstances under which we would ever find the foreign domination of our people or the economic exploitation of our class acceptable. We are convinced that capitalism, the social system, was built off the slave trade and the theft of life, liberty, and resources of African people and the non-European peoples of the world. We understand that the world's stolen resources are concentrated in Europe and the U.S., and are owned and controlled by a tiny minority of the people on the planet. Moreover, we are convinced that this capitalist system is on its deathbed.

We believe that the future belongs to the dispossessed colonized workers of the world. When armed with a revolutionary theory and led by a revolutionary party, African and other oppressed workers represent the conscious, subjective forces of history necessary for the overthrow of capitalism. This is the only way to bring about the advent of a new social system organized under the leadership of the working masses, the real producers of all material wealth.

This new social system will end production for profit and rule by a nonworking minority who maintain private ownership of our resources and control of the means of production.

We believe that the new social system that will follow capitalism is communism, a just social system based on labor according to ability and guaranteeing to each person the material resources of life and its reproduction according to need. Communism is the system that the white ruling class and all its hangers-on are attempting to suppress with the oppression of the African working class

Thus we recognize that the African People's Socialist Party, the advanced, conscious detachment of the African working class, is, like the class itself, locked in a life-and-death battle with the U.S. capitalist system. Hence, the members of our Party represent the advanced sector of the African working class. They must constantly strive for a self-motivated discipline that is steeled by conviction.

As the advanced detachment of the African working class, the African People's Socialist Party assumes the responsibility for advancing the cause of the whole class, which at any given time may be battered by ignorance, drug addiction, alcoholism, demoralization or other contradictions. The members of the African People's Socialist Party must become professional revolutionaries, individuals whose real profession is revolution with the Party as their vehicle.

The African People's Socialist Party recognizes that the colonially oppressed African workers are the most consistently revolutionary social force within the U.S. The African working class will not achieve revolutionary consciousness on its own, however. It is the task of the African People's Socialist Party, even as it is being built to full capacity, to intervene in the day-to-day struggles of the African working class, to forge deep lines in struggle and to lead the class to an ever higher, ever more precise understanding of African Internationalism, the science of black workers' revolution.

The African People's Socialist Party, a revolutionary African Internationalist Party based on a revolutionary African working class theory, is a party of professional revolutionaries. All distinctions between workers and intellectuals, laborers and "professionals," lose their significance. We are welded into one by the common cause of a proletarian future that is being advanced by the party of the colonially oppressed African working class.

On one side stand the bourgeoisie and all the institutions which serve to preserve its rule. On the other side stands the oppressed African working class, represented by the African People's Socialist Party.

Together, these two social forces represent the great contest of our time. Separately, they represent the past and the future. The conscious representatives of these two great social forces are choosing sides. Every day makes the choice by the African working class and our allies more critical.

For us the question is clear. The future will prevail. It is urgent for all those who are taking a neutral seat as spectators in this contest, to take up the call. Take the Great Leap Forward and grab the future in your hands to help shape and mold it in our lifetime, for this generation.

Those who can, must join the African People's Socialist Party; those who cannot, must support us.

Build the revolutionary Party of the African working class! Build the African People's Socialist Party!

---

1   **OY 2005**: Class, as a concept, denotes social stratification based on hierarchal relations of production tied to private ownership of property and the means of production. It has been convincingly argued by many that "class"

did not generally exist in pre-colonial Africa.

2 Marcus Garvey, 1887-1940, organized the Universal Negro Improvement Association (UNIA) and its coordinating body, the African Communities League. He published the newspaper *Negro World* in several languages and toured the Americas speaking to large audiences of African people about his vision of African independence. The UNIA had millions of members in eleven hundred branches in more than forty countries. Garvey launched ambitious business ventures, notably the Black Star Line shipping company.

3 W.E.B. DuBois, 1868-1963, was a petty bourgeois African intellectual who promoted his belief that the "Talented Tenth," an elite ten percent of the African population rises up to lead the masses. Recruited as a founding member of the NAACP, DuBois attacked Garvey's working class-identified UNIA relentlessly.

4 The African Blood Brotherhood was a black organization with ties to the Communist Party in the 1920s.

5 **OY 2005**: The relations of production in the South, which were based on labor-intensive production, placed limitations on the overall development of capitalism in the U.S., which was increasingly becoming capital intensive in this period. Segregation, Jim Crow and the prevalent white nationalist rule over the African population represented a form of Southern capitalist rule that had to be overturned in order for capitalism as a whole to develop. This is why the Northern white ruling class had different interests than their Southern counterparts. The struggle against apartheid in South Africa had analogous consequences.

6 **OY 2005:** Even though the Garvey movement organized millions of African workers around the world it was not conscious of itself as an African working class organization. It was not conscious of its own selfish working class interests.

7 **OY 2005**: Some might argue that the African Blood Brotherhood in the early twentieth century fell into this category. The African Blood Brotherhood however, was funded by and functioned as an appendage for the Communist Party USA.

8 **OY 2005:** Historically the lumpen proletariat is a European-defined social entity. It has its origin in Europe. It shares with lumpen types in the African community its character as a fierce street fighter in uprisings and rebellions.

However, its social life and mode of existence make the lumpen proletariat extremely unstable and unreliable. The lumpen is a degraded and castoff sector of society. It is parasitic in its relationship to society. It does not work and has often lost the capacity and forgotten how to work.

Because it has no relationship to social production, the lumpen is short-sighted and without the capacity for the longview. Moreover, it exists on the outskirts of society through petty criminal activities, making it vulnerable to police pressures, often resulting in collaboration with the police against the revolution as a condition for security in pursuing its own aims.

The colonial condition of African people results in huge sectors of the population being unemployed most of the time. Like the European lumpen proletariat, many of these unemployed African people resort to criminal activity to survive and are usually on the frontlines in the street fighting against the police during rebellions and uprisings.

However, unlike the European lumpen, most of these Africans have deep ties to the African community and working class. Generally speaking they go to the same churches, patronize the same bars and nightclubs and many of the same social functions.

The error of the Black Panther Party was to lower the stance of the working class to accommodate the character of the lumpen, as opposed to raising the standard of the BPP to demand that all its members uphold the highest possible stance of the African working class.

Hence, the Black Panther Party accepted the stance of the lumpen proletariat and generalized it within the party. This kept the party from developing into a party of the African working class, the only class capable of leading the struggle to destroy capitalist colonialism.

9   Wilson Goode was the mayor of Philadelphia who bombed the MOVE house on Osage Avenue on May 13, 1985, killing six adults and five children and destroying sixty-one houses in the surrounding African community.

10 The Party led a powerful campaign for the Community Control Housing Initiative. Volunteers dropped 250,000 Measure O fliers by foot on doorsteps in the flatlands of Oakland. The campaign shook the foundations of the white power structure in the city and even the state of California. One local newspaper wrote that if Measure O won in the election the governor would order air strikes on Oakland the next day.

11 **OY 2005:** Twenty years after this piece was written it is necessary to disavow any connection between African Internationalism, our worldview, and Pan-Africanism. What was described as an underdeveloped Pan-Africanism in this piece is actually the limitations of Pan-Africanism, a counterrevolutionary, petty bourgeois political concept that was given practical definition by W.E.B. DuBois in his struggles against the massive, essentially African working class-based movement of Marcus Garvey.

Pan-Africanism was further developed by George Padmore who, working with DuBois, helped to define Pan-Africanism as an anti-communist, neocolonial alternative to direct colonialism. So while there have doubtlessly been any number of courageous Pan-Africanists who have been truly committed to the liberation of Africa and the emancipation of our people, Pan-Africanism as a political manifestation in the real world, cannot provide our movement and people with the necessary revolutionary conclusion.

Moreover, it can be argued that it was the adoption of Pan-Africanist principles as developed by DuBois and Padmore that contributed to the deaths and defeats of great leaders like Nkrumah, Lumumba and Sobukwe who represented the best that Africa had to offer during their lifetimes. All three of these leaders—from Ghana, Congo and Azania (South Africa) respectively—based their movements on Pan-Africanist principles of pacifism, bourgeois parliamentarianism and mass actions without the benefit of the kind of revolutionary parties that recognition of class differentiation in Africa and the world required.

This proved to be fatal in all the above-mentioned cases as the parties they built were unequipped to lead the struggles beyond independence. In fact, in the case of Nkrumah and Lumumba, their parties were infested with petty bourgeois leaders who went over to the side of the imperialist-organized coups that overturned their governments. The bourgeois parliamentarianism and pacifism of all these leaders made them and the people they led defenseless in the face of the imperialist-inspired violence that occasioned their murderous betrayal and defeat.

African Internationalism has no relationship to Pan-Africanism. It may be said that African Internationalism owes its philosophical genesis to African Fundamentalism, the philosophy of the Universal Negro Improvement Association (UNIA) under the leadership of Marcus Garvey. The Pan-Africanist movement was founded as a direct assault on the Garvey movement and was only able to develop a mass following after Garvey was arrested and the UNIA was effectively wrecked by the U.S. government with the assistance of DuBois and others of his ilk.

Articles

On Kwame Ture

Leaders die but the Revolution must move forward

Chairman Omali wrote this article for "Point of the Spear," the editorial page of The Burning Spear *newspaper dated November 1998–January 1999. This piece sums up the life and work of Kwame Ture, formerly known as Stokely Carmichael, who as a leader of the Student Nonviolent Coordinating Committee (SNCC) in the 1960s was associated with the slogan "Black Power!" Ture died on November 17, 1998.*

In the African People's Socialist Party, we are convinced that the people are the real makers of history. This is a view that differs from those who believe that history is made by important individuals, by kings and queens or great leaders.

However, there are individuals, men and women, who, during periods of transformation, are thrust forward from among the people by the demands of the times. These individuals more than others in such times, embody the aspirations of the people in the process of making history. There is no denying the historical significance of such individuals.

We believe that the motive force of human society is the process by humans to produce and reproduce human life. This is something that we do naturally, by reproducing ourselves and by the ongoing social process of developing our capacity to produce food, clothing and shelter.

For African people—at home and around the world—the ability to produce and reproduce real life is problematic. This is shown by the fact that the average life span of an African in a

311

highly developed technological center such as the United States is, at minimum, seven years less than that of whites in the same country. The African infant mortality rate is at least twice that of whites, and in most other places in the world the statistics are much worse.

In every corner of the globe where Africans live, our ability to feed, clothe and shelter ourselves independently is marginal at best. This has been our reality for several centuries, and we enter the twenty-first century with our primary historical mission already determined by this reality.

In fact, for the past several centuries our enslavement, in one form or another, has resulted in our participation in the production and reproduction of real life for others, essentially Europeans—whites, if you will. We have produced for the imperialist system that came into existence and ascended to world hegemony on the foundation of African exploitation.

Our primary historically-determined mission, then, is to wrest away from imperialist white power our capacity for independent, self-serving production and reproduction of real life. We can judge the historical significance of individual African men and women based on their participation in this profound mission.

This is what has given significance to people like Harriet Tubman, Nat Turner, Marcus Garvey, Malcolm X, Fannie Lou Hamer, Ella Baker, Patrice Lumumba, Kwame Nkrumah and so many others. It is also what has given significance to Fred Hampton and Huey P. Newton.

It is what has given significance to Kwame Ture as well.

Kwame Ture was my friend, and at one time he was my leader. He played an important role in my political development, as I am certain he did in the development of thousands, and perhaps millions, of others, especially of our generation.

We came to know him as Stokely Carmichael during the Black Revolution of the Sixties. It was during this period that he stepped forward and boldly articulated our aspirations for power. He took us beyond the lame defensive slogans and goals of the liberal African middle class whose own desire for integration into the white nationalist capitalist system was projected onto our whole people.

Ture was a courageous man during the Black Revolution of the Sixties, but then so were other men and women. Many Africans faced the terrorism of the era with the fierce determination of a people bound to be free. It was not his courage that distinguished Ture. It was his ability to become a living representative of the anti-colonial aspirations of our people that brought him onto the world stage.

Ture came to be a symbol of the people's demand for power over our lives. He represented more than courage. He represented the boldness and audacity that were necessary for a people whose struggle had correctly come to dismiss the U.S. government as a partner in our quest for justice. Our movement now recognized that the U.S. government was the custodian of a system that is the source of worldwide African and human suffering and exploitation.

Kwame will be remembered most for his contributions during the Black Revolution of the Sixties. He was identified with the demand-slogan for "Black Power!" that mobilized Africans throughout the U.S. and the world.

Unfortunately, the Black Revolution of the Sixties was defeated by U.S. imperialism before the ideological accounts within the U.S. Front of the African Revolution itself were resolved.

Following that defeat, the Stokely Carmichael of the Sixties became Kwame Ture. He lived in Africa as a "student" of Kwame Nkrumah[1] and a guest of Sekou Ture, president of Guinea-Conakry.

Ture returned to the U.S. as a proponent of Pan-Africanism and what has been characterized as "Nkrumahism." His stature as the best recognized symbol and advocate of Black Power during the Black Revolution of the Sixties served him well in the work to bring Africa back into focus in the U.S. as the strategic core of all our revolutionary work.

I don't know when the philosophical and political differences that existed between Kwame and myself developed full bloom. I suspect that they took some time to form and take shape. The era of the Civil Rights and Black Power movements was one of rapidly emerging and shifting political and philosophical views that developed in the heat of struggle. Before the differences could be resolved, the U.S. government had effectively broken the back of the Black Revolution of the '60s.

These differences were sharply revealed in our conflicting views of what constitutes a revolutionary party and how it is built. These differences were obvious early on in Kwame's work to build the All-African Peoples Revolutionary Party (A-APRP), the organization he was affiliated with up to his untimely death. They resulted in my inability to accept his invitation to sit on the central committee of the A-APRP during the work to consolidate the organization in the U.S.

They also led to a series of polemics directed at the A-APRP in 1977 in *The Burning Spear*, our political journal, and later published in pamphlet form under the title "Smash Slander and Build Principled Unity."

Political differences based in class question

Kwame Ture was a middle class Pan-Africanist nationalist and the work he did inside the U.S. led to the creation of a middle class Pan-Africanist organization. This does not diminish his historical stature any more than the fact that W.E.B. DuBois[2] or Elijah Muhammad[3] represented middle class or petty bourgeois outlooks diminishes their historical stature.

Many people, especially liberals, correctly hold up DuBois for his tremendous intellectual contributions to our movement and his later transformation. Nevertheless, he is the father of the elitist philosophy of the "Talented Tenth," which purported that only the most "talented" ten percent of the African population rises up to lead. DuBois was one of the greatest middle class opponents of Marcus Garvey and his organization, the Universal Negro Improvement Association (UNIA), the largest working class African Internationalist organization in our history of resistance.

Likewise, who can argue the historical significance of Elijah Muhammad, with his anti-colonial philosophy of "Do-For-Self" self-reliance? More than any single force of his era, Muhammad demystified white power and white people, and raised the concrete possibility of African self-government.

His historical significance is not diminished by the fact that his vision was one of a nation of petty merchants that could come to fruition without an actual revolutionary seizure of power. Neither was Muhammad's historical significance diminished by the fact that his split with Malcolm X represented a break with the revolutionary working class impulse that had been developed by Malcolm X inside of Muhammad's organization, the Nation of Islam.

It is inevitable that in a struggle for national liberation the nationally oppressed colonial middle class will play a vital role in certain phases of our struggle while pursuing its own selfish class interests. This has been a fact in virtually all such struggles against colonial imperialism, and it makes neither the struggle nor the personality historically less significant for this fact.

However, the nationally oppressed colonial middle class does not only see its interests as requiring struggle against the colonial ruling class. The middle class is equally fearful of the independent political activity of the masses of colonial workers and poor peasants.

The Pan-Africanism of DuBois represented a middle class politic that was aligned with liberal imperialism. Objectively, the Pan-Africanism of Kwame Ture and the A-APRP does the same thing.

In fact, Pan-Africanism was consolidated as a movement influenced by the African middle class, especially W.E.B. DuBois. Most importantly, it was a movement that was conceived in contention with the millions-strong UNIA, led by Marcus Garvey.

While the A-APRP considers itself a socialist organization, it is filled with the same middle class assumptions that historically characterize Pan-Africanism. Unable to recognize the central role of the African working class in defeating imperialism and creating and leading the new revolutionary society, the A-APRP puts forth the position that students are the "spark" of the revolution. For this reason, it has based its work primarily on college campuses throughout the U.S.

While colonized students are often radical and progressive, students do not constitute a social force or class as such. Moreover, colonial education has always been viewed by the African middle class as the way to become a part of the new ruling class that emerges when independence from colonial domination is won. Education has been the vehicle through which imperialist ideology is reproduced among the colonial people. Colonial education has been seen as the way forward for those who aspire to enter the bourgeoisie.

In order to realize its aims, Pan-Africanism historically has seen itself as making some kind of deal. This takes the form of an agreement in which pre-independence colonial rulers turn over political power to an educated African elite in a country created by colonialism in the first place. Or Pan-Africanism calls for post-independence African leaders to unify Africa through mere agreement. Pan-Africanism does not require class analysis of the

African leaders who are theoretically being coaxed into unifying Africa.

In the African People's Socialist Party, our view also recognizes Africa as the national homeland of African people to be united under socialism. However, our Party understands that such unification can only happen with revolutionary struggle. Moreover, we recognize that the struggle must be led by the organized African working class in alliance with the poor peasantry. This is because it is only the workers and poor peasants who have absolutely no material interest in the continued existence of the African microstates which artificially divide us. It is the workers and poor peasants who must actually destroy the colonially-created borders to realize their aspirations for material well-being and national dignity.

We believe that this question represents the essential difference between the deal-making African middle class and the revolutionary working class.

We believe this fundamental question is also responsible for our differences in practice. For example, throughout the thirty years of its existence, the A-APRP has been opposed to any practical struggle in defense of the people. It has religiously stated that its only program is to build the A-APRP. It has characterized struggle in defense of the people as mere reformism which leaves "imperialism" untouched.

The position that the only program of the A-APRP is to build itself is the essence of careerism. There is a difference in building for the revolution and having a career of being in the movement. If the only program of a so-called revolutionary organization is to build itself—for thirty years!—then it is clear that the organization is simply a station that provides people with a career in the movement without having to build the revolution to liberate the people.

In the African People's Socialist Party we are clear: police murder of young African men is imperialism. Poverty, infant mortality, substandard housing and massive imprisonment are the ways in which imperialism articulates itself in the lives of the people. These are the manifestations of exploitation and national oppression. Imperialism is not simply a bad idea, a word to be bandied about at political conferences over the heads of the suffering masses. It is real.

Equally important, however, is the fact that struggle enhances the revolutionary capacity of the people. The organized, conscious confrontations that the people have with imperialism make the people more capable of struggling. They provide the training ground for the revolution. Nor can any organization claim a revolutionary mantle without testing its cadre in the field, on the ground in real struggle, in real confrontation with our class enemy and national oppressor.

It has been the years and years of struggle for basic democratic rights led by the Uhuru Movement under the leadership of our Party that raised the capacity for African people in St. Petersburg, Florida, for example. Those years of struggle culminated in the fact that African workers in St. Petersburg delivered a military defeat to the colonial police after the assassination of a young African man and an attack on our Party's headquarters in 1996.

We have other differences with Ture's Party as well. For example, Kwame operated in a Black United Front that did not include a single revolutionary organization. Rather, it revolved around a relationship between the National Urban League, the National Association for the Advancement of Colored People and the Nation of Islam.

Our Party opposed the way the A-APRP dodged pressure from the masses to struggle by refusing to open offices throughout the U.S. We object to the refusal of the A-APRP—the party of the "intelligentsia"—to publish a journal so it could be held accountable by the masses for its views. We disagreed with the

A-APRP's suppression of African student struggle on college and university campuses where it was based throughout the U.S. with its metaphysical policy of all political study and no struggle.

This article should not be viewed by anyone as a statement that we of the African People's Socialist Party believe that the ideological differences within our movement have now been resolved merely because we have stated our views. This is not the case. We simply believe that the resolution of these differences is necessary for the development of our revolutionary process, and that the way to resolve these differences demands that our views should contend. Indeed, the A-APRP has always been a much larger and, in many ways, more influential organization than ours. Some will view this fact as evidence of the correctness of its views in relation to ours.

But, believe it or not, this editorial is not about differences. It is about the loss of a historically significant leader of our movement—a leader who influenced at least one, and probably more, generations of African people to take up the task of liberating our people. If it appeared that this editorial was about differences, it is simply because our love for Kwame and the African Revolution makes it necessary to defend both, even though they clearly took divergent paths of development.

We mention these differences because it is necessary to project our revolutionary aims even when we mourn lost soldiers. No one understood this better than Kwame himself. People die. Even profoundly important, historically significant people die. But our movement continues. And we, those who remain in the trenches when our leaders die, continue to sum up and move forward.

Kwame Ture loved Africa and African people and so do we. We will miss him dearly.

1 Kwame Nkrumah, 1909–1972, was the first president of independent Ghana. He believed in and worked for "the total liberation and unification of Africa under an All-African socialist government" as the "primary objective of all Black revolutionaries throughout the world."

2 W.E.B. DuBois, 1868–1963, was an African intellectual who was recruited as a founding member of the NAACP. In the early twentieth century DuBois repeatedly attacked the African working class based movement of Marcus Garvey that called for "Africa for the Africans, those at home and those abroad."

3 Elijah Muhammad, 1897–1975, was the leader of the Nation of Islam when Malcolm X was a member in the 1950s and '60s."'

The crisis of Pan-Africanism

Unity and struggle with the Pan Africanist Congress of Azania

Originally published in the October 2003 issue of The Burning Spear *newspaper, this editorial was written by the Chairman to clarify both the history of unity and the political differences that the African People's Socialist Party has with the Pan Africanist Congress of Azania (PAC). Chairman Omali discusses the crisis within the PAC as well as the crisis and limitations of Pan-Africanism as a guiding political theory.*

The Eighth Congress of the Pan Africanist Congress of Azania (PAC) was held in December 2002, in Umtata in the Eastern Cape of Azania. The congress was attended by approximately twelve hundred delegates. Several other members attended as observers. It appears these numbers were negatively affected by the fact that poverty prevented many would-be delegates from attending. The PAC Constitution allows one delegate for each twenty members of the organization, and it appears likely that the PAC is the largest Pan-Africanist organization in the world. As was made clear at the Congress, the PAC is currently in the midst of a crisis, and this crisis is a reflection of the general crisis of Pan-Africanism itself.

Our Party attended the PAC Congress and I was its keynote speaker. We also had a Party delegation at the continuation of the Eighth Congress in Soweto in June 2003. This session was called because the eruption of crisis prevented the December Umtata Congress from ending on schedule.

321

The Party's participation at the PAC's Eighth Congress was a logical continuation of a relationship between our two organizations going back more than thirty years. That relationship was disrupted, though, after the formal apartheid system of direct white settler colonial domination ended a decade or so ago.[1]

Once the possibility of ascendancy to power presented itself in South Africa, the PAC, like many of the other continental African liberation organizations, appeared to have accepted the concept of a single-state solution within the white colonially established borders in Africa.

Prior to the end of the apartheid system, the African People's Socialist Party had worked with the PAC throughout the U.S. We worked with Elizabeth Sibeko, widow of slain PAC leader, David, in Atlanta, Georgia.[2] We worked with PAC representative Pulede Shoba in Oakland, California, before he was cut down by the violence of the U.S. domestic colony of African captives in the U.S.

We worked with the PAC in New York, Pennsylvania, Maryland and Florida and especially with its delegation at the United Nations where we spoke on PAC's behalf more than once. In fact, the PAC was a guest and speaker at our Party's First Congress in 1981 and attended other Congresses as well. On more than one occasion, a member of the PAC functioned as a member of a panel of judges at the annual reparations tribunal organized under the leadership of our Party in various cities throughout the U.S.

We also met and worked with several of the PAC leaders, including the incredible Zeph Mothopeng, along with John Nyati Pokela.[3] We published pamphlets of the speeches of Robert Mangaliso Sobukwe,[4] the brilliant and courageous PAC founder and leader who was imprisoned and murdered by the white settler regime because of his steadfastness in the struggle for the total liberation of Azania and all of Africa.

Moreover, unlike many who refused to take a principled stand of support for a specific liberation organization in Azania, preferring to claim support for both the Pan Africanist Congress and the African National Congress (ANC), the two leading organizations there, our Party stood squarely with the PAC.

Our newspaper, *The Burning Spear*, became the unofficial organ of the PAC. We wrote and published supporting articles as well as PAC speeches and documents, and printed articles written by PAC leaders. We toured their members throughout the U.S. and provided PAC with a multitude of forums when the ANC, darling of white liberals and the Moscow-related communist parties, refused to allow them space on podiums of the white left and some black radical groups.

Our stance with the PAC was based on principle. It was determined by PAC's commitment to national liberation, its declaration of an all-African solution not only for Azania, but also for Africans worldwide, and the intent to expropriate the expropriators, the white settler oppressors who had robbed our people of liberty and land. Moreover, for the duration of our relationship, we had struggled with the PAC and its leadership to join our efforts to build the African Socialist International (ASI), a single worldwide organization of revolutionary African socialists. We have always believed that the African Socialist International is necessary for the liberation of Africa and African people.

However, it must also be said that our Party's relationship with the Pan-Africanist Congress of Azania was one of unity *and* struggle. We united with the PAC in its contest with the white-settler colonial capitalist regime and the black liberal ANC, whose guiding document, the Freedom Charter, had long ago allocated the land of Azania to all who lived there—white oppressor and black oppressed alike.[5] Nevertheless, there were fundamental disagreements that did not go unmentioned by us.

These disagreements included:

- The nature of the organization. We strongly disagreed with the concept of the "congress." Various African-based organizations were characterized similarly—as conventions, fronts, movements, etc. We argued that these kinds of formations allow for the African primitive petty bourgeoisie or middle class to hide its class aims, winning power for itself, while exploiting the misery and energy of the mass of African workers and poor peasants. We argued, and still do, that while these types of mass formations are sometimes permissible and tactically useful, our struggle must be *led* by the advanced detachment of the African working class, aligned with the poor peasantry. This is the only social force capable of taking the liberation struggle to its revolutionary conclusion. Hence, what is needed to lead the struggle is a revolutionary party that has struggled for and achieved a revolutionary theory and line that will liberate the people and elevate the working class to power.

- The concept of socialism. Like many Pan-Africanists, PAC was vague on its concept of socialism. It talked about socialism as if it were simply a concept that society in general could be won to, that once one came to power all one had to do was to declare its existence. Hence, PAC never talked about socialism as a contest between classes, as something that can never be accomplished without the ascendancy of the African working class to the position of ruling class. It could not talk about socialism as the armed ascendancy to power of the mass of African workers aligned with the poor peasantry.

- The question of class struggle in African society. Like many other African liberation organizations, PAC refuses to recognize the role of class in African society. This leaves PAC, like many others, trapped into personality politics, where judgments are made of African movements and leaders based on the personalities of those involved, rather than on the class forces that they serve. No doubt this stems in part from the fact that the historical engine of our struggle as a people was fueled by foreign aggressors taking Africa from us and taking many of us from Africa. For a few hundred years now, our efforts have been directed at winning all-African unity in the struggle against white imperialist thugs. However, it has been the success of the struggle against direct white power in the form of open colonialism that has led our white oppressors to disguise their rule through the elevation of black faces to positions of nominal power. This indirect rule is called "neocolonialism" and is a product of the collaboration between the primitive petty bourgeoisie and white power. The attack on Africa by Europe was a condition for the rise of capitalism as white power in the world. But, having come into being, capitalism has established new relationships and a new context within which our struggle must be fought.

Many PAC members want organizational transformation

It was the efforts of PAC's young Secretary General Thami Ka Plaatje that resulted in a delegation of our Party attending the PAC's Eighth Congress. Plaatje represented the tendency in the PAC that is clamoring for a transformation within the organization that would make PAC capable of leading a struggle to alleviate the suffering of the masses. Plaatje had attended the 2002 conference in London to build the African Socialist International, sponsored by our Party. Already busy making efforts to reenergize PAC's international connections, Plaatje, impressed by our efforts and politics, then invited me to make the keynote presentation to the PAC's Congress.

We have reported on the significance of that visit in previous issues of *The Burning Spear.* While there our Party, comprised of delegates from London and the U.S., toured the shantytowns, hostels and townships where the vast majority of our people live and suffer under wretched conditions in a land where we are supposedly free.

It is a land where the African primitive petty bourgeoisie in the form of the African National Congress holds nominal power. The destruction of the white regime's atomic weapons was a condition of transferring nominal power from white to African hands.

It is a land where the white population, which makes up only ten percent of the total population, controls eighty-seven percent of the land, an actual territory that is four times larger than England and Northern Ireland combined. Additionally, the unemployment rate for Africans is more than forty percent. Millions of our people live in shanties—hovels put together by ingenious people taking scraps of zinc and other discarded materials to put together shelter to protect themselves from the elements.

In this land, where, according to official statistics, the poverty of the African masses has increased by nineteen percent and the wealth of whites has increased by fifteen percent over the last five years, the crime rate has gone off the charts in the African community. The Negro revolution of the ANC has solved the material needs of the petty bourgeoisie only, leaving the masses to extraordinary means to meet simple basic needs.

In this land, everywhere we visited we would ask the African workers, young and old, employed and unemployed, to express their hope for the future. Time after time, we would be told, "There is no future. There is no hope." While we expected mass cynicism toward the ANC, the crime and the recurring refrain of hopelessness also spoke volumes about the fact that no political organization in this extremely volatile and ripe political situation, not even the PAC, had given the masses a vision of a liberated future. It was as if the people in Azania had come to the end of history.

Our discussions and observations prior to the December Umtata Congress convinced us that not only was there a crisis simmering just below the surface in Azania but there was also a crisis within the Pan Africanist Congress of Azania. The level of opposition to the leadership of President Stanley Mogoba, a Christian bishop, was revealed in the fact that three other PAC members, including Plaatje were running against him for the presidency of the organization.

The ranks of the organization, though growing because of increasing popular opposition to ANC and the legacy of the PAC as the organization of the steadfast Robert Sobukwe, were nevertheless roiling with discontent. Many saw the Eighth Congress as the make-or-break congress that would rescue the PAC from its demoralizing electoral ineffectiveness and offer an analysis and strategy for liberation.

I was aware of these contradictions when I stepped to the podium to make the keynote presentation to the Umtata Congress. I was also aware that the PAC base suffered demoralization because the organization's work revolved around an electoral strategy for achievement of power. So, I spoke to this and other contradictions and, walking a delicate balance between the divided leadership and the masses, offered up an analysis and strategy for moving forward to power. [For a transcript of that presentation, see "Izwe Lethu i Afrika!" on page 173.]

The tumultuous response to this presentation by the congress attendees made it clear that the PAC rank and file heard the analysis and general direction they were looking for.

The speech was interrupted over and over again by spontaneous applause and I received an extended standing ovation, punctuated by revolutionary song and dancing.

The presentation was the only one at the congress that addressed the general contradictions the Azanian masses and the PAC itself are facing. It was the only presentation that presented the struggle of the masses of our people and the PAC within the context of the overall struggle against imperialism.

The report from Deputy President Dr. Motsoko Pheko, dealt essentially with the land issue and the desire of PAC to gain back land for the African people. President Mogoba made a call for unity within the organization and especially within the leadership of the organization. He also talked about the need for harder work by the organization to achieve the aims it set for itself.

Fierce struggle inside the PAC

The Congress exploded in crisis during the closed session because of struggles around the credentials report. This was the report that would determine who could vote during the election of officers of the organization. The controversy emerged because of challenges to the delegates from the Free State, the base of Deputy President Pheko.

Claims were made that Pheko had gone to a village and slaughtered a cow for a feast in order to get people to sign up as delegates who would vote for him during the congress. When delegates were challenged, it is said that some of Pheko's delegates, as young as thirteen years old, knew nothing of PAC's politics and began to cry, pleading to be allowed go home.

The intensity and duration of the struggle around the credentials report allowing Pheko's questionable delegates to participate in the election finally made it necessary for the veterans of PAC's armed wing during the liberation struggle to intercede and halt the vote for PAC officers for fear that it would destroy the organization.

None of the other reports and business of the congress was possible under the circumstances. A visibly shaken PAC President Stanley Mogoba made the announcement to the delegates, expressing concerns about fraud and promised that the congress would be reconvened only after an audit of the membership to determine the legitimacy of the Free State delegates in question.

It was not until June 2003, six months later, that the congress reconvened, this time in Soweto. Again, our Party was present. The atmosphere was measurably different from Umtata. For one thing, the congressional leadership had determined that security for the congress's leaders would be provided by the South African police, an assumption that the membership was a threat to the leadership and that PAC's own security could not be trusted with the task. The spontaneous, celebratory spirit was gone. Even efforts by the leadership to get the delegates to sing the freedom songs so freely done in Umtata were generally ignored by suspicious delegates.

Patricia de Lille, one of the three PAC members elected to parliament[6] along with Mogoba and Pheko, had quit the organization to form her own organization, thereby depriving PAC of one of its paltry parliamentary seats. The National Executive Committee (NEC) had expelled Maxwell Nemadzivhanani, a contender for PAC office of president. Cameroon Tabane, a contender for the office administrator and leader of PAC's youth organization, was expelled as well because he had allegedly made public statements supporting both Nemadzivhanani and Plaatje for the office of presidency.

The air was rife with rumor. Aware of the desire of the rank and file for new leadership, Mogoba had made a pact with Pheko to support Pheko against Plaatje with the condition that Pheko as president would allow Mogoba to keep his seat in the parliament as a PAC representative.

It was assumed by many that the expulsion of Nemadzivhanani was done to eliminate him as a challenge to Pheko's bid for the organizational presidency. The expulsion of Tabane was seen as an attempt to deny both Nemadzivhanani and Plaatje the support from the youthful PAC base during the election.

The open session consisted of solidarity messages that included a demagogic presentation by Lester Lewis. A London based Pan-Africanist, and ally of Pheko, Lewis openly sang the praises of Mogoba. Following the statements, the congress went straight to the heart of the matter. The intent of the leadership was to elect new leadership and all other issues were to be deferred. However, to get to the issue of an election, the congress still had to leap the hurdle of the credentials question.

Fierce struggle from the floor ensued. The membership demanded that before the issue of credentials could be entertained, a report had to be made by the leadership on the results of the investigation into the fraud at the Umtata congress. From the floor, delegates also demanded the audit of the membership necessary to determine the legitimacy of Free State delegates.

For long, excruciating hours the chair of the session refused to discuss the report, claiming that the congress could not legitimately move forward without first approving the delegates, including those suspected of being fraudulent from Free State. Even as the debate was occurring, Free State delegates were complaining about irregularities within its delegation.

Finally, through the use of procedural rules to crush political discussion and through use of the police to break up struggles from the floor, the credentials report was accepted by the congress only to learn that no investigation of fraud and no audit of membership had been carried out.

For more than twenty-four hours, the PAC congress was a political battleground, with its membership fighting for the future of the organization of Sobukwe. Recesses were called and attempts to broker deals were made. At one point, it is said that an offer was made to Plaatje to accept the post of deputy president, allowing Pheko to ascend to the presidency.

However, it was clear that although the delegates lined up behind specific leaders for president of the organization, the issue was not simply one about power within the organization, but about what kind of organization PAC would be and what policies it would pursue in the struggle for state power

Many of the leaders wanted to reduce the contradictions in the congress to a question of procedure. They used the power of the organization to squelch political struggles necessary for PAC to elevate itself to a position of real revolutionary leadership. Under these circumstances, it was clear to Plaatje that even if he were to consider a deal to become Deputy President, he would never be able to accomplish anything within a leadership that had so disregarded the wishes of its own membership. This leadership had clearly pre-determined who would become president of the organization and had covered up the contradictions that made it necessary to halt the Umtata congress.

After twenty-four hours of unrelenting struggle on the congress floor, Plaatje supporters were barely allowed to begin reading the statement announcing the withdrawal of Plaatje's name as a candidate for president and announcing the slate of names of his supporters for other posts in the leadership. Plaatje supporters believed this slate would rescue PAC and kick start the revolutionary process in Occupied Azania.

The National Executive Committee leadership had its way. Pheko was elected president and a new administration assumed the reins of the organization. PAC missed this opportunity to harness the incredible energy of what was a growing member-ship base for the Revolution.

But the struggle has not yet ended. Plaatje has since been expelled from the PAC after the new leadership was inundated with calls for its own resignation. The provinces of Western Cape, Eastern Cape, Free State and parts of Gauteng have openly stated that they do not recognize the current leadership. This led the veterans and the former president to call a well-attended all-Africanist conference, where a call was made for Plaatje's rein-statement.

How the PAC will respond to this current situation is anyone's guess.

Years ago Robert Mangaliso Sobukwe was faced with the contradictions of the organization he belonged to at the time. This was when he was with the youth branch of the African National Congress. After so many struggles and betrayals, including the adoption of the notorious Freedom Charter, Sobukwe determined that there was no longer room within the organization for the advancement of the revolutionary aspira-tions of the oppressed and dispossessed Azanian masses. This prompted him to break away and found the Pan Africanist Congress of Azania.

Today, conscious revolutionaries everywhere are faced with the question of whether the philosophy and organizational for-mations they are currently involved with hinder or advance the struggle to liberate Our Africa. Inside the PAC these questions are pressing.

Izwe Lethu i Afrika!

---

1   The apartheid system was ended in 1994 when African National Congress leader Nelson Mandela became the first African president of South Africa.

2   David Sibeko was the Permanent Observer from the Pan Africanist Congress of Azania to the United Nations from 1975 until his assassination in Tanzania in 1979. His wife Elizabeth was a PAC activist in the U.S. until she returned

to South Africa following the end of apartheid. Elizabeth died in 1999.

3 John Pokela was Chairman of the Central Committee of PAC, based in Dar es Salaam, Tanzania, from 1981 until his death in 1986. He is credited as the man who unified the party following a period of crisis for the organization. Zephaniah Mothopeng, popularly known as Uncle Zeph was imprisoned three times during the liberation struggle, the last time for ferrying arms and recruiting into APLA when he was seventy-five years old. He was elected PAC Chairman in 1986 while in prison. He was released in 1988 and confirmed as PAC president in 1990 before dying the same year.

4 Robert Mangaliso Sobukwe was instrumental in the break with the ANC in 1958 that led to the birth of the Pan Africanist Congress. He was PAC's first president. Sobukwe died in 1978.

5 The Freedom Charter was adopted by the ANC in 1955.

6 Patricia de Lille, a long-time activist and leading member of the PAC, was elected to the South African parliament in 1997.

Live like our African martyrs
Death in the struggle is better than life on our knees

This is a very inspiring call to action written by Chairman Omali on the occasion of African Martyr's Day, designated by the African People's Socialist Party to be February 21, the anniversary of the assassination of Malcolm X. This article appeared in the Chairman's Point of the Spear column in the February 2004 issue of The Burning Spear *newspaper.*

On February 21, 1965, at a community meeting in Harlem, New York, several gunmen stood and in short order took the life of Malcolm X. Slamming round after round of flesh-tearing, bone-shattering projectiles into his body, his assassins attempted to hold back our future as a liberated people by removing one of our bravest and clearest champions.

The murder of Malcolm X was one of the many assassinations carried out by the U.S. government or other representatives of imperialist white power during the crucial Black Revolution of the Sixties that shook the foundations of the world capitalist system.

On January 17, 1961, a few years before the assassination of Malcolm X, several thousand miles away on the continent that Malcolm X recognized as his homeland, Patrice Lumumba, Prime Minister of newly liberated Congo, was murdered. Lumumba was also killed through the connivance of the U.S., along with Belgium, England and other white imperial powers.

In 1968, in Memphis, Tennessee, three years after the assassination of Malcolm X, Martin Luther King became another

African victim of imperialist murderers. In 1969, the killing of King was followed by the assassination of Black Panther leader Fred Hampton in Chicago, Illinois.

These were among the more notable leaders of our struggle for liberation who were marked for death by the imperialists. They were targeted because of their success in mobilizing Africans in pursuit of our liberation. Many other leaders were assassinated as well. In Africa, imperialism did everything possible to destroy our movement for liberation, destabilizing our victories with coups, such as the one in Ghana in 1966 that led to the overthrow of Kwame Nkrumah.

Death was the ultimate deterrent to revolution and liberation. J. Edgar Hoover, former head of the FBI, then the primary domestic secret political police of the U.S., is said to have declared his intent to demonstrate to young Africans in the '60s that should they become revolutionaries they would be dead revolutionaries.

The imperialists have depended on our fear of prison and death being greater than our love of freedom and the liberation and unification of Africa, our Motherland. Hence, not only do they kill our leaders, they often do so with great flair and spectacle.

As easy as it would have been for killers with the expertise of the U.S. and other imperial powers to kill inconspicuously, the public executions of King, Malcolm X and Fred Hampton and the murder of Patrice Lumumba, make it clear that the attacks on our leaders were also attacks on the will of our people to resist and to win our freedom.

The 1960s was an era of revolutionary insurgency throughout the world. The Cuban revolution of 1959 followed on the heels of the Mau Mau insurrection against British colonialism in Kenya and Ghana's independence in West Africa. These victories opened up the whole great era of revolutionary successes of the sixties. Others emulated the Cuban Revolution throughout

South America, and Viet Nam became the symbol of the revolutionary determination of the masses to overthrow imperial colonial domination everywhere.

Imperial white power rests upon a base of the oppressive exploitation of the masses of peoples worldwide. Its material wealth, social institutions and even its much vaunted "democracy" require as a foundation the brutal expropriation of the material and human resources of Africans and others of the so-called Third World.

Despite the assassinations and setbacks, human progress is today measured by our liberation movements. Even as the imperialists and most oppressor nation denizens would deny it, it is a simple fact that the cumulative effect of our successes over the past half century is generally responsible for the present crisis of imperialism. This crisis is often expressed popularly as the "war against terrorism," which is really nothing more than a response to the anti-colonial, anti-imperialist efforts of today.

In the U.S., the imperial white power government has attacked the African community with chemical warfare in the form of a drug economy. At least one of every ten African men, a potential revolutionary, is in prison.

But it is too late for imperialism's efforts. More and more Africans are stepping into the ranks of the Revolution. They are following the examples of and learning the lessons left them by our murdered leaders like Malcolm X, Fred Hampton and Patrice Lumumba. That is as it should be, because our oppressors intended to teach a lesson with the assassinations of our leaders: that struggle against white power is futile.

In September 1981, our Party resolved to take away the power of our enemies to use the death of our leaders as weapons against our struggle. We took February 21, the day of the assassination of Malcolm X and declared it the "Day of the African Martyr."

That resolution from our Party's Congress, included this passage:

"The African People's Socialist Party calls on all African revolutionaries of all countries to raise high, in a revolutionary manner, the heroic memory of all our fallen martyrs, of all those in every city, village, community and country where they fell, as evidence of the determination of our people to fight every battle on every front until liberty has been won."

"The African People's Socialist Party calls on all African revolutionaries of all countries to initiate special ceremonies and programs in every community where an African revolutionary has fallen and to raise the memory of our fallen freedom fighters to its proper revolutionary and historical significance."

The crisis of imperialism is real and cannot be underestimated. It is the crisis of imperialism that is responsible for the U.S. attacks and interventions in Iraq, Afghanistan, Colombia, Venezuela, the Philippines and so many other places around the world.

The weakness of our enemy does not automatically translate into strength for our revolution. Nevertheless, there are places where the people's resistance has defeated imperialism's threat of death as the ultimate deterrent to struggle. In some places in the world, slavery is seen as being worse than death and martyrdom is held in the highest esteem. It is in these places that imperialism is facing its biggest challenge, partially because the fear of death has been neutralized.

While this is not a call to martyrdom, it is a call to recognize our power to take away the imperialist weapon of the threat of death. It is a call to our movement to hold up for emulation the courage of our leaders who were willing to make the ultimate sacrifice in the struggle for our liberation.

It has been said that one of the criteria necessary for revolution is an oppressed people who have concluded that even death is better than being on our knees. This is not a call to death, but a call to an appreciation that life for our people in freedom and in possession of our dignity and all our resources is more important than the death of an individual who fights to make it possible.

Long Live the African martyr!
Izwe Lethu i Afrika!

Hands off Haiti!

African workers everywhere must defend our sisters and brothers

Chairman Omali Yeshitela wrote this editorial for the March 2004 issue of The Burning Spear *newspaper. The paper went to press just days before the U.S. overthrew the Haitian government on February 29, 2004 and kidnapped President Jean Bertrand Aristide, taking him to Africa.*

This article is an excellent summation of the struggle in Haiti and how the contradictions there are tied to the conditions that African workers experience all over the planet.

The island-country where Toussaint L'Ouverture and Jean-Jacques Dessalines successfully waged the first anti-colonial, democratic revolution in the Western Hemisphere in 1804 is now the poorest country on earth. The Chairman makes the call for African workers everywhere to build the African Socialist International so that we can defend our brothers and sisters wherever they are under attack.

By the time you read this article, Jean Bertrand Aristide, president of Haiti, may be overthrown by U.S.-trained and supported thugs, or he may be dead. As of this writing, Port Au Prince, Haiti's capital is in turmoil. It is being encircled by killers who are intent on dragging Haiti back into an era of terror not unlike that of the era of the Duvaliers or the terrorist reaction in the wake of the U.S.-backed coup that first unseated Aristide in 1991.

The current situation in Haiti is a consequence of two crucial factors. The first factor is the absolute hostility of the U.S.

government to any semblance of an independent African government any place on earth. The second is the weakness of the African Liberation Movement, reflected in its poverty of ideology and organization.

The island called Haiti, where Columbus first landed in 1492 and in short order decimated the Indigenous peoples, is known as the most impoverished place in the world. It has been recognized as such for so long that many have come to believe that poverty and violence are natural to the land and people. However, such is not the case.

The occupants of Haiti are Africans who are there as a result of being kidnapped from Africa and put there under the gun and whip for Spanish and French profits. The Africans in what was then called Hispaniola were part of the overall process of European looting, annexation and slavery that gave birth to the capitalism and white power that now dominate the world at the expense of the rest of us.

Late in the eighteenth century, Haiti became a symbol for oppressed peoples of the world when Africans began the struggle that would eventually lead to Haiti's independence in 1804. It was the first successful slave rebellion and workers' revolution in the world.[1]

When the African Revolution against colonial slavery began in Haiti, the colonial powers of the day, which included the U.S. and France, trembled at the thought of what a successful revolution would mean. They feared this example to all the oppressed peoples of the world, in particular the Africans and Indigenous people throughout the Americas.

Indeed, as late as 1822 when Denmark Vesey[2] was planning a rebellion against colonial slavery in Charleston, South Carolina he encouraged the Africans he was organizing by telling them they would be joined in the rebellion by Africans from Africa and from Haiti.

Napoleon Bonaparte[3] was so concerned about the Haitian uprising that he sent several thousand crack French troops to Haiti in an attempt to put it down. The French were soundly defeated at the hands of the Haitian revolutionaries. Napoleon was quoted as saying during the time that, "The freedom of Negroes, if recognized in St. Domingue [as Haiti was then called] and legalized by France, would be the rallying point for freedom seekers of the New World." For the first fifty-eight years of Haiti's existence as a free country the U.S. refused to recognize the island-country

Haiti's resources repeatedly stolen

To achieve international recognition, Haiti had to pay France one hundred fifty million francs in gold as "reparations" to the slave owners and to cover the cost of the war of liberation. The U.S supported this demand by France. By the end of the century, Haiti was paying more than eighty percent of its budget towards this debt and its interest. This is the origin of Haiti's role as a debtor country. It is not unlike that of Africa today or of the Southern U.S. sharecroppers who worked for the landowners all year and at the end of the year found themselves in debt, notwithstanding all they had earned for the owner.

Haiti has a rocky history of political instability and international intrigue. Much of it was generated by the mulatto elite who, accepting the common ideological assumptions of the day that exist up to now, saw themselves as superior because they were the light-skinned children of the slave masters.

In 1915, the island was invaded by the U.S. Marines who occupied the country until 1934 when they left after looting the treasury. This left the people in even deeper poverty and under the authority of a military trained and organized by the U.S.

From 1957 to 1986, the country was ruled by the vicious François Duvalier (Papa Doc) and his son and successor, Jean

Claude (Baby Doc), both of whom were supported by the U.S. Jean-Bertrand Aristide played a major role in mobilizing the people against the Duvalier regime. His efforts against the regime—as a priest in some of the poorest parishes around Port-au-Prince—propelled him into the leadership of the impoverished masses and resulted in several assassination attempts against his life.

With Baby Doc exiled in France, living off hundreds of millions of dollars stolen from the Haitian people, elections were finally held in 1990. The elections were held by the military junta that assumed power and which, on orders from the U.S., intended to legitimize the next era of terrorist rule of the island. It was expected that CIA-backed Marc Bazin would become the next elected president and would give a democratic cover for the continued oppression and exploitation of the African masses.

When Aristide announced his entry into the presidential race on the last day to apply, the impoverished African masses were instantly mobilized. His liberation theology, sprinkled with socialist concepts of empowering the laboring masses, captured the imagination of the people and raised their hopes of a better future for themselves and their children.

His election threw a monkey wrench into the plans of the U.S. and they immediately went to work to overthrow him. Within seven months after the election, a coup by the Haitian military, organized and trained by the U.S., overthrew Aristide, sending him into exile. The military then went on a murderous rampage that resulted in thousands of Aristide supporters being killed and thousands more being driven underground. More than five thousand Africans fled the island in rickety boats, often resulting in death or, if they reached the U.S., imprisonment in concentration camps in Miami.

Nevertheless, the U.S. was left with a mess. Because Aristide had been a candidate independent of U.S. support, his base among the poor people, who constitute more than eighty percent of Haiti's population, was ungovernable. Having become a darling of the liberals during his exile, Aristide worked tirelessly to expose the anti-democratic machinations leading to his overthrow.

In 1994, the U.S. deployed twenty thousand troops to Haiti to reinstate Aristide. However, his reinstatement was conditioned by his agreement to step down in 1995. The U.S. would give the appearance of a democratic solution with the reinstatement of Aristide, but hoped that replacing him before he could continue with his reforms would allow them to install a docile puppet. Instead Aristide was replaced as president by René Préval who was a member of Aristide's own Lavalas party.

Aristide was re-elected again in 2000. He accepted neoliberal "free market" reforms dictated by Washington, the supreme imperial white power. U.S. terms included opening a free trade zone on the border with the Dominican Republic, the U.S. neocolony where most of the U.S. armed thugs now attacking Haiti were based. The free trade zone is being funded by a World Bank loan that supports sweatshop owners. He also agreed to pay back debts to the International Monetary Fund that stem from the period of the U.S.-imposed dictatorship.

These conditions led to the growing emiseration of the African masses. The growing poverty was accompanied by a series of military assaults on police stations in various sections of the country by thugs crossing over from the Dominican Republic. Some of the assaults were obviously connected to well-known CIA and U.S. Special Forces-trained assassins and torturers who played prominent roles in repressing the people after Aristide was overthrown in 1991.

There was a coup attempt in 2001 by former members of the military and increasing numbers of anti-government protests that escalated in violence. Claims of election irregularities led to the withdrawal of loans and grants from the government by the

U.S. and U.S.-dominated institutions. All of this set the conditions for provocateurs to turn Aristide's impoverished base against him or at the least, to undermine their support for the floundering government.

As the U.S.-led assault is meandering toward the capitol, Aristide is calling on the international community to help. France, the former colonizer and darling of the white left because of its self-interested opposition to the U.S. attack on Iraq, has told Aristide to surrender his democratically-elected position to the thugs, popularly called the "opposition" by the imperialist media.

The U.S., currently flexing its muscles worldwide as the new empire, has echoed France's position, showing the world how meaningless the idea of democratic elections is when African freedom is at issue.

African impoverishment creates white wealth

This brings us to the real issue, and that is our weakness as a people dispersed throughout the world. We are bereft of the organization and philosophy necessary for our liberation and security.

In the real world, none of us should be surprised by the role being played by the U.S., France or any other white imperial power in Haiti or any other place in the world. Our conditions of existence as a people, wherever we are located, are due to the fact that all of European white power propelled itself into power off our enslavement and dispersal throughout the world.

The permanent poverty and dispersal of our people are absolute conditions for the ongoing wealth, power and unity of the white imperialist world. We, therefore, must accomplish our liberation with no illusions of support by white power.

Nor will we be liberated by any kind of theology—liberation or otherwise. We must embrace a philosophy born of an examination of our real history and place in the world. That philosophy is African Internationalism. African Internationalism explains the world as it is, not as we would wish it to be. It teaches us that capitalism, the world system with which we are locked in a life and death embrace, was born of the theft of our resources in Africa and the trade in African bodies. It was this reality that created, for the first time in history, a world economy that was the condition for the rise of capitalism in the world.

African Internationalism teaches us that our poverty and oppression are due to the fact that wherever we are we have been deprived of our own resources—both human and material. For all of Africa's wealth, all Africans are impoverished. For all our labor around the world, Africans are poor. Yet Africa's resources and our labor have made and continue to make the white world wealthy and secure.

When the U.S. and France function as they do in Haiti or any place else, they do so to protect a system that requires Africans and others to remain as hosts to parasitic white power. We are not poor because we are poor. We are poor because white power sucks our blood and must do so as a condition of its own continued existence.

Moreover, regardless of where we are located—in Haiti, the U.S., Africa, Europe or elsewhere—we cannot win our freedom alone. Our condition has a single origin. The slavery and colonialism that impoverish Africa are responsible for our presence and oppression in Haiti, Brazil, Europe, the U.S. and throughout the world.

Haiti, with a population of seven million or so, cannot sustain a national economy. Nor can most of the microstates in Africa created for us by white power. We must organize as one people. We must recognize that we are Africans and Africa, the richest continent in natural resources in the world, is central, strategic to our liberation worldwide. This must not be understood as mere Pan-Africanism that dismisses the need for revolutionary struggle wherever we are. Africans around the world should be doing all within our means to defend Haiti.

A genuinely organized and philosophically clear African population would have resulted in Aristide calling on the African working masses—especially in the U.S., but worldwide—to defend Haiti. A genuinely organized and philosophically clear African population would have forced the U.S. and other imperial white powers to pay a consequence for their interventions in Haiti.

We would even send organized military forces to beat back the U.S.-supported thugs. It has been suggested that the notorious street gangs of Los Angeles would be sufficient to defeat the armed aggressors. African Internationalism teaches us that the only social force to rely on is the African working class aligned with the poor peasantry.

Aristide is in a weak position because he disbanded the army, which had been the base for much of the U.S.-led attacks on the people. It is true, the State is an organ of repression and the army is a part of the State apparatus, having been created to protect the interests of the mulatto elite and their imperialist masters. Therefore, the neocolonial army should have been smashed. But, in order to truly replace the neocolonial army, all power has to be seized by the armed masses who become a workers' State ready to fight and die for the country. Only then can African workers in Haiti become the ruling class and the collective owners of the means of producing life's necessities.

The African People's Socialist Party is consumed with the intent of becoming a worldwide Party, an African Socialist International, which can give leadership to every struggle we are involved in as a people and a class.

We call on the laboring masses of the world to support their sister and brother workers of Haiti, workers who have heroically done so much for the emancipation of toilers everywhere. We especially call on the African workers to do all within our means to protest the imperialist attack on our brothers and sisters and to join us of the African People's Socialist Party in creating the African Socialist International.

In July of this year, Africans will be traveling to London from throughout the African world to participate in the conference of the African Socialist International. We cannot say for certain what will have occurred in Haiti by that time, but we are determined to take the future of our people out of the hands of imperialist white power. We must assume our responsibility to rescue Africa and ourselves and to build a new world where we can have the advantage of the wealth of Africa and our own labor.

African workers and poor peasants of the world, unite! Izwe Lethu i Afrika!

1 Toussaint L'Ouverture, along with his generals Dessalines and Christophe were former slaves who led the African revolution in Haiti, which began in 1791. By 1804, Africans had driven French and British colonialism out of Haiti.

2 Denmark Vesey was born in West Africa in 1767 and was named Telemanque. He was kidnapped and enslaved in Virginia as a young boy. In 1800 he won a lottery prize and was able to leave the plantation and set up a successful carpentry business. Despite his personal success, Vesey was committed to fighting the system of enslavement. In 1822 he built a literal army of over 9,000 enslaved and "free" Africans in the Charleston area to instigate an insurgency. On June 23 of that year Vesey was hanged for the "crime" of attempting to overthrow the slave system.

3 Napoleon Bonaparte, 1769-1821, was emperor of France.

Interviews

A revolutionary vision

Chairman Omali was interviewed by Doug Tuthill on January 27, 2004. Tuthill is a St. Petersburg resident and the Chief Operating Officer of Creative Loafing Media. In this relaxed setting, the Chairman has an opportunity to express some of his deepest observations and convictions about the revolutionary process which will liberate African and oppressed peoples everywhere.

You call yourself a "revolutionary." What does that mean?

It means that I don't believe the conditions that confront African people in this country can be resolved through reform. It's going to take an absolute overturning of the current social system. This is true as it relates to rights and justice for African people, and for most other people who experience colonialism in this country—Mexicans, Puerto Ricans, folk like that. Ultimately it is going to be necessary to rescue white working people themselves.

A revolution that goes beyond reform is necessary. Reform serves only to perfect the process of expropriating value from people's labor and resources. A total transformation, a total over-turning of the existing social system is absolutely necessary if Africans and other people here and all over the world are ever to know freedom.

Assume your revolution is successful. What will that look like? What is your vision?

I don't think there is a blueprint for that. There are so many

351

elements that go into creating this future. Central to it all will be the realization of the informed aspirations of oppressed human beings. The revolution that I'm talking about will begin with a process central to African people. We may be seeing it unfolding now. This revolution is not going to be nice, clean and pristine like many thought in the past, with the "magnificent workers" in the lead. It is poor and oppressed people working with what they have at the moment, trying to change their situation, perhaps not even being informed by a scientific process. Such a process may already be happening in the Middle East and throughout the Americas in places like Venezuela and Colombia.

I am convinced that we are living in a whole new era. We refer to this era as the "Final Offensive." We mean this in historical terms, not in terms of a battle that would be waged and everything would be changed. The imperial order that we are experiencing now has no dynamic character. It's no longer a matter of imperialism growing stronger and capturing more resources. It's a matter of it hanging onto everything it has stolen over the past four or five hundred years.

Obviously you can't make a revolution for the whole world, but part of what informs me strategically is a belief that central to this process is a struggle for African people spread across the world to achieve freedom and independence. Central to that is the Continent of Africa—its unification and liberation. This will contribute to the unraveling of the existing social system.

We believe in a social system where production is not for profit, where people will be able to produce and share collectively. I am not capable of producing a blueprint for how it will look because that will be determined by the revolutionary process and by all kinds of people participating in this process. This will not be a revolution created by a single group of people.

We probably saw a hint of this revolution in this country in the 1960s. We saw the unleashing of the democratic aspirations of groups such as women, homosexuals, Mexicans, Native people and Africans. This time around there is more unity among the colonized peoples. We have a greater unity and capacity to work collectively to define what is going to happen. There is also a greater unity among oppressed peoples worldwide and a greater ability to communicate with each other—to talk about a joint strategy to effect our freedom and liberation.

Is the revolution you are talking about a process that changes how people relate to each other and how they produce and share their production?

Yes. We have some assumptions—we aren't just involved in an open-ended struggle. We talk to the African community here and throughout the world. We have regular conferences in England, France and now in Belgium where Africans worldwide come together to discuss what this revolution will look like. We are trying to come to some conclusions about what is necessary to make it happen. We know that central to this process is the emancipation of the working people. The producers—the people who work and produce to sustain themselves—have to have authority. All value comes from their work. There is no value or wealth outside of their work. They produce wealth but they are always on the bottom, and their futures are always most tenuous. That's upside down. The producers must have control of the future because the producers create wealth. So central to our revolution is the authority and emancipation of the working people—the producers.

What is the role of power in this transformation?

Power is an absolute necessity. The democratic future we seek is only a dream without the power to make it happen. Someone said of Marcus Garvey[1] that he gave us backbone when we used to have wishbone. The struggle for power is real.

Our oppressors tell us that what we really need is to be accepted and liked and appreciated by the oppressor. That's taught in every institution.

The people need power. The people need to have the ability to deliver a consequence. If you don't have power then you are just a dreamer. Some oppressed people are afraid of power, of the thought of exercising power. That's something they have been taught, but power is absolutely necessary. Otherwise you're relying on the good will of folks, who, if they had good will, we wouldn't be in the situation that confronts us today.

How would this change in power relations affect race relations?

I don't think people can have a good relationship if there is a large disparity in power. People need to go into relationships as equals. The reality is white people in America are accustomed to power and the possession of power, even if it's something they've never given any thought to.

Africans in America are accustomed to not having power and being in this unequal relationship with white people. It is common to hear Africans aspire to becoming assistants. This is an incredible thing! That is their highest aspiration, to be an assistant. For good relationships to emerge, based on equality, it is going to require the acquisition of power by the oppressed. At that juncture you can have a decent relationship between equals.

The fact is white people will never know what African people think as long as this unequal relationship exists, because you don't tell powerful people what you really think when they can do something to you if they don't like what you say. Sometimes you don't have the courage to discover what you really believe if you lack power. You don't even have the courage to think it or allow it to really surface. That's why we sometimes see these explosions that come from oppressed people—finally they dare to think and look at relationships in ways they never have before.

Many whites are frightened by the idea of a more equal power distribution. Is this a false fear?

It is a false fear. There is the fear in the back of the minds of many white people that if black people ever have power they are going to do to white people what white people have done to us. The reality is that there is greater likelihood for violence or revenge in our current unequal relationship. Africans have been maids and servants in white homes, taken care of white children, and we have not been violent or sought revenge. There have been instances when people have been oppressed and come to real power yet there has been no revenge or violence. The only time people are looking for revenge is when they are being oppressed. When people are no longer oppressed they no longer look for revenge. What they are looking for is a decent future. Power opens up the possibility for good relationships.

I live with the certainty in my own mind that revolution will occur, and dues will need to be paid, but ordinary people will not pay those dues. At the juncture white people can capture their own consciousness they will want to participate in exacting dues from the oppressors as well. Whites will have the opportunity to recognize their kinship with the rest of humanity, as opposed to this foul ruling class that sits on all of us.

You refer to yourself as a democrat. Is the revolution you've described a democracy?

The revolution I've described is the way through which lasting and genuine democracy can occur. A real revolution is actually a democratic process. I've heard people like Lenin[2] say otherwise, but I think a real revolution requires the participation of masses of people. It's not something that takes place because a small group of individuals or an organization wants it to happen.

What we refer to as democracy is the ability to restrict the capacity of the State to impact on the lives of the people. We define the State as an oppressive institution that essentially serves the purpose of maintaining the status quo and protecting the interest of those in power. The arms of the State are the police and military, the jails and courts. Democracy is our capacity to restrict the State's ability to impose its will upon the people, thereby freeing the people to exercise their free and informed will.

I believe that revolution, in the final analysis, is the way through which we'll have this democratic process. The times when the African community has known most democracy in this country have been during the height of revolutionary struggle. In the 1960s we saw an explosion of democracy. As a consequence, we saw less crime in the community. In St. Petersburg after TyRon Lewis[3] was killed and the rebellions occurred, there was an explosion of democracy. All the people at all levels were exercising a level of freedom and free will that you don't find ordinarily.

You're a leader of the African People's Socialist Party. What does it mean to be an African socialist, and how does African socialism relate to democracy and the revolution?

We actually call ourselves African Internationalists. African socialism is phony. Historically, African socialism has meant that a sector of the colonially-created petty bourgeois leadership came to power—particularly after the independence movements throughout Africa—and called themselves African socialists in order to avoid real socialism. Genuine socialism assumes that the working people, the producers, are in power, not some elitist groups or individuals. African socialists after independence continued to use the State as a tool of oppression against the workers and peasants.

We call ourselves African Internationalists because white socialists and Marxists[4] ask us to ignore our unique history of oppression in order to be socialists. All people need to have an analysis that is born of their experiences as a people—their history of struggle. We are Africans. But to say we are Africans is not to say that we are narrow nationalists. We are internationalists. We have solidarity with all the oppressed peoples on earth. While we understand the strategic necessity of unifying and liberating Africa, we recognize that ours is a struggle for a world without borders. We concentrate on Africa because that's who we are and where we are.

White Marxists—and sometimes Negro Marxists as well—have a theory of the development of human society. But it's not a theory of human social development; it's a theory of *European* social development. They attribute their theories to everybody, but their theories don't fit Africa. We can be Africans and internationalists and stand on our own history and experiences and draw our own conclusions about human social development. We are defining our condition from our historical perspective.

When you talk about Black Power and African Liberation, you're not simply satisfied with Africans being in power. You've talked about African leaders being in power who are undemocratic, contrary to the revolutionary principles you are articulating. So you're not simply looking for black faces in positions of power as opposed to white faces. Is this why you are as critical, if not more critical, of undemocratic African leaders as you are undemocratic white leaders?

Right. In fact, the greater problem is those undemocratic African leaders because they stand as ideological transmission belts from the imperial powers into our communities, and they are armed. Their weapons are not to fight external enemies; they are to keep the African masses oppressed inside their communities and countries.

The fundamental struggle we are having now at the international level is with the Pan-Africanists. Pan-Africanists hold up the line of all Africa being united. But Pan-Africanism represents what we are struggling against.

A man named Marcus Garvey built an incredible organization, millions and millions strong, with a steam ship line, black dolls, black pride and black dignity. W.E.B. DuBois from the same period is loved by liberals of every stripe. DuBois was a very brilliant man, well educated and erudite, and he hated Garvey and the Garvey Movement. DuBois put forward the theory of the Talented Tenth when he was with the NAACP (National Association for the Advancement of Colored People). This talented ten percent of the black community would, with the permission of the white ruling class, give leadership to the rest of us.

DuBois fought the Garvey Movement. He said black people in America cannot live in Africa. DuBois worked with the Ashcroft[5] of his time, the attorney general of the United States, to destroy the steamship line that Garvey had created. DuBois was one of those forces who created the ideological and political conditions for the U.S. government to wipe out Garvey.

Garvey called himself an African Fundamentalist. The masses of African poor people, workers and all kinds of folk joined the Garvey Movement, while DuBois led the Negro intellectuals—the proper Negroes. In 1919, DuBois convened a Pan-Africanist conference, pulling the Pan-Africanist movement together and giving it structure. DuBois worked with colonial forces in Africa, such as France, which helped him set up his conference. The French and British hated Garvey and moved to destroy him and his movement. The Pan-Africanist movement held up the idea that the smarter, more educated Africans would oversee certain places in Africa and work with the colonial powers.

The Pan-Africanist movement could only emerge as influential among Africans after the Garvey Movement was destroyed. Pan-Africanism then became the only movement that had an all-African view. Many people who saw Africa as central and fundamental ended up joining the Pan-Africanist movement, despite its contradictions. My dear friend Stokely Carmichael became a Pan-Africanist and died a Pan-Africanist. But it's a petty bourgeois movement that relies essentially on agreements between the African leaders. It talks about a socialism that does not require the workers and peasants to come to power. It's a charity kind of socialism.

When you criticize these African leaders as petty bourgeois, are you saying that they do not embrace a distribution of power that you think is necessary for democracy?

Yes. This redistribution of power is absolutely necessary. It's not just necessary for democracy in the abstract; it's necessary for the reunification of Africa. Africa cannot unite because these petty bourgeois elitists benefit from the balkanization of Africa. They can be prime ministers, generals, etc. It facilitates their own capacity to extract wealth for their own benefit. Africa cannot develop a healthy economy balkanized as it is, but these guys can live well and they do live well. Mobutu was one of the richest men on earth when he died. It was a small price for the imperialists to pay to allow him to do that.

Some people criticize your views by saying that you are romanticizing human nature and are overly idealistic. There are always going to be people who are only interested in power and there will always be people without power. There are always going to be people who will use their power advantage to exploit others to acquire more and more wealth. You have a view of human nature that is very

optimistic, that we can transcend our current condition and reach a better place.

I believe human beings are capable of constructing and living in a just society with equitable production and distribution of wealth. I am guilty of believing that. I don't think there is any real evidence that disproves this capacity. I am not talking about something that has not existed.

The first stage of the Marxists' theory of social development is called "primitive" communism. They know about this primitive communism because of a man named Lewis Henry Morgan,[6] who was an anthropologist in the nineteenth century. Morgan's studies showed Marx and Engels[7] what socialism looked like. His studies looked at Indigenous societies on this continent in which women were not oppressed—they were equal. There was no exploitation; there was absolute equality and people shared collectively everything they had.

Like all historians, Morgan, Marx and Engels had to work backwards in an attempt to understand the development of human society. They did that based on their own European-centered experience and worldview, coming to the conclusion that European society represented the "highest" level of human development while other societies were more "primitive." Their error was in generalizing the traits of the communistic societies that they observed among the Indigenous peoples. There is little evidence that such collective and non-oppressive societies ever existed in the general history of Europe.

One of the criticisms often made of the African community is our unwillingness to think and act like individuals. Instead we act collectively. We need to get rid of this collective thing, they tell us, because you can't have development unless you go for yourself. Greed and self-interest are what create our development, they say. That criticism reflects our different worldviews, and stems from the fact that historically our societies were ordered quite differently. The organization of the State has not looked the same in all societies. In Europe, the State developed with a fixation on private property and the private ownership of land, whereas many other societies were organized around kinship.

As a child I was always disturbed by the story of the grasshopper and the ant. The grasshopper was carefree and never worked hard but the ant was busy all the time working. The ant was always warning the grasshopper that if you don't work now when the winter comes you are not going to have anything: "I'm working and storing all my stuff. When the winter comes I'm not going to give you anything, and you're going to die." Sure enough the ant's prediction came true and the grasshopper was left with nothing. I was blown away by that as a child. I could not believe that the ant would not give the grasshopper anything to live. I think that's part of the explanation of how different societies developed in the world. Europeans think like the ant, but not Africans.

Things happened independent of the will of human beings. Where we developed and how we developed have a lot to do with the character and culture of a society.

Slavery has historically occurred across many geographically diverse societies. Doesn't this suggest that there is something about human nature that forbids us from embracing your notion of democracy?

Colonial slavery inflicted on African people by Europeans was not the same thing as slavery in other times or places. You won't find anything—even the terrible things done by the Romans—that compares with the chattel slavery endured by Africans. It damn near underpopulated an entire continent and dispersed us throughout the world. That was unique in human history and gave rise to a whole new social system. I believe that the slave trade was fundamental to the emergence of the whole new era of capitalism. I more than believe this. It's something that can be shown empirically. Fighting slavery does not resolve the contradictions that confront us. Capitalism created a whole new context for the struggle we are involved with now.

Critics of your analysis say there is a role for free markets in creating a context for innovations and development.

Your question assumes that free markets work. They don't. The reality is that we live in a world today where over half the people on earth live on less than two dollars per day, so where is the success of free markets? It doesn't exist. Some say it exists because America is wealthy and the greatest place on earth, but America is wealthy not because of free markets but because it has the weapons and force to keep the rest of the world suppressed so that it can take their resources.

Free market capitalism is a theory that does not work. Just look around the world. Capitalism doesn't only exist in the U.S., England and France. It's a world system. In one part of this system the vast majority of people's human and material resources are being sucked up by imperial powers. This is a "free" market that's not free at all. If you want to see how not free it is, look at the five million people who died in the Congo since 1998 so that the U.S. and other forces could get coltan, a mineral necessary for cell phones and computers.[8] The theory of free markets does not work for the majority of people on earth.

Is there a role for free markets within the context of your revolutionary process?

I don't know what that means. I know the history of free trade originates with the slave trade. The whole concept of free trade came from the emerging bourgeoisie demanding free trade in opposition to the monopoly of the slave trade that was held by nobility, by the monarchy. Your question assumes that human beings will not work to uplift their collective condition. It implies that somehow individual greed has to play an essential role. If that were the case then impoverished Cuba would not have the best medical system in the world. Cuba sends medical people all over the world and tells us that if we can get black people to Cuba they will make them doctors.

Cubans are motivated to treat and cure disease. But here in America, where more money is spent on health care than anyplace on earth, the health care system is something like twenty-fifth in the world. The problem is that the objective of the U.S. health care system is not to treat and cure disease; it's to make money. So the truth is the other way around, as long as greed and money are the incentive, we will *not* progress.

I believe, yes, that human beings can care enough about our collective well-being that we will work toward that, and we will be better off. If we worked for our collective well-being, we would not have paved parking lots on every corner because we'd have decent public transportation and the ozone layer would be less threatened. If workers had something to do with planning the places where they worked you wouldn't have all these work-related health problems.

I believe there is a material incentive in all of us to make informed determinations to work for the collective good. The problem is that this free market where profit has to be the motivating factor is an ill-informed notion because of the contradictions the free market creates. If people had an opportunity to access good information they would make better choices. When people act against their own best interest it's because of ignorance. I think it was Engels who said that freedom is the recognition of necessity. That's what we have to help make happen. This notion that only intellectuals can grasp reality and envision the future is a farce. Ordinary people can, and that's our obligation. People will do what's in our collective best interest. Oil spills, nuclear waste and toxins are not in our best interest.

Are there any other comments you'd like to make?

Yes. History is written by the so-called victors. I think ignorance is a terrible burden on human society in general. It's a terrible disservice to human beings to be deprived of knowledge and information. Ignorance enables people to applaud their own oppression. It deprives people of an ability to know of their own human significance. That is one of the things that has happened to Africans. We suffer from an imposed veil of ignorance all over the world. The world has been defined by colonialists and imperialists in a fashion that holds up white people's civilization in a very vulgar, superior fashion. That is a terrible disservice to everybody.

I don't know how many people die because people in Africa, Asia and Latin America are unable to get information and knowledge that could cure disease and build decent places to live. This imposed ignorance and poverty is just incredible. What a terrible toll it takes on the human spirit to wake up every morning, look at yourself in the mirror and to see yourself as a despised person who has made no contribution to human development or human society. It doesn't do African *or* white people any good.

One of the reasons that white people have such difficulties looking at truth and reality is because for the last four or five hundred years the African, the Mexican and other oppressed peoples have been the objects of history and not the subjects of history. Increasingly, though, Arabs, Chinese, Japanese, Mexicans and Africans are now writing history with ourselves as the subjects of history and white people as the objects of history. This is something that white people have a real serious difficulty dealing with, never having been the objects of history before.

We go to Europe every year for our African Socialist International conference with Africans from around the world. During this trip we go to the British Museum and museums in Paris and

Belgium. In these places we find incredible evidence of African civilizations. We walk down the main boulevard of Paris and see on one end of this boulevard the obelisk with the golden pyramid at the top and hieroglyphic writing on it. On the obelisk is a plaque saying it was given to France by the viceroy of Egypt in the nineteenth century. Of course the viceroy of Egypt was a Frenchman.

The Louvre Museum in Paris has the greatest collection of African art in the world, but Africa does not have access to its own art. Africans are demanding that France give our art back, and the French president says that Africans ought to be happy that the art is worth being in the Louvre!

In Paris, we visit what used to be called the Museum of the Colonies—it has another more politically correct name now.[9] On the front of the building is a raised sculpture with ivory on the outside depicting a huge scene of rubber coming from Congo, of loot coming from Indochina and all over the world. All of it comes into the hands of this plump white woman at the very top who represents France.[10] You see this kind of art all over Europe, evidence of where all their wealth and resources come from.

When Christians in America pray and end the prayer with Amen, they are talking about Amen-Ra who was an important Egyptian God. You see all the evidence of what Africa has been and it is just an incredible experience. It's enough to break someone down into tears. We've taken Africans living in France to see this. They had never seen this before—they did not know their own art existed. They did not know their own history was there in Paris.

I think information, knowledge and history are such powerful weapons that need to be put back into the possession of the people. When the masses of African people have possession of this history and this knowledge, we become invincible. When a people know what we have done, we realize what we are capable of doing.

1 Marcus Garvey, 1887–1940, organized the Universal Negro Improvement Association (UNIA) and its coordinating body, the African Communities League. He published the newspaper the *Negro World* in several languages and toured the Americas speaking to large audiences of African people about his vision of African independence. The UNIA had millions of members in eleven hundred branches in more than forty countries. Garvey launched ambitious business ventures, notably the Black Star Line shipping company.

2 V.I. Lenin, 1870–1924, revolutionary, political leader and theoretician, was the driving force behind the Russian revolution of 1917 and the formation of the Union of Soviet Socialist Republics (USSR).

3 TyRon Lewis was eighteen years old when he was killed by the St. Petersburg, Florida police during a traffic stop on October 24, 1996. His murder sparked rebellions in the African community of St. Petersburg. In response to these events, the Uhuru Movement led a dynamic movement of the African working class community for economic development and an end to the policies of police containment.

4 Followers of Karl Marx 1818–1893, the German philosopher, political economist and revolutionary, author of the *Communist Manifesto*, *Capital* and many other theoretical works.

5 John Ashcroft was the right wing U.S. attorney general during George W. Bush's first term in office, 2000–2004.

6 Lewis Henry Morgan, 1818–1881, was a North American anthropologist who studied Indigenous society in the U.S.

7 Friedrich Engels, 1820–1895, worked and wrote political theory with Karl Marx. Engels was the co-author of the *Communist Manifesto.*

8 Coltan, short for Columbite-tantalite, is a metallic ore found mainly in the eastern regions of the Democratic Republic of Congo. When refined, coltan becomes a vital component for the capacitors that control current flow in cell phone circuit boards. More than five hundred tons of refined coltan is used in the United States yearly. U.S.-backed wars to control coltan have killed and made homeless more than five million Africans in eastern Congo since the late '90s.

9 Museum of African and Oceanian Arts.

10 The official Paris tourism website says of this museum: "Its facade contains a frieze depicting the contributions made by France's overseas colonies."

Our African culture and the drive for independence

This is a follow up interview with Chairman Omali by Doug Tuthill on February 12, 2004. Tuthill is the Chief Operating Officer of Creative Loafing Media, and a resident of St. Petersburg, Florida.

What is it about the communal nature of African culture that causes Africans to view democracy differently than Europeans?

I'm not sure this is uniquely African. It exists in other cultures as well. What is peculiar, historically, is the European attachment to private ownership of land. The circumstances under which European culture, personality and consciousness were born and developed, the harshness of these northern conditions, caused the development of their individualism. In the southern cradle of civilization, which includes Africa, we did not have such a hostile confrontation with nature.[1] I think the necessities of surviving in these northern climates caused this individualism. So individualism in the north and collectivism in the south emerged as central to their respective cultures.

How does the communal nature of African communities manifest itself today?

In recent years the whole desegregation effort has undermined collectivism in the African community. During my childhood—and this still occurs in some rural African communities today—you could eat wherever you were at dinnertime. It wasn't like, "I've got to go home to eat." We called other African children cousins even though we weren't related. That was an ongoing tradition in our community.

Any parent, any adult, assumed responsibility for the children—all the children. If I were being bad, an adult would snatch me up, spank my butt and tell me to go tell my mother what he or she did. Of course I didn't tell my mother because if she found out I'd get another spanking. It was real collectivism. There was no such thing as an orphan. That was just a ridiculous concept to us. We just couldn't imagine it. Any time a parent died or something else happened, there wasn't even a second thought—someone in the community would take the child. It wasn't as if they were doing a favor, it was just how things were done.

When a child was born, a group of women would always go to the house, take care of the mother and take care of the house. That was just the natural kind of collective existence we had.

There is the tradition of the Tree in our community. Men—and it is especially men—like to gather around the tree. You can find them there in the coldest times of the year, north and south. Sometimes they have a fifty-gallon drum with a fire in it. It's a cultural legacy that's been there forever. That's where we come together.

In the African community family reunions are huge. It is the community; it is collectivism of a sort. If you look at some of the traditional African villages you see them designed around a central courtyard with all of the houses opening onto this yard. This is very much woven into the culture of African people.

Our collective African way of life began to break up, and welfare contributed to its demise. We used to have a collective poverty—we even shared that. But welfare individualized poverty and caused the person to look to the mailbox once a month, as opposed to having a relationship with the community.

A condition for getting welfare was that there couldn't be a man in the house. Welfare was a real assault on our families. African families were originally much broader than the current acceptable family structure. Families were collectives. That's why even today Africans still call each other brother and sister. We used to always refer to any older person as an uncle or aunt. In Africa today children I meet refer to me as uncle.

Welfare defined a family much more narrowly. The man was no longer the provider, and the provider is now this mysterious entity that sends signed checks once or twice a month. This is when the erosion of African families really began. Welfare devalued African men, both in the men's eyes and in the eyes of the women. The man was no longer a needed provider, a key factor in European culture.

This is ironic because these 1960s war-on-poverty programs were created by white liberals who thought they were doing good by helping poor people. But you are saying those programs actually undermined African extended families, and had a negative effect.

Yes. We had things like community burial funds. The first black insurance companies came out of burial funds. Eventually those sorts of initiatives were outlawed, and this way of creating collective wealth for the community was undermined. Instead we were given the liberal solution that individualizes every problem and success. This was an assault on the community's capacity for creating collective wealth and growth.

In the early twentieth century, Marcus Garvey[2] created African-owned enterprises by collecting nickels and dimes, but this is no longer possible. We can no longer sell stock to only black people. The collective achievement of wealth by the community is no longer possible. More than a hundred thousand people came out in 1919 in New York to see Garvey launch his

Black Star steamship line. We all owned those ships and that was a beautiful thing. That was 1919 and Africans haven't owned anything anywhere since.

White liberals said they were going to provide resources but to access these resources blacks need to fit into the white community's definition of family and how communities should behave. Most whites today see instances of collectivism in the African communities as weaknesses.

Historically women have played strong leadership roles in the African community. The problem is that the European definition of family goes all the way back to the fact that their societies were organized around land and property. In other societies, including Africa, we organized around kinship. That's where the concepts of clans and tribes came from. Even the way warring groups treat each other is different when they are organized around kinship rather than individual control of territory.

I'm not sure liberals with good intentions created all these welfare programs.

There is another side to this. The more educated an African becomes the more alienated that African becomes from himself and his community. The black middle class is so full of self-alienation because the world is defined from the perspective of those in power. So here you have the slave seeing himself from the point of view of the slave master. The more educated a person is the more he is likely to have that kind of assumption.

It is an illogical response to oppression by educated sectors of the African community in the face of lynchings and bombings to say that the way we can resolve this is to move next door to the ones doing the lynching. It's an absolute self-abnegation. So you have this minority in the African community for whom the solution is being with and like white people. Many Africans are in distress because they want to be like whites. They accept white definitions of beauty, family, materialism and success. But then that alienates them from their African history and culture.

I have been giving presentations on the church in our community. As part of this discussion I have been looking at how the Jews resisted Roman oppression, and how Jesus resisted oppression. They had the same tensions in their community that we have in ours. Some Jews identified with the Romans, and came into conflict with their own Jewish people. Jesus was a Jew who was trying to lead his people against the Romans, and came into conflict with the Jewish neocolonialists. That's the same struggle we are having in our African communities. We are resisting while other Africans are saying let's join with the oppressors. Sometimes these forces become better oppressors than the oppressors themselves.

Where does the black separatist movement come from?

Separatism was labeled by the NAACP (National Association for the Advancement of Colored People), which wanted to assimilate into white society. They defined those who did not want to assimilate as separatists. But if the NAACP was trying to assimilate, then the African community was already separate!

When the white colonials wanted to create a country they did not issue a declaration of separation, they issued a declaration of independence! The accusation of separatism is negative, but independence is positive.

There has never been a time when the desire for independence was not strong in the African community here. After the Civil War and the betrayal of the Africans by the Republican party, many Africans left the South to set up all-black cities. There was a move to set up an independent state for black people in Madagascar, and in Oklahoma in this country.

There has never been a time when there was not a tendency for Africans to be self-governing in response to the violence and oppression imposed on us. I don't think that's an unnatural urge. It's been characterized as negative, as a sign of hopelessness in the black community. That's a liberal idea, but they think the greatest thing is for us to be one of them. It's interesting, some white people want to kill us for trying to integrate. But when we say we want to be independent, we don't want to integrate, we are accused of being negative separatists who are full of hopelessness. Damned if you do, damned if you don't.

When you talk about revolution and democracy, it's all tied to the drive for independence.

The drive for independence is the highest expression of democracy. We are a whole people who were brought into captivity. Africans are the only people who did not come to this country looking for a better way of life.

This drive for African independence got momentum through Marcus Garvey. He created this incredible international movement. Freedom movements in Cuba and Nicaragua, and throughout Africa and the Americas sprang from the Garvey Movement.

Today we are building the African Socialist International, which enables us to meet with Africans worldwide. It's such an emotional thing. Africans from everywhere who've never been in touch with each other finally find themselves in the same room defining our experiences and our reality. It's a magnificent reunion. We take people from housing projects in this country and reunite them with other Africans from all over the world. It's just an incredible experience.

1   Chairman Omali is referring to the theory of the African anthropologist Cheikh Anta Diop, 1923–1986. Diop showed that the severe climate and environment of Europe (the northern cradle) resulted in the development of an individualistic, xenophobic, aggressive, nomadic culture among the white isolates, in contrast to the cooperative, xenophillic, peaceful, sedentary culture among Africans who inhabited the more benign climatic and environmental zones (the southern cradle).

2 Marcus Garvey, 1887–1940, organized the Universal Negro Improvement Association (UNIA) and its coordinating body, the African Communities League. He published the newspaper the *Negro World* in several languages and toured the Americas speaking to large audiences of African people about his vision of African independence. The UNIA had millions of members in eleven hundred branches in more than forty countries. Garvey launched ambitious business ventures, notably the Black Star Line shipping company.

Index

375

Made in the USA
Columbia, SC
12 April 2021